JOHN CUTHBERT FORD, SJ

Moral Traditions series

James F. Keenan, SJ, series editor

American Protestant Ethics and the Legacy of H. Richard Niebuhr
William Werpehowski

Aquinas and Empowerment: Classical Ethics for Ordinary Lives
G. Simon Harak, SJ, Editor

Aquinas, Feminism, and the Common Good
Susanne M. DeCrane

The Banality of Good and Evil: Moral Lessons from the Shoah and Jewish Tradition
David R. Blumenthal

Bridging the Sacred and the Secular: Selected Writings of John Courtney Murray
J. Leon Hooper, SJ, Editor

A Call to Fidelity: On the Moral Theology of Charles E. Curran
James J. Walter, Timothy E. O'Connell, and Thomas A. Shannon, Editors

The Catholic Moral Tradition Today: A Synthesis
Charles E. Curran

Catholic Social Teaching, 1891–Present: A Historical, Theological, and Ethical Analysis
Charles E. Curran

The Christian Case for Virtue Ethics
Joseph J. Kotva Jr.

The Context of Casuistry
James F. Keenan, SJ, and Thomas A. Shannon, Editors
Foreword by Albert R. Jonsen

The Critical Calling: Reflections on Moral Dilemmas Since Vatican II
Richard A. McCormick, SJ
Foreword by Lisa Sowle Cahill

Defending Probabilism: The Moral Theology of Juan Caramuel
Julia A. Fleming

Democracy on Purpose: Justice and the Reality of God
Franklin I. Gamwell

Ethics and Economics of Assisted Reproduction: The Cost of Longing
Maura A. Ryan

The Ethics of Aquinas
Stephen J. Pope, Editor

The Evolution of Altruism and the Ordering of Love
Stephen J. Pope

The Fellowship of Life: Virtue Ethics and Orthodox Christianity
Joseph Woodill

Feminist Ethics and Natural Law: The End of the Anathemas
Cristina L. H. Traina

❀ JOHN CUTHBERT FORD, SJ ❀

Moral Theologian at the
End of the Manualist Era

Eric Marcelo O. Genilo

Georgetown University Press
WASHINGTON, DC

As of January 1, 2007, 13-digit ISBN numbers have replaced the 10-digit system.
  13-digit   10-digit
  Cloth: 978-1-58901-181-6   Cloth: 1-58901-181-3

Georgetown University Press,
Washington, DC
www.press.georgetown.edu

Library of Congress Cataloging-in-Publication Data

Genilo, Eric Marcelo.
John Cuthbert Ford, SJ : moral theologian at the end of the manualist era / Eric Marcelo Genilo.
    p.   cm. — (Moral traditions series)
Includes bibliographical references and index.
    ISBN-13: 978-1-58901-181-6 (cloth : alk. paper)
    ISBN-10: 1-58901-181-3 (cloth : alk. paper)
    1. Ford, John C. (John Cuthbert), 1902– 2. Christian ethics—Catholic authors.
3. Christian sociology—Catholic Church. I. Title.
BJ1249.G46 2007
241′.042092—dc22   2007011197

14 13 12 11 10 09 08 07   9 8 7 6 5 4 3 2
First printing
Printed in the United States of America

CONTENTS

FOREWORD

For many years, John Cuthbert Ford, SJ, and Weston School of Theology were synonymous: he was the embodiment of moral theology at the Jesuit seminary in the Massachusetts town of Weston. Gracious, big-hearted, and opinionated, Ford was the face of the institution.

His decision in January 1969 not to accompany the school as it moved from Weston to the city of Cambridge resulted in a kind of a divorce. Ford did not want to see the seminary outside its Catholic setting; he was set against the decision to have Weston rent classroom space on the campus of Episcopal Theological Seminary (ETS, later Episcopal Divinity School) while participating as a member of the Boston Theological Institute (BTI). He especially did not want to see Jesuit students taking courses at ETS, or worse, at Harvard Divinity School and Boston University. In Ford's mind, ecumenical ventures were not pertinent to Catholic priestly formation.

Ten years after John Ford's resignation I began my master's of divinity degree at Weston. The moral theology faculty at the time was Mary Emil Penet, IHM, David Hollenbach, SJ, and Edward Vacek, SJ. The two Jesuits, Hollenbach and Vacek, had done their doctoral studies at American universities, Yale and Northwestern, respectively. Sr. Mary Emil, or SME as we called her, taught the fundamental moral theology course and, before coming to Weston, had worked for a year in Rome with Josef Fuchs, SJ, arguably the most prominent Jesuit moralist of his time. In a sense, she brought Fuchs to Weston Jesuit. The high point of any lecture was when she shared with us a moral conundrum, and would recount how she went and asked Fuchs what he thought. She would begin the narrative, "So I asked Fuchs . . . ." At Weston, in 1979, Fuchs was a legend, and Ford was simply a memory. Or so it seemed.

The irony of this shift should not be lost on the reader. Fuchs and Ford represented polar constituencies that dominated the papal commission on birth control in the mid-1960s. Fuchs authored the majority report calling for change; Ford countered with the minority report and apparently persuaded Pope Paul VI that he could not change the teaching on birth control. It is hard to imagine any senior moralist having greater influence in the writing of *Humanae vitae* than John Ford. It is equally hard to imagine any senior moralist more influential than Fuchs in galvanizing cardinals and bishops to consider changing the teaching on birth control. In Fuchs' Rome, Ford won; in Ford's Weston, Fuchs won.

Moreover, had Ford come to Cambridge in 1969 and taught in the Weston classrooms, in all likelihood he would have encountered ETS's own moral theologian, Joseph Fletcher, the father of situational ethics, whose landmark book on the topic in 1966 eventually sold one million copies. What would Weston and ETS have been like in its first year together, if the "father" of *Humanae vitae*, who insisted on the absolute universal applicability of Church teaching on birth control, met the "father" of an ethics that denied the universal and insisted on the radical uniqueness of the particular situation?

Though Ford resigned from Weston with considerable anger and resentment, it is noteworthy that this is the first book about the work of a Weston faculty member. Even more ironic is that its author, Eric Genilo, SJ, was once a Weston student mentored by me, Josef Fuchs's last student. In 1991, I succeeded SME and assumed the very teaching position held by John Ford at Weston.

Contradictions and ironies are very much a part of John Ford. On the one hand, he was the most important American Catholic moral theologian to oppose the obliteration bombing of the Allies during World War II, to insist on understanding alcoholism more as a medical condition than a moral one, and to defend Catholics who believed in selective conscientious objection. On the other hand, he practically single-handedly constrained Pope Paul VI from changing Church teaching on birth control, routinely acted as censor of the "new moral theology," and opposed any real ecumenical venture in theological education. Eventually someone would have to grapple with this legacy.

Five years ago Georgetown University Press published Mark Graham's splendid account of *Josef Fuchs on Natural Law* in its Moral Traditions series. With this work, the study of that enormous period of debate and development in the life of the Church becomes certainly more complete and inclusive. It also becomes more reconciled, because Eric Genilo, a Filipino Jesuit, offers a deeply favorable treatment of John Ford. The fact that a Filipino, who very much loves the local context of his own nation replete with its distinctive casuistry, sympathetically captures the intransigent defender of universals should not be missed.

Ford might look at Weston Jesuit School of Theology today and see exactly what he feared: a mix of clerical and lay students trying to read ecumenically the signs of the times. He may also find in theological ethics today what he feared would happen, that inevitably followers of "the new morality" of Fuchs and others would see a need to find moral truth not only in the universal but also in the personal and the local.

Still with Genilo's work we can see that Ford very much belongs to the tradition, as alive and as diverse as tradition is. Though Ford labored to keep the tradition from becoming what it became, he has today his rightful place in it. With this book his legacy may finally enter more comprehensively into mainline theology. Perhaps in this, a certain reconciliation occurs not only between Ford and Weston but also on a larger scale between those who followed Ford and those who followed Fuchs. And in this, today's moral tradition offers us much hope.

—James F. Keenan, SJ

PREFACE

John Cuthbert Ford, SJ, was a major figure in the history of moral theology in the United States from the early 1940s up to the late 1960s. Contemporary references to Ford's work, however, have been limited to his writings on obliteration bombing, contraception, and alcoholism. The absence of any comprehensive examination of his contribution to moral theology provides the rationale for this study of Ford's writings and method as a moral theologian.

The main documentary resource used for this study is Ford's collection of personal papers. After his death in 1989, Ford's papers were entered into the Archives of the New England Province of the Society of Jesus, located at Campion Center (formerly Weston College, in the town of Weston, Massachusetts) where Ford lived and taught for many years. In 1997, the New England Province Archives were relocated to Holy Cross College in Worcester, Massachusetts. Ford's papers were processed in 2000; they comprised sixty-two boxes of indexed folders containing materials related to Ford's work in moral theology. Along with published materials, the collection includes handwritten notes, correspondence, clippings, pamphlets, personal photographs, and original poems and musical compositions by Ford. Some of the more notable items in the collection include Ford's correspondence with colleagues, his handwritten notes during his private meetings with Paul VI and his Roman diary, a detailed journal of his behind-the-scenes interventions during the discussions on marriage and contraception during the sessions of Vatican II.

The point of departure of this study is the insight that Ford had two modes in his method of moral theology: a standard mode and a crisis mode. Ford and his two modes can be situated in the context of the manualist tradition as it was practiced in the last three decades before Vatican II and as it was challenged by the renewal of moral theology shortly after the Council. Focusing on three themes, this study compares Ford with a figure against whom Ford described himself: John Noonan on the development of doctrine in history, Josef Fuchs on moral objectivity, and Oliver Wendell Holmes Jr. on morality and law.

The study begins with a brief description of the life and career of Ford, highlighting his significant contributions in moral theology. The main body is divided into three major parts. Part I presents aspects of manualism and their influence on Ford's practice of moral theology. Ford's two modes of doing moral theology are illustrated by moral cases resolved through probabilism in the standard mode and the case of contraception in the crisis mode. Ford's approach to doctrinal development is contrasted with the approach of the historian John Noonan.

Part II examines Ford's approach to moral objectivity. While Ford defended objective moral norms in response to situational ethics, his defense was counterbalanced by his consideration of diminished subjective culpability of penitents. Ford's approach to moral objectivity contrasts with that of his contemporary Josef Fuchs.

Part III explores Ford's approach toward morality and law and in particular his use of moral theology to defend vulnerable persons. Ford's critique of Oliver Wendell Holmes's legal philosophy was typical of his concern about the separation of law from morality and the danger of totalitarianism. A number of moral cases illustrate Ford's pastoral efforts to protect a range of threatened individuals or groups in society.

This study concludes with an evaluation of Ford's legacy as a moral theologian. A time line of Ford's life and career provides a chronology of his participation in various moral debates.

ACKNOWLEDGMENTS

To those who have contributed to the completion of this book I offer my heartfelt thanks.

I would like to thank Fr. Paul Nelligan, the archivist of the New England Jesuit Province during the time of my research. I also thank Heidi Marshall for her help in photocopying and cataloging my research and Alice Howe for her assistance in facilitating permission for publication.

A number of Jesuits have provided valuable personal information about John Ford through interviews and emails. I wish to thank Bro. Edward Babinski, Frs. Robert Manning, Paul Lucey, Maurice Walsh, John Broderick, and Charles Currie.

I thank Richard Brown, director of Georgetown University Press, and the Press staff for their assistance and support.

Most of all, I wish to thank my director, editor, and friend Fr. Jim Keenan. He introduced me to the writings of John Ford and encouraged my interest in Ford's manualist method. Without his inspiration, guidance, personal care, and humor I probably would not have persevered long enough to finish. He believed in my work, sometimes even more than I did. Jim, I am truly, truly grateful.

CHAPTER ONE

THE LIFE AND CAREER OF JOHN C. FORD, SJ

John Cuthbert Ford was born on December 20, 1902, in Boston, Massachusetts. He graduated from Boston College High School and, at the age of seventeen, entered the Maryland–New York Province of the Society of Jesus. He was ordained to the priesthood in 1932.[1] He received his doctorate in moral theology in 1937 from the Pontifical Gregorian University in Rome and began teaching moral theology at Weston College, the Jesuit house of formation in Weston, Massachusetts. While at Weston, he also earned a degree in civil law from Boston College Law School. He taught at the Gregorian University in Rome (1945–47), at the Catholic University of America in Washington, DC (1958–66), and at West Baden College in Indiana and St. Mary's College in Kansas.[2]

A prolific writer and popular public speaker, Ford combined an extensive knowledge of moral principles with a creative pastoral sense. He made his expertise accessible to the general public; his personal papers give evidence of numerous inquiries from both clergy and laity who sought his advice on a variety of moral topics such as medical and sexual ethics, war, religious governance, psychology, and addictions.

With Gerald Kelly, SJ, Ford coauthored a widely used two-volume work, *Contemporary Moral Theology Vol. I: Questions in Fundamental Moral Theology* and *Contemporary Moral Theology Vol. II: Marriage Questions*.[3] Ford and Kelly also invented the genre of "Notes of Moral Theology" currently used in the journal *Theological Studies*.[4] For six years Ford wrote the journal's "Notes" where he reviewed and critiqued current literature on moral theology.[5]

Ford is recognized for his significant contribution to the Church's teaching on three moral issues: obliteration bombing, alcoholism, and contraception. On the issue of obliteration bombing, Ford is widely praised for writing "The Morality of Obliteration Bombing" in the September 1944 issue of *Theological Studies*.[6] This article is considered one of the best moral critiques during World War II of a particular strategy of waging war against Germany and is cited as the most influential article in the journal's history.[7] Translated into various languages, the article is still used by the US Army in its international training center in Europe.[8] Ford's article is considered one of the inspirations for the Vatican II statement condemning attacks against civilians as a crime against humanity.[9]

On the issue of alcoholism, Ford campaigned for alcohol education for both clergy and laity and introduced a pastoral approach aimed at assisting alcoholics both in the confessional and in counseling situations. His approach to alcoholism combines rigorous moral theology and attentive listening to the stories and experiences of alcoholics, leading to the development of a nuanced understanding of the freedom and responsibility of persons addicted to alcohol and other drugs.[10]

Ford also contributed significantly to the development and promotion of Alcoholics Anonymous (AA). His first-hand experience of recovery from alcoholism through the help of AA led him to attend the Yale Summer School of Alcohol Studies, where he eventually became a regular summer lecturer and where he came into contact with the pioneers of the AA movement.[11] Through the invitation of Bill Wilson, cofounder of AA, Ford helped edit two books, *Twelve Steps and Twelve Traditions* and *Alcoholics Anonymous Comes of Age*[12] in order to present AA to Catholics in a manner that avoided any theological disputes.[13] Ford's pastoral approach became the basis for many church-based alcohol treatment and prevention programs.[14]

Ford's contributions to moral theology are overshadowed by his involvement in the Papal Commission on Population, Family, and Birth Rate during the 1960s. This commission, commonly referred to as the papal birth control commission, was given the task of studying the issues of population in order to advise the pope on the state of the teaching of the Church on birth control. Even before Ford was appointed to the commission, he had been vocal in his objection to any change in the magisterium's teaching on contraception. In this context, Daniel Callahan compares Ford (and his coauthor Gerald Kelly) to "civil servants" in his review of their book *Marriage Questions* in *Commonweal*.[15] During the commission deliberations, Ford was one of the most unyielding defenders of the traditional teaching on birth control; he also helped draft the commission's *Minority Report*.[16]

Ford's identification with the conservative group in the papal birth control commission affected his reception as a moral theologian by new generations of Jesuit seminarians at Weston College. Although Ford's expertise and competence were still held in high esteem by his colleagues and peers, younger Jesuits were less receptive to his style of moral theology.[17] When the decision was made in 1968 to transfer Weston College to Cambridge, Massachusetts, Ford asked to resign as an active member of the faculty.[18] In a letter to his provincial superior, Ford explained that it was too late for him to change his fundamental ways of thinking, and he was convinced that his usefulness as a teacher of moral theology was at an end.[19] After his retirement from teaching, Ford remained active in the field of alcoholism studies and maintained his pastoral ministry counseling alcoholics. He also continued providing moral advice to individuals and institutions through correspondences and consultative work.

In 1956 Ford received the Cardinal Spellman Award for outstanding contribution to sacred theology from the Catholic Theological Society of America.[20] In 1988 he received the Cardinal O'Boyle Award for the Defense of the Faith from the Fellowship of Catholic Scholars.[21]

John Ford died on January 14, 1989, at the age of 86.

Notes

1. In 1926, John Ford became a member of the New England Province of the Society of Jesus, which was established as a separate province from the Maryland–New York Province.
2. Biographical information on John Ford was provided by the Province Archives of the New England Province of the Society of Jesus. Additional information was supplied by Ed Babinski, SJ, of the New England Jesuit Province Office.
3. Ford and Kelly, *Contemporary Moral Theology*, Vol. I (1958); *Contemporary Moral Theology*, Vol. II. (1963)
4. Fahey, "Farewell" (2005), 737.
5. Ford, "Current Moral Theology" (1941); Ford, "Patriotic Obedience" (1942); Ford, "Notes on Moral Theology" (1943); Ford, "Notes on Moral Theology" (1944), Ford, "Current Theology" (1945); Ford and Kelly, "Notes on Moral Theology, 1953" (1954).
6. Ford, "Morality of Obliteration Bombing" (1944), 261–309.
7. Langan, "Catholic Moral Rationalism" (1989), 34.
8. Fahey, "Farewell" (2005), 736.
9. *Gaudium et spes*, 80.

10. Morgan, "'Chemical Comforting'" (1999), 50.

11. Ibid., 34–35.

12. Wilson, *Twelve Steps and Twelve Traditions* (1953); *Alcoholics Anonymous Comes of Age* (1957).

13. B., *Recovery Today* (1999).

14. Morgan, "'Chemical Comforting'" (1999), 53.

15. Callahan, "Authority and the Theologian" (1964), 321.

16. McClory, *Turning Point* (1995), 110.

17. Interview with Maurice Walsh, SJ, Campion Center (formerly Weston College) at Weston, MA, April 29, 2003.

18. Weston College became the Weston Jesuit School of Theology when it transferred to Cambridge, Massachusetts in 1969.

19. Ford, Letter to Guindon (1969).

20. Catholic Theological Society of America, *Recipients of the Cardinal Spellman Award* (2006).

21. Grisez, "Presentation of the Cardinal O'Boyle Award to John C. Ford" (1988), 14.

PART I

METHOD

I think one of the things I would be thankful for was that I started moral theology at a time when we had to teach from the manuals. I got to know the manuals very thoroughly. I read six or seven manuals for every single presentation of every single subject. I got to know the tradition as it was presented in those manuals very thoroughly. I am grateful for that because it exposed me to a point of view which I think had an awful lot of good balance to it. The major defects of the manuals include the fact that they are heavily concerned about sinfulness and the degree of sinfulness. They are confession-oriented. This slanted the whole moral view. There wasn't the grand view of the moral life that you hoped to find in moral theology. Granted all these limitations, I think there is a great deal of wisdom in the way the manuals went about their casuistry and their qualification of moral obligation. They were very careful.

Richard McCormick in
Odozor, *Richard McCormick*

 JOHN FORD'S MORAL THEOLOGY AND THE MANUALIST TRADITION

Richard McCormick described the manualist moral theology of the 1940s and 1950s as "all too often one-sidedly confession-oriented, magisterium-dominated, canon law-related, sin-centered, and seminary controlled." Nevertheless, he qualified these comments, characterizing the moral theology of the manuals as also "very pastoral and prudent, critically respectful, realistic, compassionate, open and charitable, and well-informed."[1]

McCormick gave particular praise to John Ford and Gerald Kelly as "the two dominant American moral theologians of the '40s and '50s." He notes that they "had such towering and well-deserved reputations that most of us regarded their agreement on a practical matter as constituting a 'solidly probable opinion.' It is easy to understand why their experience, wisdom, and prudence were treasured by everyone from bishops, college presidents, moral theologians, physicians, priests, and students to penitents and counselors."[2]

John Ford's method in moral theology expressed strong elements of the manualist tradition, combining these with casuistry, ascetic theology, and a guarded approach to ecumenism. The manualist tradition and its expression in Ford's own method is explored first. The role of confession in the manuals, their preoccupation with sin, and their use of the virtues all influenced Ford. Ford's casuistic method went beyond the manuals, however, as did his self-understanding as an interpreter of the magisterium. The chapter concludes with an analysis of Ford approaches to ascetics and ecumenics.

Context: The Significance of the Sacrament of Confession

The most influential factor in the evolution of the practice and the discipline of moral theology was the development of the sacrament of confession, according to moral theologian John Mahoney.[3] In the thirteenth century, the Fourth Lateran Council obliged church members to go to confession at least once a year. Lay ignorance about this sacrament, combined with a lack of competent confessors, resulted in infrequent reception of the sacrament of confession. In the sixteenth century, the Council of Trent attempted to address this problem by reaffirming the requirement of yearly confession and instituting the seminary system for the formation of priests. Moral theology as a distinct discipline was introduced in seminaries to train competent confessors. At the beginning of the seventeenth century, the first manuals appeared. Simultaneously seminary textbooks and practical guides for pastors in the administration of the sacrament of penance, such manuals were in use until Vatican II.

Confession and the Formation of Conscience

In *Questions in Fundamental Moral Theology*, Ford and Kelly remind their readers that Pius XII, in his encyclical *Mystici Corporis*, had insisted that the formation of the Christian conscience is "an apostolate of the confessional."[4] In his own teaching and pastoral ministry, Ford considered the confessional as a privileged place for the formation of a penitent's conscience. For example, in the case of alcoholic penitents, Ford urged confessors to gradually form the consciences of the penitents to recognize and acknowledge their addiction to alcohol. He offered, too, concrete prudential guidance to the confessor:

> But if you have a case of a priest who confesses drunkenness, I think a good question might be, "Is this getting to be a problem of some kind, Father?" And I think a good confessor ought not let these things slip by. He ought to ask a question of that kind, when he suspects a problem—even if it is only partial drunkenness that is confessed.
>
> I think it is a mistake tactically to tell a priest then and there, "You are an alcoholic; you need AA" That just won't work. You can't stuff that

down anybody's throat. Besides, how do you know? But by the right kind of questioning and the brief instructions, you can give him some information about what alcoholic drinking means. For instance, tell him that there are some alcoholics who never get theologically drunk, and many alcoholics who rarely get theologically drunk. Bringing that point home to a priest in confession may wake him up.[5]

Ford emphasized the serious responsibility of the confessor to form the penitent's conscience with great care. He wrote, "When integrity of confession is all that is at stake, if the confessor doubts whether to ask a question or how to ask it, it is better to remain silent. He can study or consult afterwards and be ready for another occasion. It is better to omit material integrity than to risk bringing odium on the sacrament of penance. One's absolution will be valid even if the penitent has not made himself clear."[6] Confessors were to avoid embarrassing penitents when inquiring about sexual matters in the confessional. It was more prudent to sacrifice the integrity of a confession (i.e., that all mortal sins be confessed in kind and number) rather than cause distress to a penitent.

Ford's solicitude toward penitents can also be seen in his pastoral approach toward contraception in 1964, when the birth control commission was still in session and the question of contraception was still under study. Despite his consistent opposition to contraceptive use by married couples, Ford recommended that confessors must not refuse absolution to penitents who chose to continue using contraceptives. Ford was aware that reputable theologians such as Bernard Häring and Louis Janssens had been publicly voicing their opinions in favor of a change in the teaching on contraception.[7] At this period in the birth control controversy, when there was public confusion regarding the certainty of the teaching on birth control, Ford chose to respect the conscience of penitents who chose to follow the opinions of reputable theologians. Writing to a fellow Jesuit, Ford argues that "perhaps we have here a sort of good faith to which we should yield."[8]

A Preoccupation with Sin

The moral theology of the manuals had been criticized for placing most of its emphasis on sin, and giving too little attention to growth in

Christian perfection. The roots of manualism's preoccupation with sin can be traced back to the two councils that shaped confessional practice. The Fourth Lateran Council required confessors to diligently inquire about the circumstances of the sins being confessed. The Council of Trent also urged each penitent to make a thorough disclosure of his or her mortal sins in confession. John Mahoney asserted that this obligation to make an examination of "the nooks and shadows of conscience" had brought about a preoccupation with sin and its different forms.[9]

A crucial matter that needed to be established in confession was whether a particular sinful act was mortal or venial. This task fell to the confessor, guided by the manuals and aided by moral theologians. In 1943, Ford stressed the importance of the distinction between mortal and venial sins: "Heaven and hell are at stake in the decision whether a man's guilt is mortal or not. Fortunately, the decision is in God's hands. But the moralist and confessor cannot shirk the responsibility of making the estimate as well as they can."[10]

The attention given to sin and its distinctions was not meant to emphasize the sinfulness of penitents. On the contrary, the diligent cataloguing of sins by manualists was meant to aid both the confessor and the penitent. The more precise and comprehensive a confessor's knowledge of what constituted mortal and venial sin, the more he would be able to determine the penitent's state of sin and provide appropriate moral advice to form the penitent's conscience.

An example can illustrate Ford's method of drawing distinctions in a moral case. In the May 1941 issue of *Theological Studies*, Ford published his response to a letter sent by a high school principal inquiring about the morality of cheating in examinations. The letter writer asks:

What is the moral guilt of a person who cheats in the following kinds of examinations?

    (a)   A common term examination through which the teacher checks the work done by the student.

    (b)   A competitive examination for a medal, a scholarship.

    (c)   A professional examination to obtain a license to practice law, medicine, etc.

    (d)   An accumulation of deceptions of class (a)

What is the nature of the sin if any? Is it against justice, obedience, etc.?

Ford consulted the current manuals and discovered that the matter had not yet been thoroughly discussed by moralists at that time. He offered his moral opinion on the case:

> (a) To cheat in a common term examination is ordinarily venially sinful, the sin being that of lying. The student who submits work as if it were his own unaided effort, when in reality it is not his own, is lying, not by his words but by his deeds. . . .
>
> (b) . . . In a competitive examination for a medal or scholarship cheating is a sin against justice. The other competitors have a strict right in justice that they should not lose their chance of winning or have their chances diminished by such means. . . .
>
> (c) . . . In the case of an examination to obtain a professional license (e.g., to practice law or medicine), cheating involves the sin of lying, as in any examination. I do not believe it ordinarily involves a sin of disobedience. . . . However, it would be sinful—both against charity and justice—for a person who was not properly qualified for law or medicine to attempt to *practice* those professions. . . .
>
> (d) Finally, you submit the question of an accumulation of deceptions in ordinary class and term examinations. I do not believe that the accumulation of such sins of itself amounts to a grave sin.

In Ford's mind, the most serious matter in the case was the acquisition of two bad habits, namely, the habit of lying and dishonesty in action, and the habit of grafting—that is, trying to get something from nothing. At the end of his letter Ford recommended that school authorities should avoid discussing the problem of cheating with students in a manner that would give the impression that it was a mortal sin.[11]

Moral Minimalism and Mediocrity

The manualist focus on the boundary between mortal and venial sins led to criticisms that the theology of the manuals promoted moral minimalism, that is, the manuals were only concerned with the avoidance of sin and not the pursuit of Christian perfection.

Thomas Slater, who wrote the first English-language moral manual in 1908, warns his readers that the moral manuals were not meant for edification.

Here, however, we must ask the reader to bear in mind that manuals of moral theology are technical works intended to help the confessor and the parish priest in the discharge of their duties. They are as technical as the textbooks of the lawyer and the doctor. They are not intended for edification, nor do they hold up a high ideal of Christian perfection for the imitation of the faithful. They deal with what is of obligation under pain of sin; they are books of moral pathology. They are necessary for the Catholic priest to enable him to administer the sacrament of Penance and fulfill his other duties.[12]

Ford's own seminary students shared the impression that moral minimalism was the predominant theme of manualist moral theology. He wrote, "What is the first thought that comes to the mind of a seminarian when the moral theology course is mentioned? Is it the practice of virtue and the pursuit of Christian perfection? Or is it perhaps, 'Thou shalt not commit adultery'? Is it the preaching of the good news of the Christian way of life? Or is it the sad news that there are sinners, Christians, legions of them, waiting to have their confessions heard, waiting to be absolved from mortal sin?"[13] Ford recommended that seminary professors present moral theology with a more comprehensive approach to the Christian moral life, and avoid concentrating on the minimal requirements of the moral law.

Despite his concern for moral minimalism in the seminary, however, Ford was hesitant to address the tendency toward moral mediocrity among ordinary Christians.

It is a good thing to be impatient with spiritual mediocrity—especially in one's own life. And it is a good thing to be impatient with it in the lives of others, if this impatience is the burning zeal which animated the saints and urged them on to inspire others to spiritual heroism like their own. But it would not be a good thing if it consigned to outer darkness the millions of mediocre men, the millions upon millions of ordinary Christians, who follow Christ, as it were, from afar. No matter what method of teaching or preaching we use, no matter what aspect of Christianity we stress, whether it be the fear of sin, the love of virtue, or the perfect love of God through Christ, it will always remain true that the vast majority of Christians will not be spiritual heroes. To demand of them that they strive for perfection just as the saints have done, insisting on the gravity of this obligation, and even denying the state of grace to those who fail so to strive, would be a type of rigorism not unknown in the history of the Church and lethal in its effects.[14]

Ford's defense of the "mediocre Christian" may have been intended to avoid rigorist perfectionism in moral theology, but it may have also encouraged a morality that was satisfied with minimal observance of the objective norms of morality.

The Use of Virtues

Thomas Aquinas defined habits as dispositions directing a person to act in a certain way, either good or evil. The most important virtues in Christian life are the theological virtues of faith, hope, and charity. These virtues are not acquired by human effort but are infused by God into a person. Through these infused virtues, the human faculties of intellect and will are perfected. The four cardinal virtues of prudence, justice, temperance, and fortitude are called acquired virtues. These virtues are attained by constant practice and are perfected by the presence of the theological virtues.

The infused virtues can be lost by mortal sin, while the acquired virtues are weakened but not lost in the presence of mortal sin because they can be maintained by habitual practice. The cardinal virtues observe the prudent middle course or mean, avoiding the extremes of excess or deficiency that make a particular moral act imperfect or tend toward evil. The Christian life is a life of growth toward human flourishing, perfection, and closer union with God through the virtues.[15]

Although the virtues were present in the manuals, they were regarded more as a remedy for vices rather than as a means to perfection. Ford treated virtues as means to counter vices, but he also gave importance to the virtues as an important spiritual aid for persons striving to avoid the harmful effects of addictive substances and maintain a balanced Christian life.

For example, he wrote frequently on the virtue of sobriety as a response to the problem of alcoholism. Following Aquinas' definition of the virtue of sobriety as the special virtue for the regulation of the appetite for strong drink, Ford advised those who were prone to abusing alcohol to apply the virtue of sobriety in their lives similar to the way the virtue of chastity should be applied. Both sobriety and chastity can be lived out in two ways: total abstinence or moderate use, depending on the state of a person. For a nonalcoholic, moderate use would be a proper mean for living out sobriety, while for an alcoholic total abstinence would be the only reasonable option, to prevent falling into the spiral of alcoholism's negative effects.[16]

On another occasion, in his article "Chemical Comfort and Christian Virtue," he addressed the human need for "chemical comforting" and the danger of falling into chemical addiction. He recognized the widespread use of chemicals in everyday life to kill pain, relieve tension, escape fatigue, restore energy, and so on. Noting the increasing use of substances such as caffeine, nicotine, aspirin, barbiturates, and tranquilizers, he asks the question, "What is the virtue which regulates the use of these drugs and chemicals, and the pleasures and comforts they provide?" He proposes a new virtue: "In the medical dictionary I found the word *pharmacophobia* to describe a morbid fear of drugs and chemicals. And I found the word *pharmacophilia* for a morbid love for drugs and chemicals. But I found no word to describe the *medium virtutis* in this matter. If we must have a good name, resounding and technical, for the virtuous, temperate attitude towards chemical comfort, the proper title and *mot juste* is obviously: *pharmacosophrosyne*. It means moderation and reasonableness where drugs are concerned. It means good sense about drugs, or drug-sense."[17]

Though one can see the possibility of chemical comforters being abused, Ford avoided making a list of prohibitions to accompany his newly coined virtue. Respecting the capacity of human reason and trusting in God's grace, he left to every individual the responsibility to find the virtuous mean in the use of chemical comforters.

How does one find the *medium virtutis* in the use of these chemical comforters which provide minor satisfactions for minor human needs? The answer is an appeal to good sense, common sense, drug-sense, the sweet reasonableness of Christian virtue. This is a highly personalized exercise of judgment. A man must use his own reason to settle his own case. He must study the scientific facts, look around him, compare and evaluate, select and reject, in this matter as in any other if he wants to find the permissible course, the wiser course, the more perfect course for himself.

No one can do it for him. He cannot even do it for himself without the enlightenment of God's grace.[18]

Method: Casuistry, Rhetorical Pleas, and Practical Wisdom

John Ford's method of moral argumentation was characterized by a creative use of casuistry, rhetorical pleas, and cumulative arguments.

High and Low Casuistry

Casuistry has two forms, high casuistry and low casuistry. High casuistry, which flourished from 1556 to 1656, is an inductive method of moral reasoning applied to new moral cases that could not be resolved by currently held moral principles and precepts. This form of casuistry compares a new moral case with other cases that have already been resolved with certainty. This method of comparing cases, called taxonomy, brings to light important similarities and differences that can be relevant to the solution of the new case. The resolved cases against which new cases are compared are called paradigm cases. The new cases that are compared with paradigm cases are called hard cases.[19]

Through time and frequent usage, paradigm cases eventually were distilled into abstract moral principles. With these principles at hand, moralists shifted from inductively comparing new cases with paradigm cases to deductively applying abstract moral principles to new cases. This principle-based method of case resolution is called low casuistry and it was the method of casuistry often used in the manuals. In certain cases, however, manualists combined both methods of casuistry.[20]

As a manualist, Ford would usually turn to moral principles in resolving a moral case. At times, Ford would use high casuistry to supplement and strengthen his principle-based arguments if the seriousness of the case necessitated a multiplicity of arguments. An example of Ford's use of both methods of casuistry was his treatment of the possibility of hydrogen bombing of cities.[21] When the hydrogen bomb was developed after World War II, Ford anticipated the possible military use of the hydrogen bomb similar to the use of the atomic bomb in Hiroshima and Nagasaki. Using manualist casuistry, he analyzed the case by applying the principle of double effect, and the just war principles of noncombatant immunity and proportionality. The principle of double effect prohibited an actor to directly intend the evil effect of an action that simultaneously had good and evil effects. Using this principle, Ford argued that military leaders cannot use a hydrogen bomb on a military target within a densely populated area and deny any direct intention of causing harm to the civilians. Citing the Allied bombing of Rome in World War II when precision bombing was used to ensure hitting only military targets and avoiding damage to monuments, Ford argued that if it was possible to conduct precision bombing to save monuments, military leaders should also choose a less destructive and less indiscriminate weapon than a hydrogen bomb if they truly do not intend the death of civilians. The use of a hydrogen bomb on a military target located in a city directly intends the deaths of innocent citizens and violates not only the principle of double effect but also the just war principle of noncombatant immunity. It also violated the just war principle of proportionality, both because of the great disproportion between the intended destruction of the military target and the widespread devastation and death it would cause and because of the all-out war it might precipitate. Using principle-based manualist casuistry, Ford declared the hydrogen bombing of city targets to be gravely immoral.

To strengthen his principle-based argument, Ford also used high casuistry by comparing the case of hydrogen bombing of cities with two paradigm cases. The first case was the use of a hydrogen bomb on an enemy fleet in the high seas. In this paradigm case, the principle of double effect was applicable. It was possible to have direct intention to destroy the enemy with a hydrogen bomb and having the foreseen but unintended death of civilians onboard the ships in the fleet. The destruction was limited to the military target. Comparing the two cases, he judged that the harm caused by bombing a military target in a city was disproportionate and unjustified compared to bombing an enemy fleet at sea.

The second case was the use of a sledgehammer to kill a spider on a neighbor's head. For Ford, the use of the hydrogen bomb on a city was similar to this case. The case highlighted the absurdity of hydrogen bombing a city—how could one say that one intended only the death of the spider, considering the injury or death of the neighbor as merely incidental? One could kill a spider without harming the neighbor just as one could hit a military target in a city while minimizing civilian deaths. The grave and unjustified harm inflicted on the neighbor by killing the spider with a sledgehammer was comparable to the unwarranted destruction caused by the hydrogen bombing of a military target in a city.

Rhetorical Pleas

Ford also used rhetorical pleas to support his casuistic arguments. Just as a good physician would seek to persuade his fellow physicians of the appropriateness of his diagnosis by identifying the points of similarity and dissimilarity of his medical case with other known cases, a casuist would seek to persuade his peers of the validity of his conclusions by pointing out the similarities and dissimilarities presented in his taxonomy of cases.[22]

Ford's article on obliteration bombing during World War II is a good example of his use of rhetorical pleas to persuade an audience. In that article, Ford addressed fellow Americans about the immorality of the obliteration bombing then being conducted by Allied planes on German cities. This type of bombing involved the systematic destruction of a city section by section through aerial bombing. Sometimes called "carpet bombing" or "area bombing," this military tactic was indiscriminate in its destruction because not only military targets were destroyed but also residences, schools, hospitals, and other civilian structures.

To drive home the point that this form of bombing gravely violated the principle of noncombatant immunity, Ford wrote up a list of 109 different classes of persons who lived and worked in the targeted cities. The list was exhaustive and inclusive, both in order to give a human face to the German civilians who were threatened with obliteration bombing and to evoke a sense of empathy for the victims and a strong reaction against the bombings. The full quote is presented below to preserve the rhetorical effect that Ford wished to convey.

> Read the list. If you can believe that these classes of persons deserve to be described as combatants, or deserve to be treated as legitimate objects of violent repression, then I shall not argue further. If, when their governments declare war, these persons are so guilty that they deserve death, or almost any violence to person and property short of death, then let us

forget the law of Christian charity, natural law, and go back to barbarism, admitting that total war has won out and we must submit to it. The list:

Farmers, fishermen, foresters, lumberjacks, dressmakers, milliners, bakers, printers, textile workers, millers, painters, paper hangers, piano tuners, plasterers, shoemakers, cobblers, tailors, upholsterers, furniture makers, cigar and cigarette makers, glove makers, hat makers, suit makers, food processors, dairymen, fish canners, fruits and vegetable canners, slaughterers and packers, sugar refiners, liquor and beverage workers, teamsters, garage help, telephone girls, advertising men, bankers, brokers, clerks in stores, commercial travelers, decorators, window dressers, deliverymen, inspectors, insurance agents, retail dealers, salesmen and saleswomen in all trades, undertakers, wholesale dealers, meatcutters, butchers, actors, architects, sculptors, artists, authors, editors, reporters, priests, lay brothers, nuns, seminarians, professors, school teachers, dentists, lawyers, judges, musicians, photographers, physicians, surgeons, trained nurses, librarians, social and welfare workers, Red Cross workers, religious workers, theatre owners, technicians, laboratory assistants, barbers, bootblacks, charwomen, cleaners and dyers, hotel men, elevator tenders, housekeepers, janitors, sextons, domestic servants, cooks, maids, nurses, handymen, laundry operatives, porters, victuallers, bookkeepers, accountants, statisticians, cashiers, stenographers, secretaries, typists, all office help, mothers of families, patients in hospitals, prison inmates, prison guards, institutional inmates, old men and women, all children with the use of reason, i.e., from seven years up. (After all, these latter buy war stamps, write letters of encouragement to their brothers in the service, and even carry the dinner pail to the father who works in the aircraft factory. They all co-operate in some degree in the aggression).[23]

Another example of Ford's rhetorical pleas to reinforce a moral argument is a portion of his defense of the teaching on contraception during the fifth and final session of the papal birth control commission on June 20, 1966. Speaking before cardinals and bishops, Ford explained why the Church had always taught that human intrusion into the act of conception was a violation of natural law. Making dramatic reference to Michelangelo's *Creation of Man* on the ceiling of the Sistine Chapel, Ford argued his case:

God stretching out his finger to touch the finger of Adam and transmit new life to him. This is the moment we are talking about—the *fieri* of a new life. This is the moment of conception. Contraception (that is contraception) involves a will which is turned against new life at this moment. It is against this life, in advance, that is, against its coming-to-be, its *fieri*. Your conception is your very origin, your link to the community of living persons before you. The first of all gifts received from your parents, your first relationship with God as he stretched out his finger to touch you.

In my opinion, there are different ways of expressing the underlying substantial truth: like life itself, the inception of life belongs to God. To attack it is to attack a fundamental human good, to intrude in God's domain.[24]

Cumulative Arguments

Although Ford was a manualist moral theologian, his method of presenting his arguments was occasionally similar to the high casuists of the sixteenth and seventeenth centuries. Rather than rely solely on the deductive method of low casuistry, he utilized a diverse array of arguments to support a particular moral position. The words used by Jonsen and Toulmin to describe the kind of cumulative argumentation of the high casuists can also apply to Ford's method of presenting arguments: "Casuistical argument resembles the rhetorical and commonsense discourse that piles up many kinds of argument in hopes of showing the favored position in a good light. The 'weight' of a casuistical opinion came from the accumulation of reasons rather than from the logical validity or the arguments of the coherence of any single 'proof.'"[25]

A good example of this is found in his treatment of the case of the scarred uterus or "hysterectomy with repeated cesarean section." The case is also historically noteworthy because his conclusions allowed Catholic health care facilities to assist women with this medical condition. In this case, Ford used the principle of double effect as well as a taxonomy of medical cases to argue his position. He also utilized rhetorical pleas, papal teaching, and appeals to common sense to persuade his audience about the rightness of his position.

The case of the scarred uterus is described as follows:

A woman is now pregnant for the fourth (or fifth, sixth, or seventh, etc.) time. All her previous deliveries were by cesarean section, and her obstetrician now believes that when he does the next section he will find the uterus so much weakened that he cannot repair it adequately. In a word, his fear is that the uterus will be in such a condition that, even after repair, it will very likely rupture in a further pregnancy. The question proposed by the obstetrician and the mother is this: should this fear prove to be well-founded when the next section is performed, may the irreparably damaged uterus be removed as a seriously pathological organ?[26]

The debate among moralists over this case revolved around whether the removal of such a weakened or scarred uterus constituted a direct or indirect sterilization. Those who claimed it was a direct sterilization argued that the primary intention of the operation was to prevent a future pregnancy.

Ford admitted a development in his own thinking regarding the case. In his "Notes on Moral Theology" in 1942, Ford evaluates the case and concludes that the removal of a weakened uterus was an illicit direct sterilization. His argument was based on a consideration of the intention of the act.

> To the present writer it seems that such an operation is an illicit contraception procedure. The objection may be offered that we should decide the objective morality of the operation independently of the woman's intention (to prevent future conception), for that is a subjective element. The answer is that the intention which governs a human act is part of the objective morality of the act. The adequate moral object is made up of the proximate object, circumstances, and intention. It is impossible to judge the complete objective morality of a given act independently of the intention of the agent. The decree of a year ago against *direct* sterilization certainly must include any sterilization the *purpose* of which is to prevent future conceptions, even if this is intended only as a means to the health of the whole body.[27]

By 1944, however, new scientific data had convinced Ford to change his position. A study by the physician Cornelius O'Connor showed that mothers who undergo an operation to remove their weakened uterus immediately after a cesarean operation had a 1 percent mortality rate compared to 2 percent mortality rate for mothers who, after a cesarean operation, did not have their weakened uterus removed. This meant that the danger of death doubled for a woman retaining a weakened uterus after a caesarian operation because of a future pregnancy that could rupture the uterus. This 1 percent difference in mortality was sufficient reason to justify the removal of the weakened uterus:

> Theologians recognize that a 1% danger of death is a very real danger and teach that persons who are undergoing an operation involving that amount of danger, or even less, are to be given the sacraments as persons who are truly in danger of death. Such persons are entitled to all the privileges which canon law allows in *periculo mortis*. Now, it seems to me that a danger of death twice as great as that is objectively a very important and serious matter, constituting a sufficient reason for permitting sterilization.[28]

In a letter to the editor of the *American Journal of Obstetrics and Gynecology*, Ford gave tentative approval to cesarean hysterectomy on the condition that the object of the operation was to safeguard the patient's health here and now and not to prevent future dangerous conceptions.[29] In another correspondence, Ford admitted "I formerly believed that the damaged uterus case could not be defended, but after careful thought for many years I am now convinced that it is a solidly probable application of the principle of double effect."[30]

The key to Ford's change in position was his recognition that the weakened uterus was already in a pathological condition. Using the principle of double effect to justify his new position, Ford argued that it was licit to intend the good effect of preserving the health of the patient by removing a presently pathological uterus while at the same time not directly intending the resulting sterilization. To prove this point, Ford used a technique called "supposition."

> The supposition here would be that a woman has a double uterus (a condition that occasionally exists), one damaged, and one healthy. Granted the supposition, the removal of the damaged uterus would eliminate the source of danger without at the same time inducing sterility. This indicates very strongly that the damaged uterus is a separate cause of danger and that it may be made the precise object of surgical intervention even in the normal case without at the same time any direct intent of sterilization.[31]

Using this hypothetical case or supposition, Ford was able to separate the pathological condition of the weakened uterus from the sterilizing effect of its removal. The good effect intended is the prevention of the rupture of a damaged uterus, not the prevention of conception. The removal of the weakened uterus, with its sterilizing effect, was no different from other cases of legitimate use of the principle of double effect in which the evil effect produced was foreseen but unintended.[32]

Ford also used taxonomy to contrast the case with paradigm cases. A paradigm case of direct sterilization is the case of cutting a woman's fallopian tubes to prevent a dangerous pregnancy due to her condition of cardio-renal disease. Sterilization was directly intended in this paradigm case because the fallopian tubes were healthy and were only being cut for the purpose of avoiding pregnancy. A paradigm case of indirect sterilization is the case of a cancerous uterus. Sterilization in this case was indirect because the reproductive organ had a pathological condition that presented a danger to life independent of any pregnancy. The scarred uterus case is different from both paradigm cases. Unlike the first case, where the healthy fallopian tubes are cut, the case of the scarred uterus is considered already to have a pathological condition. Unlike the second case, where the cancerous uterus is dangerous apart from any pregnancy, the scarred uterus, although weakened, presents no imminent danger to the life of the mother except in the case of a future pregnancy. While she is not pregnant, her uterus would be unlikely to rupture.[33]

Ford acknowledged that the application of the principle of double effect was "notoriously slippery and open to dispute" in complicated cases such as the scarred uterus case. However, he believed that there was less danger of abusing such a principle if its results coincided with common sense. Ford raised an important pastoral question: "Is it in accord with common sense to tell a woman who has had many cesareans: 'You have worn out this uterus in the service of motherhood. Nevertheless you must keep it; and if you wish to protect yourself against the danger inherent in using it, you must abstain from marital intercourse.'?"[34] This question addressed the objection of some moralists that a present danger to the patient was needed to justify a mutilation of an organ, such as the scarred uterus. In response, Ford cited Pius XII who allowed mutilations "to avoid or, naturally, to repair serious and lasting damage which cannot otherwise be avoided or repaired." He noted that moralists have regularly allowed mutilations when serious medical conditions cannot be avoided or repaired by other means, and that papal documents have not prohibited such an interpretation of the principle of totality.[35]

In Ford's view, the weakened uterus presented an existing danger in the normal circumstances of married life. He defined danger as consisting "in a set of circumstances from which one can foresee with certainty or probability a future impending evil." Taking into consideration the married life of a woman with such a damaged uterus, Ford concluded that such a woman was in danger of conceiving again. Ford rendered this judgment: "To say that she can avoid this danger by imposing perpetual abstinence on herself and her husband is to require a degree of heroism to which our moral principles do not oblige her."[36]

The wide array of arguments that Ford used in the scarred uterus case established a solidly probable opinion for moral theologians, pastors, physicians, and patients. He used manualist casuistry through the principle of double effect and through the interpretation of papal teaching. He applied high casuistry through the use of taxonomy, supposition, rhetoric, and common sense.

The masterful use of argumentation by Ford on the scarred uterus case, using the best of the Catholic moral tradition, makes more ironic the 1993 statement of the Congregation on the Doctrine of the Faith (CDF) regarding the case of "uterine isolation." The CDF made a distinction between the case of a damaged uterus, which posed an immediate threat to the life of a mother after a delivery, and a weakened uterus that did not present an immediate danger to the life of a mother but was foreseen to be incapable of carrying a future pregnancy without danger to the mother. The CDF allowed the removal of the uterus in the former case but did not in the latter case. The CDF argued that the removal of the weak uterus in the latter case did not have a properly therapeutic character but was aimed at preventing future pregnancies and was therefore a direct sterilization. Such a procedure is therefore no longer practiced in Catholic hospitals.[37] The CDF made a distinction between present and future danger to the mother, and only allowed removal of a pathological uterus that endangered the patient in the present.

The difference between the moral judgment produced by the deductive logic of the CDF document on uterine isolation and the solidly probable opinion formed by the cumulative arguments used by Ford on the scarred uterus case indicates how the methods of high casuistry can

significantly shape pastoral solutions to moral problems. Ford's use of a
great diversity of arguments in his treatment of cases reveals that he was
not an ordinary manualist limited by the deductive method, but rather
a skilled casuist who could shift and combine methods to construct a
solid wall of argumentation.

The Magisterium and Moral Theologians

In a 1978 issue of *Chicago Studies* devoted to the historical development
of the relationship between the magisterium and theologians, Michael
D. Place states that "the manner in which the Church understands itself
determines the manner in which it perceives the relationship between
the theologian and the magisterium."[38] During the first millennium of
the Church's history, the Church understood itself primarily as a community of believers. Matters of faith and discipline were submitted to
councils and there was great effort made to achieve consensus. During
this time, there was frequent collaboration between bishops and theologians.[39] From the time of the Gregorian Reform in the eleventh century
to Vatican I in the nineteenth century, there was a gradual shift in the
self-understanding of the Church, from a communal model to a more
juridical model. From a self-understanding as a community of believers,
the Church gradually moved toward thinking of itself more as a political
and hierarchical entity.[40]

Beginning with Gregory XVI (1835) the papacy began to speak of the
magisterium, along with Scripture and tradition, as a source of Christian truth. The papacy began to assert the magisterial interpretation of
the faith as the norm for the Church. Matters which were previously
resolved by theologians were now resolved by the pope or by the Holy
Office, the successor to the Inquisition.[41]

John Mahoney writes that no single event was more dramatic in the
making of moral theology than in the solemn definition of papal infallibility in Vatican I.[42] This definition of the pope's infallibility in his
exercise of extraordinary magisterium did not result in a flurry of infallible teachings from the pope. Instead, there was an increase in the use
of the pope's ordinary, noninfallible magisterium through encyclicals,
allocutions, and other interventions in the life of the Church—which
had the effect of making these papal pronouncements infallible by
association.[43]

Joseph Komonchak, in a study of manuals from 1891 to 1963, points out that when the pope uses his ordinary teaching office, he teaches in a manner that does not express a clear intention of making a definitive judgment on a matter. The manuals, however, regard the pope's ordinary teaching office as "authoritative," which meant that the pope had been given authority to teach in such a way that his pronouncements required assent even if the arguments used were not compelling. Unlike other teachers whose teachings were judged by the merit and strength of their arguments, the pope, in his exercise of the ordinary magisterium, required from those he taught the obligation of internal religious assent. The manualists distinguished this internal religious assent from mere external conformity or respectful silence. The person assenting must internally and sincerely affirm that what was taught by the magisterium was true. This assent is "religious" in the sense that it involves an act of faith that recognizes the pope as a teacher given authority by Christ.[44]

John Ford was trained in the manualist tradition to regard the magisterium as the authentic interpreter of the moral law, and to render internal religious assent to ordinary papal teaching. His sense of obedience to the magisterium was reinforced by the teachings of Pius XII, whose papacy began almost at the same time as Ford's teaching career as a moral theologian. The influence of Pius XII is evident in Ford's works. In the first pages of Questions in Fundamental Moral Theology, Ford and Kelly lay down the basis and starting point of their investigation of contemporary moral issues of their time. They began with the premise: "The Church has the authority to teach the laws of God."[45] Quoting Pius XII, these two authors state that the laws of God, found in natural law and revelation, were given to the Church as "the moral treasure of humanity in order that she might preach them to all creatures, explain them, and hand them intact and safeguarded from all contamination and error from one generation to another."[46]

It was during Pius XII's pontificate that the interpretative role of the moral theologian was clearly defined. In his encyclical Humani generis, Pius XII quoted Pius IX regarding the task of the theologian: "it belongs to them to point out how the doctrine of the living Teaching Authority is to be found either explicitly or implicitly in the Scriptures and in Tradition."[47]

To emphasize the interpretative role of theologians, Ford and Kelly note that in the course of the first fifteen years of his papacy Pius XII made one thousand public addresses, allocutions, and radio messages.[48] The authors comment that "even if the Holy See were now to remain silent for ten years, the theologians would have plenty to do in classifying and evaluating the theological significance of Pius XII's public statements."[49]

To fulfill the task of interpretation, the theologian was expected to be familiar with verbal formulations used in papal texts. The theologian must also know the context of a papal text (e.g., on what occasion and to what audience the text was read) and apprehend the papal intention for the pronouncement. If, for example, the pope was trying to settle a controversy or correct an erroneous belief, the words of the texts must be interpreted only in light of the controversy or error being addressed and not generalized to other areas.[50]

Ford's familiarity with the texts, contexts, and intentions of papal teachings enabled him to judge whether or not an authoritative teaching had already been given on a moral issue. Aware of the different levels of authority of papal pronouncements, Ford insisted that in the absence of an authoritative church teaching, "no prelate, preacher, spiritual adviser, or confessor is justified in imposing the stricter view on others."[51] Richard McCormick attests to Ford's careful reading of papal teaching. "Prior to *Humanae Vitae*," McCormick wrote, "both Ford and Kelly challenge moral theologians who claim that Rome prohibits more than Rome does. For instance, at the 1959 convention of the Catholic Theological Society of America, a theologian argues that 'documents of the Holy See have convinced me that "rhythm" cannot be recommended as a Christian solution for overpopulation. In my opinion Rome has spoken and the case is settled.' John Ford responds; 'Rome has not spoken.'"[52]

Although Ford acknowledged that papal pronouncements might at times be vague, obscure, or imprecise, and further refinement and clarification were sometimes necessary, he was very careful not to give the impression that the papacy could ever be in error in its pronouncements. In keeping with the manualist tradition, Ford firmly believed that the Holy Spirit protected the magisterium from grave error. To account for revisions made to the formulation of papal pronouncements, he explained that the words of papal texts might at times fail to express fully the mind of the Holy See. Previous popes did not have the intention to be obscure in their writings; they simply were not able to express themselves adequately. Revisions to papal pronouncements would be necessary at times in order to express more clearly a pope's original intention.

An example to illustrate a refinement of a papal teaching was the case of punitive sterilization. In the 1930 encyclical *Casti connubii*, Pius XI implies that he was condemning punitive sterilizations in general. Ten years later in 1940, the Holy Office, with the approval of Pius XII, condemned direct sterilization without qualification. However, in 1951 and 1953, Pius XII spoke of this condemnation of sterilization but restricted it to the direct sterilization of the innocent. To explain this restriction of a previous general condemnation, Ford proposed that Pius XII had realized that the formula previously used was broader than Pius XI's intention.[53] Ford's explanation presupposed that successive popes were generally consistent in intention, and when a pope made a change in the teaching of a previous pope, he was not correcting an error but rather he was expressing more clearly an original intention.

The magisterium determined the boundaries within which theological investigation must be conducted, and it had the prerogative to withdraw from theological discussion any moral issue that it considered already defined by a papal teaching. Once the pope had decisively settled a moral question, theologians could no longer speculate on the matter. Pius XII insists on this prerogative in *Humani generis*: "But if the Supreme Pontiffs in their official documents purposely pass judgment on a matter up to that time under dispute, it is obvious that that matter, according to the mind and will of the Pontiffs, cannot be any longer considered a question open to discussion among theologians."[54]

The freedom that Ford allowed for theological investigation depended on the state of the Church's teaching on a particular moral issue. If there was no authoritative teaching to guide theologians in resolving a moral case under investigation, Ford encouraged his fellow theologians to formulate and propose probable opinions that would provide laypersons and confessors with moral options on how to proceed with the case at hand. If, however, the moral issue had already been defined by a body of authoritative magisterial teachings, Ford only allowed theological investigations that were aimed at clarifying the application of the current teaching. Any theological discussion directed toward a substantial revision of an authoritative papal teaching was unacceptable. In *Marriage Questions*, Ford and Kelly declare: "authority is the supreme guide of the moral theologian."[55]

Ascetic Theology

In 1879, Leo XIII initiated the revival of Thomistic thought in the Church, particularly in seminary formation. However, there was a difference between Aquinas' original synthetic vision of theology in the thirteenth century, when ethics had not been separated from dogma and spirituality, and the narrower perspective of nineteenth and twentieth century confession-oriented moral theology, which had developed separately from dogmatic and ascetic theology.

By the nineteenth century Aquinas' original unified view of theology had become fragmented into different fields of study in theology. John Gallagher asserts that "when Aquinas' doctrine of law and grace was separated by the neo-Thomist manualists from the doctrine of providence, it became almost inevitable that moral theology would become a legalistic discipline verging toward positivism."[56]

Ford was aware of the criticisms made against manualist moral theology regarding its disconnection from other areas of theology:

> What has become of the revealed sources? What has become of the inspiring moral appeals of the fathers? Where does one find the spiritual food with which to nourish the practical lives of the faithful? In fact, where does one find the spirit of the Sermon on the Mount, the specific charter of Christian morality? Where is it translated in terms of modern life and proposed to the faithful as the dynamic and controlling force in their lives? These are the questions asked by the modern critics of moral theology. They say they look in vain for all this in a modern manual of moral theology—or else when they look they find it with difficulty, because the emphasis is all on casuistry, on legal distinctions, and on the human reasonings of philosophy.[57]

There were practical reasons why Aquinas' treatises were separately taught in the seminary. The subject matter of theology had grown so vast that no single course or professor in the seminary could teach it comprehensively. The division of courses in the seminary enabled the professors and students to study the different aspects of theology in manageable units.[58] This fragmentation of the study of theology had also adversely affected the study of moral theology; Ford believed that it was the moral professor's responsibility "to repair the damage done by fragmentation, to integrate the contents of the course with other parts of theology, with dogma and ascetics, with Holy Scripture, canon law and pastoral, and with ecclesiastical history."[59]

If one were to look for an integration of moral theology with spirituality in the works of John Ford, the best place to find it would be in his writings on alcoholism. Oliver Morgan observes that in the course of forty years, Ford's writings on moral and pastoral responses to the problem of alcoholism show a transition from a legalistic, sin-centered approach to an approach that was grounded in both "a biblical, creation-centered perspective and in Christian ascetical sources that spoke in a more modern idiom of virtue and attention to rightly-ordered and disordered relationships."[60]

Ford introduced a threefold description of alcoholism as a disease: a disease of the body, of the mind, and of the soul. Ford made an important contribution to the pastoral treatment of alcoholism as a disease of the soul. To assist alcoholics who suffer moral and spiritual deterioration because of their condition, he advised confessors to help prepare the alcoholics' souls to receive God's grace. "I don't think that anything but the grace of our Lord Jesus Christ overcomes that kind of blindness, and our role as priests is to bring that grace to the alcoholic. Our role as priests, of course, in general, is to bring the soul back to God, to bring him closer to God. But I think more particularly our role in the case of the alcoholic is to help to penetrate his blindness with regard to his own problem and his own self."[61]

Following St. Ignatius' "Principle and Foundation" Ford viewed alcohol as a good creature of God; its prudent use would depend, then, on whether it helps or hinders the human journey toward God.[62] Recognizing the debilitating effects of alcoholism on a person's body and mind, Ford invoked the biblical concept of stewardship to support his moral argument against the abuse of alcohol. "Christians do not believe that man is master and owner of his own body and mind, to do with as he pleases. He is a steward, who is obliged by the terms of his stewardship to take care of his own health as the gift of God, to respect the integrity of his physical members as the property of God, and, above all, to preserve intact his own reason, lest he destroy within himself the image of God."[63]

Taking into serious consideration modern society's seemingly limitless and diverse use of chemicals, including alcohol, to provide physical comfort and to avoid various pains, Ford encouraged persons to develop of a spirituality of "right comforting."[64] Nevertheless, he wrote, "the final and highest answer of Christianity to these problems is not the discovery of better and greater pleasures. It is to be found only in the doctrine of the Cross, which is not a doctrine of comfort and self-indulgence but of self-renunciation."[65] He presented the cross of Christ as the answer to society's pursuit of comfort and pleasure.

Ecumenical Cooperation

The moral theology of Ford's time viewed cautiously any cooperation with Protestants. Danger to the integrity of the Catholic faith was to be avoided whenever possible. Ford exercised two modes of dialogue with Protestants. Whenever Ford perceived that a moral or pastoral issue had not yet been defined by an authoritative teaching, and there was a high level of agreement among Catholic and Protestant thinkers on the issue, he easily collaborated with Protestant peers. On the other hand, when Ford perceived that a moral or pastoral issue had already been addressed by an authoritative teaching by the magisterium, and there was a radical difference between Catholic and Protestant positions on the issue, Ford vigorously defended the Catholic position, at times negatively portraying the Protestant position as erroneous or at least misguided.

Ford's most extensive ecumenical collaboration was in the area of alcoholism education and treatment, especially in his involvement with Alcoholics Anonymous. From his own recovery experience and from his observations of other recovering alcoholics, Ford was convinced that AA's twelve–step program was the most effective way of helping persons with alcohol-abuse problems. He also observed that AA's initially explicit Protestant orientation might be perceived as a "danger to the faith" which could deter Catholics from participating in AA's programs.

Bill Wilson, cofounder of Alcoholics Anonymous with Robert Smith, had sought Ford's editorial assistance for two AA books, *Twelve Steps and Twelve Traditions* and *Alcoholics Anonymous Comes of Age*. Wilson praised Ford's editorial work: "He [Father Ford] went over *Twelve Steps and Twelve Traditions* with a fine-tooth comb and is most solicitous that we never get into a jam with the [Roman Catholic] church. He is one of our very best under-cover agents."[66]

Aside from his involvement with AA, Ford was also a team member in The North Conway Institute (NCI), an ecumenical organization committed to shaping public policy on alcoholism and educating people about alcohol abuse. Ford's innovative pastoral approach to alcoholism became the basis for the 1966 interfaith consensus statement by The Ecumenical Council on Alcohol Programs (TECAP), an interdisciplinary board involving Protestants, Catholics, Jews, and secular agencies.[67]

In contrast to this positive ecumenical collaboration, Ford exercised a more partisan approach on the issue of contraceptives. Until 1930, Catholic and Protestant leaders had both officially rejected the use of contraception by married couples for birth regulation. However, the 1930 Lambeth Conference of the Anglican Church broke with the tradition and allowed couples to use of contraceptives when there was a morally sound reason to do so.

Ford's strong objection against the procontraceptive position of the Anglicans was expressed in his defense of the teaching of the encyclical *Casti connubii*, which was promulgated by Pius XI in 1930 as a direct and opposing response to the Lambeth Conference's break with tradition. In his *Minority Report* presented at the papal birth control commission in 1966, Ford argued that to change the traditional teaching on contraception would damage the value and dignity of the Church's teaching authority, and would cast doubt on the guaranteed assistance of the Holy Spirit that the magisterium presumes to enjoy. It would also imply that the 1930 Lambeth Conference was correct while *Casti connubii* was wrong.

> This change would inflict a grave blow on the teaching about the assistance of the Holy Spirit, promised to the church to lead the faithful in the right way toward their salvation. For, as a matter of fact, the teaching of *Casti Connubii* was solemnly proposed in opposition to the doctrine of the Lambeth Conference of 1930, by the church "to whom God has entrusted the defense of the integrity and purity of morals . . . in token of her divine ambassadorship . . . and through our mouth." Is it nevertheless now to be admitted that the church erred in her work, and that the Holy Spirit rather assists the Anglican church![68]

Another instance concerns Ford's decision not to participate in the 1969 transfer of the Jesuit theological school, Weston College, from the town of Weston, Massachusetts, to the campus of the Episcopal Theological School (ETS) in the heart of Cambridge, Massachusetts. One of the reasons he gave for his decision was his objection to Jesuit seminarians being allowed to take courses under non-Catholic professors in theological schools such as ETS and Harvard Divinity School. He expresses this sentiment in a letter to a fellow Jesuit: "Here at Weston we are in the throes of reorganization with a strong drive to move us to Cambridge where we would be closely affiliated with Episcopal Theological School, and where there is contemplated an unspecified amount of interconfessional undergraduate theological training during the first three years of theology and probably still more for the fourth year. Nobody pays attention to me when I insist that this is not proper ecumenism, and that our students should be thoroughly trained in their Catholic theology before trying to engage in serious ecumenical discussion."[69]

The degree of Ford's ecumenical collaboration was conditioned by the circumstances surrounding the moral issue involved. Whenever he did not perceive collaboration as diminishing the integrity of the authority of the magisterium, Ford was willing to actively engage non-Catholics in common endeavors. If, however, collaboration seemed to pose a "danger to the faith" that might promote indifferentism, or might undermine church authority or church teachings, Ford chose to disengage from ecumenical cooperation. Authority again made the difference.

Notes

1. McCormick, "Moral Theology 1940–1989" (1989), 3–4.
2. Ibid., 4.
3. Mahoney, Making of Moral Theology (1987), 1.
4. Ford and Kelly, Contemporary Moral Theology Vol. I (1958), 99.
5. National Clergy Conference on Alcoholism 1999, 45–46.
6. Ford and Kelly, Contemporary Moral Theology Vol. II (1963), 232.
7. Ford, Letter to Cosgrove (1964): Ford, Journal notes (1964).
8. Ford, Letter to Furlong (1964), On absolution (handwritten notes) (1966).
9. Mahoney, Making of Moral Theology (1987), 30–31.
10. Ford, "Notes on Moral Theology" (1943), 564.
11. Ford, "On Cheating in Examinations" (1941), 252–56.
12. Slater, Manual of Moral Theology (1908), 5–6.
13. Ford and Kelly, Contemporary Moral Theology, Vol. I (1958), 42.
14. Ibid., 81–82.
15. Pope, "Ethics of Thomas Aquinas" (2002), 37.

16. Ford, *Man Takes a Drink* (1954), 49.
17. Ford, "Chemical Comfort and Christian Virtue" (1959), 366–67.
18. Ibid., 374–78.
19. Jonsen and Toulmin, *Abuse of Casuistry* (1988), 14; 252.
20. Keenan, "Return of Casuistry" (1996), 130.
21. Ford, "Hydrogen Bombing of Cities" (1957), 6–9.
22. Jonsen and Toulmin, *Abuse of Casuistry* (1988), 257.
23. Ford, "Morality of Obliteration Bombing" (1944), 283–84.
24. Kaiser, *Encyclical That Never Was* (1985), 209.
25. Jonsen and Toulmin, *Abuse of Casuistry* (1988), 256.
26. Ford and Kelly, *Contemporary Moral Theology*, Vol. II (1958), 329.
27. Ford, "Notes on Moral Theology" (1942), 592–93.
28. Ford, "Notes on Moral Theology" (1944), 514–17.
29. Ford, "Letter to the Editor" (1947).
30. Ford, Letter to Forsyth (1959).
31. Ford and Kelly, "Notes on Moral Theology, 1953" (1954), 70.
32. Ford and Kelly, *Contemporary Moral Theology*, Vol. II (1963), 333.
33. Ibid., 329–30.
34. Ford and Kelly, "Notes on Moral Theology, 1953" (1954), 71.
35. Ford and Kelly, *Contemporary Moral Theology*, Vol. II (1963), 335n27.
36. Ibid., 335–36.
37. Congregation for the Doctrine of the Faith, *Responses to Questions* (1993).
38. Place, "From Solicitude to Magisterium" (1978), 225–27.
39. Lynch, "Magistery and Theological Reforms" (1978), 207–8.
40. Place, "From Solicitude to Magisterium" (1978), 226.
41. Ibid., 236.
42. Mahoney, *Making of Moral Theology* (1987), 143.
43. Ibid., 156.
44. Komonchack, "Papal Magisterium and Religious Assent" (1982), 70–71.
45. Ford and Kelley, *Contemporary Moral Theology*, Vol. I (1958), 4.
46. Ibid., 6.
47. Pius XII, *Humani generis* (1950), 21.
48. Ford and Kelly, *Contemporary Moral Theology*, Vol. I (1958), 20n3.
49. Ibid., 21.
50. Ibid., 31.
51. Ibid., 157.
52. McCormick, "Moral Theology 1940–1989" (1989), 5.
53. Ford and Kelley, *Contemporary Moral Theology*, Vol. I (1958), 29–30.
54. Pius XII, *Humani generis* (1950), 20.
55. Ford and Kelley, *Contemporary Moral Theology*, Vol. I (1958), 3.
56. Gallagher, *Time Past, Time Future* (1990), 70.
57. Ford and Kelley, *Contemporary Moral Theology*, Vol. I (1958), 46.
58. Ibid., 100.
59. Ibid., 102.
60. Morgan, "'Chemical Comforting'" (1999), 42–46.

61. Ford, "Clergy's Role" (1959), 51–53.

62. Ford, *What About Your Drinking?* (1961), 51.

63. Ibid., 79–80.

64. Morgan, "'Chemical Comforting'" (1999), 46.

65. Ford, "Chemical Comfort and Christian Virtue" (1959), 379.

66. B. 1999.

67. Morgan, "'Chemical Comforting'" (1999), 52,

68. Ford, "State of the Question" (1968), 60.

69. Ford, Letter to Molinari (1968).

CHAPTER THREE

JOHN FORD'S
TWO MODES OF
RESOLVING MORAL CASES

John Ford had two ways of proceeding in resolving moral cases: a standard mode and a crisis mode. I begin by presenting his interpretation of church teaching and his use of probabilism in the standard mode; then I show how Ford made selective use of probabilism and unconventional methods in the crisis mode. Case examples illustrate both modes.

The Standard Mode

Ford approached moral cases that were neither grave nor urgent in the standard mode, using a manualist approach to interpreting papal teaching and a straightforward application of probabilism. In this mode, he assessed the authority of papal pronouncements, weighed the probability of various moral opinions, and offered his own opinion and pastoral solution. He engaged other theologians in dialogue and was willing to reconsider his moral position if other moralists disagreed with him. In this mode, he acted as a surveyor of probable opinions.

Interpreting Papal Teaching in the Standard Mode

Two cases illustrate Ford's method of interpreting papal teaching in the standard mode: his interpretation of Pius XII's 1956 Christmas Message on the subject of Catholic conscientious objection, and his interpretation of the 1955 letter of the Holy Office on artificial onanism. Both cases demonstrate Ford's careful interpretation of magisterial teachings.

PIUS XII'S 1956 CHRISTMAS MESSAGE

In his 1956 Christmas message, Pius XII states that a Catholic citizen "cannot invoke his or her own conscience in order to refuse to render the services and perform the duties established by law."[1] This means that if a Catholic were drafted to fight in a war of self-defense declared by a legitimate authority, the draftee could not claim exemption as a conscientious objector.

The U.S. Department of Justice sent a letter to Patrick Cardinal O'Boyle of Washington, D.C. requesting the bishops of the United States to interpret the pope's message and to apply it to Catholics seeking exemption from military service on the grounds of conscientious objection. John Ford was asked to give his theological opinion on this matter.[2]

Ford offered two reasons why the bishops should not give an interpretation to the U.S. Justice Department. First, as a matter of protocol and propriety, the proper interpreter of a papal message is the Holy See itself, not the bishops. It would not accord with ecclesiastical protocol for regional bishops to attempt to clarify a papal pronouncement that had worldwide implications. Such an interpretation could have unforeseen impacts, and only the Holy See has the competence to settle a controversy that would be universally binding to all Catholics. The Church's teaching on conscientious objection during this time was still indefinite. Ford explains the state of the teaching in 1956:

> During the past thirty or forty years there have been certain pacifist writings in various parts of the world by Catholics, priests, and theologians in good standing, whose works have borne an *imprimatur*, and who have not been officially condemned by the Holy See. These writers have tried to justify to a greater or lesser extent conscientious objection to modern war. The vast majority of theologians have opposed these views. But a few of the Catholic faithful, erroneously but in good faith, have embraced them, sincerely believing that their Catholic religious principles require them to be conscientious objectors.[3]

Second, Ford argued that from the perspective of civil law this question could not be settled simply by appealing to the Church's teaching on conscientious objection. The good faith of the objector should also be considered by government officials. A Catholic who believes in good faith that it is his or her religious duty to refuse participation in war must still have protection under law, even if his or her conscience is in error.

Is not the law meant to protect persons who erroneously but in good faith cherish a certain religious belief? Could not a Catholic erroneously but in good faith cherish such a belief and be entitled to the protection of the law? I do not know the law and cannot say. But I do think the Bishops should not allow themselves to be drawn into a position where they would equivalently be giving or favoring an opinion on this legal point, where they would be, as it were, supplying the Department of Justice with ammunition to fire at a Catholic conscientious objector whenever litigation arises about the right of the Catholic objector, or whenever criminal proceedings are instituted against him . . . . Our theology requires us to protect the rights of an erroneous conscience, and when the just laws of the land protect these rights, we should do nothing which might prejudice the administration of such laws with equal justice to all citizens, whether Catholic or not.[4]

The papal message only reiterated a common teaching of theologians that "when a legitimate government engages in a just defensive war which is objectively and in reality a just defensive war, a private citizen cannot refuse to take part in it by appealing to his conscience." Ford noted that the message did not address two issues: (a) whether, subjectively, a Catholic may be justified to refuse participation in war and (b) what authority determines whether a given nation is engaged in an objectively just war.[5]

In any war, if one nation is fighting unjustly, then conscientious objection by its Catholics citizens is considered morally obligatory. In most cases, however, it is difficult to determine which side in a conflict is fighting justly. Ford gave a hypothetical example: if the United States and Italy should engage in a war against each other, both sides could not be objectively justified at the same time. If the bishops of both nations declare that their cause was just and that no Catholic on their side could appeal to conscientious objection, then one group of bishops would have to be objectively mistaken. The papal message did not help determine which conscientious objector would be justified. Ford concluded that the 1956 Christmas message could not be applied to settle practical issues of conscientious objection in a real situation of war.[6]

Ford was particularly apprehensive about providing the U.S. government with additional means to force its citizens to go to war. He pointed out that the United States would not necessarily be on the just side of every war it might undertake. "It would be wrong, therefore, to encourage the Department of Justice to attribute to it [the papal statement] a force, which it does not actually possess," he wrote, adding, "We must not be naïve enough to believe that the United States will always be on the side of the angels in every war it wages."[7]

Ford also reminded the Bishops of the modern weapons of mass destruction available to the United States at that time. Catholic conscientious objectors who refuse to engage in a war that uses such weapons could be presumed to be in good faith.[8]

Mindful of the evolving state of the teaching on conscientious objection, Ford was careful that the Christmas message of 1956 be treated only as a general principle and not as a strict rule that denied conscientious objection in every case. Sympathetic to the position against war held by conscientious objectors, as a moral theologian he was also aware that conscientious objection had not yet received universal acceptance in the Church, and that it was far from being a defined teaching. Therefore, the best protection he could offer to Catholic conscientious objectors was respect for the erroneous conscience.

The absence of a definite teaching on Catholic conscientious objection delayed the bishops' response to the issue until after Vatican II. In 1965, The Pastoral Constitution on the Church in the Modern World provided the opening for a development of a Church position on selective conscientious objection for Catholics. "It seems right that laws make humane provisions for the case of those who for reasons of conscience refuse to bear arms, provided however, that they agree to serve the human community in some other way" (Gaudium et spes 79).

In November 1968, the U.S. bishops addressed the issue of Catholic conscientious objection in a pastoral letter "Human Life in Our Day." The bishops urged the U.S. government to allow selective conscientious objection for those who refuse to serve in wars they consider unjust. These objectors should not be sanctioned by the government and they should be allowed to substitute some form of community service for military service. In 1971, the bishops issued a more direct statement in their Declaration on Conscientious Objection and Selective Conscientious Objection:

> It is clear that a Catholic can be a conscientious objector to war in general or to a particular war "because of religious training and belief." It is not enough, however, simply to declare that a Catholic can be a conscientious

objector or a selective conscientious objector. Efforts must be made to help Catholics form a correct conscience in the matter, to discuss with them the duties of citizenship, and to provide them with adequate draft counseling and information services in order to give them the full advantage of the law protecting their rights . . . As we hold individuals in high esteem who conscientiously serve in the armed forces, so also we should regard conscientious objection and selective conscientious objection as positive indicators within the Church of a sound moral awareness and respect for human life.[9]

The statements from the Second Vatican Council and the U.S. bishops enabled Catholics to form their consciences regarding selective conscientious objection, thus making Ford's appeal to the protection of an erroneous conscience unnecessary.

LETTER OF THE HOLY OFFICE ON ARTIFICIAL ONANISM

The Holy Office sent a letter in 1955 to bishops in the United States concerning the use of chemical and mechanical devices that prevent conception. The letter reads:

The Supreme Congregation of the Holy Office is seriously alarmed about the ever-growing practice of so-called artificial onanism, which consists in having recourse to the use of various chemicals and mechanical devices to rob the natural act of generation of its powers to beget new life. In its solicitude to safeguard the sanctity of married life, it directs the attention of all Ordinaries to the duty of exercising constant vigilance, lest in speech or in writing in this regard the consciences of the faithful become perverted and purity of morals be contaminated by this depraved vice.

The sacred Congregation particularly raises its voice utterly to condemn and reject as intrinsically evil the application of pessaries (Sterilet, diaphragm) by married couples in the exercise of their marital rights.

Furthermore, Ordinaries shall not permit the faithful to be told or taught that no serious objection may be made according to the principles of Christian Law, if a husband cooperates materially only with his wife who uses such device.

Confessors and spiritual directors who hold the contrary and thus guide the consciences of the faithful are straying far from the paths of truth and moral righteousness.

> Further publications, public discussions, conferences, etc. about the lawfulness of such cooperation on the part of the husband are strictly forbidden, and Ordinaries shall take the necessary measures that this prohibition is religiously complied with.[10]

Ford noted some peculiar aspects of the letter that point toward a less forceful interpretation: the letter's official text was in English, not Latin; although addressed "to all Ordinaries" it was not received by all the bishops in the United States.[11] Comparing the letter with similar statements from the Holy Office on material cooperation in contraceptive practices, Ford commented that the language used in the letter relayed "a strong warning to confessors against the unqualified exculpation of material cooperation on the part of the husband." The language avoided any explicit declaration that material cooperation in the sexual practice was always and in all circumstances immoral, however.[12] Ford concluded, on the basis of his evaluation of the letter's language, that its author did not intend to give a condemnation: "No body on earth knows better than the H.O. [Holy Office] how to condemn an opinion in clear and unambiguous language. When they fail to do so, one may legitimately presume that they did not intend to do so."[13]

Ford also disagreed with the letter's instruction that the faithful must not be taught that there was no serious objection to a husband's material cooperation with his wife who uses contraceptive devices. He asserted that material cooperation "can be allowed for proportionate cause, as a general rule, unless there is some positive prohibition."[14] Ford noted that the Catholic Theological Society Association (CTSA), in its June 1955 meeting, had issued a consensus position declaring that absolution cannot be denied to a husband who, for grave reasons, only materially cooperated with the use of contraceptive devices by his wife. Regarding the prohibition against any discussion on the lawfulness of cooperation on the part of the husband, he noted that the Canon Law Society and the CTSA had already conducted discussions on the matter. Ford's opinion was that the letter did not substantially change the teaching on artificial onanism, and that it did not exclude absolution of husbands involved only in material cooperation.[15]

Ford acknowledged the power of the Holy Office to condemn unacceptable theological opinions, but he did not accept the text of this letter from the Holy Office without careful analysis. Using manualist norms of interpretation to measure the force and applicability of the letter, Ford analyzed the wording of the text, the language used, and the manner of dissemination. He did not wish to interpret an intention of condemnation where there were few indications for it.

The cases on conscientious objection and artificial onanism demonstrate Ford as a careful interpreter of church teaching in the standard mode.

Ford's Use of Probabilism in the Standard Mode

In moral theology, probabilism is applied to situations where there is doubt regarding the applicability of a law to a particular moral case. The word "probable," as used in moral theology, means "arguable" or "possibly true." A moral opinion is "probable" when it has good arguments to support it. A moral opinion is considered "more probable" when it has stronger and more plausible arguments to justify it compared to other moral opinions on the same matter. Conversely, a moral opinion is "less probable" when it has less compelling arguments.[16] The doctrine of probabilism holds that, in the case of a doubtful moral law, one can follow the solidly probable moral opinion of a reputable moral theologian even though an opposite moral opinion may be more probable.

Bartolomeo Medina, a Dominican professor in Salamanca, introduced the doctrine of probabilism in 1577. Medina writes in his commentary to Aquinas' Summa theologiae, "It seems to me that, if an opinion is probable, it is licit to follow it, even though the opposite opinion is more probable."[17] Medina is careful to state that an opinion is probable not "merely because it has proponents who state apparent reasons, but because wise men propose it and confirm it by excellent arguments."[18] Gabriel Vasquez (1551–1604), a Jesuit, introduced a distinction into Medina's statement that an opinion can be considered probable on the authority of "wise men with excellent arguments." Vasquez proposed that an opinion may be "intrinsically probable" (founded on excellent arguments) or "extrinsically probable" (founded on the authority of "wise men"). The intrinsic probability of a moral opinion is based on the reasonableness of the arguments that support the opinion. A moral opinion gains greater intrinsic probability when it "makes more sense" than other moral opinions. Extrinsic probability, on the other hand, is measured by the number and reputation of the moralists who support a particular moral opinion. Traditionally, if five or six theologians of notable prudence and learning independently adhered to a particular moral opinion on a case, their opinion can be considered solidly probable. The opinion of just one exceptional authority might also be sufficient to make an opinion solidly probable.[19]

Ford looked to the pope for guidance in determining the parameters for the application of probabilism. If the pope remained silent regarding a controversy, Ford would interpret this as an indication that theologians had the liberty to form probable opinions. In standard mode cases, Ford surveyed the opinions of reputable theologians and assessed the weight of extrinsic probability of each of these opinions. Ford insisted that moralists cited as extrinsic authorities must be manualists who have explicitly recommended their opinion for use in confessional practice.

> When a moralist, writing for other moralists, merely reports that a certain opinion is held by someone, he himself cannot be quoted to show its extrinsic probability. But when he writes a manual for the use of confessors to help them hear confessions, and includes such an opinion without condemning it, one can generally conclude that he recognizes its probability for practice, or at least he would not refuse absolution to a penitent who wants to follow it.[20]

Two cases illustrate Ford's use of probabilism in standard mode: (1) the case of double vasectomy, and (2) the case of live machine-gun fire for military training.

THE CASE OF DOUBLE VASECTOMY

In 1955, there was a debate among theologians whether a man who had undergone a permanent and irreversible double vasectomy before marriage was impotent and thus had a natural impediment against contracting marriage according to the Code of Canon Law of 1917. A double vasectomy involves the cutting of a portion of both ducts (vas deferens) through which sperm pass from the testes; this procedure prevents sperm from reaching the prostate and the seminal fluids. Canonists and moralists were divided among themselves between a majority and a minority opinion on the matter.[21]

The majority opinion held that the man with a double vasectomy was incapable of acts proper for procreation because he could not produce "true seed" (i.e., ejaculated seminal fluid that contained matter from the testicles), rendering him impotent and unable to contract marriage. This opinion, held by numerous reputable canonists and moralists (e.g., Gasparri, DeSmet, Wernz-Vidal, Ojetti, Capello), was also supported by a series of judicial rulings on marriage cases by the appellate tribunal of the Holy See, the Roma Rota. Pius XI and Pius XII had also granted dispensations in a number of marriage cases that appeared to support this majority opinion.

The minority opinion held that a man with a double vasectomy, even if permanent and irreversible, was only doubtfully impotent and is therefore allowed to contract marriage. This opinion is based on the observation that the canon law basis for judging male impotency was not scientifically sound. Although the number of canonists and moralists who held this view were relatively fewer, their reputation and authority gave the opinion at least extrinsic probability. Among the supporters of this opinion were Versmeersch, Schmitt, Gemelli, and Kelly.

It is notable that neither opinion required the presence of any spermatozoa in the ejaculate in order for it to be "true seed." Even though the presence of spermatozoa in the seminal fluid was necessary for procreation, canon law only required the presence of testicular matter in the man's ejaculate (i.e., matter that directly came from the testicles, even if it did not contain any spermatozoa) for the seminal fluid to be true seed. The majority opinion judged a man with double vasectomy to be impotent, not because he lacked spermatozoa but because there was a physical obstruction that prevented any testicular matter from being included in the man's seminal fluid.

Citing current medical knowledge, Ford questions the logic of this canonical requirement:

> It is generally thought that the vast majority of the sperm found in a given ejaculate have come from the terminal ends of the vasa, and few if any have come all the way from the epididymides. Indeed the journey from the testicles would be a rather long one to take place in the time during which an orgasm lasts, which is a matter of seconds. The coiled tubes of the epididymides through which the sperm would have to travel to reach the beginning of the vasa deferentia are from sixteen to twenty feet long,

and the vasa deferentia themselves are two feet long. Furthermore, there is reason to believe that in a given orgasm it is the first impulse of the ejaculation that contains the heaviest concentration of sperms. These considerations make it unlikely that that in a given orgasm anything travels all the way from the testicles and epididymides out to the external world.[22]

Although the majority opinion had greater extrinsic authority, it had less intrinsic authority because its physiological presuppositions were inconsistent with medical knowledge at that time. "They [the supporters of the majority opinion] find themselves in the embarrassing position of accusing the vasectomized man of impotence for a reason that, if valid, would make everyone impotent, because it is much more probable scientifically that the testicles do not play a part in any marriage act by contributing to it during the act itself the transmission of sperms or anything else through the vasa."[23]

Ford made his own survey of ten canonists and theologians in Rome and nine professors in American seminaries on their position regarding the double vasectomy case. His survey revealed a significant number of respondents willing to consider the minority opinion as probable. Ford contributed his opinion after his survey: "I consider the minority opinion probable and safe in practice."

Ford observed that the Church's teaching on impotence was still in a process of evolution, and new scientific discoveries continued to correct previous misconceptions about the reproductive system. The discussion among theologians regarding probable opinions on the case of double vasectomy remained open because the pope had refrained from definitely settling the controversy. "The only thing which will bring about satisfactory settlement of the controversy and satisfactory norms of practice will be an explicit official decision by competent Church authority. While awaiting such a decision discussions like the present one serve a useful purpose," he wrote.[24]

In this case, Ford both surveyed and evaluated probable opinions and participated actively in the theological discussion.

THE USE OF LIVE MACHINE-GUN FIRE FOR MILITARY TRAINING
This case involved a form of military training requiring soldiers to crawl under live machine-gun fire. In his 1943 "Notes on Moral Theology,"

Ford expresses his concern about this dangerous training practice.[25] The object of the training exercise was to teach soldiers the importance of staying low during wartime. Actual deaths and injuries resulting from the training practice helped reinforce this lesson. Ford questioned the use of the principle of double effect to justify this practice, and asserted that the machine gunner could not in good faith say: "I intend to teach a lesson, I do not intend to kill." He believed that there was a conditional direct intention to kill in this training practice. The direct purpose of the firing was to kill or wound soldiers if they raised their bodies too high. Ford pointed out that the live machine-gun training was even worse than the death penalty meted out to a sleeping sentry. The sentry would at least get a trial before being put to death, while the crawling soldier who raised his head would receive instant death without any due process. Ford further argued: "A soldier guilty of robbery and rape would get a better hearing than the unfortunate individual who, perhaps through some spasmodic motion induced by fear, is jerked above what may be called appropriately the dead line. Life is cheap at wartime. But we cannot afford to make it that cheap, without being tainted with the ruthlessness of which we accuse our enemies."[26]

Acknowledging that other theologians did not share his objection to the use of the principle of double effect to justify such a dangerous training practice, Ford refrained from making a moral judgment of persons involved in the training practice. Two years after his discussion of live machine-gun training, Ford mentions the case again in the 1945 "Notes on Moral Theology." Recognizing that the weight of extrinsic authority lay with the view opposite his own, Ford did not insist on his opinion. "I condemned in these Notes two years ago the practice of training soldiers by having them crawl under live machinegun fire. Hardly anyone of those I heard from agreed with my solution of the case. Naturally, I am not so convinced of my opinion as to insist on it in the face of such opposition. But it makes me believe that the question of directly intending danger of death requires further study."[27] Since there was no authoritative teaching on the matter that could settle the matter, Ford deferred to the opinion of other moralists who disagreed with his position. When dealing with such standard cases, Ford respected the differing opinions of other moralists, even deferring to the weight of their cumulative opinion.

The Crisis Mode

When Ford perceived that a moral case involved a grave and imminent threat to a basic good or value, his approach was significantly different. He would approach the case in the crisis mode taking a firm moral stand and make selective use of probabilism to defend his position. He would confront, correct, and even challenge persons in authority, whether civil or ecclesiastical, and forcefully tell them what was right or wrong. He would invoke of the authority of the magisterium, and exert his influence to control the direction of theological discussions. In this mode, Ford acted as an arbiter of orthodoxy.

Several cases illustrate Ford's crisis mode approach to grave and urgent cases: (a) the case of the infallibility of *Casti connubii*; (b) the case of obliteration bombing; and (c) the case of contraceptives. The first two show Ford's selective use of probabilism, while the third demonstrates Ford's willingness to use unconventional methods to defend his moral position in what he saw as a crisis.

Ford's Selective Use of Probabilism in Crisis Mode Cases

Probabilism cannot be applied to those cases where a definite object, such as salvation, real Baptism, valid Orders, has to be secured beyond possibility of doubt; for the actual and objective attainment of such an object can be secured only by the actual and objective fulfillment of certain specified conditions. Such conditions are absolutely essential, and it is obvious that no amount of probability on the side of any opinion will avail, unless that which is necessary is actually done. . . .

Probabilism cannot be applied to cases which have speculative probability in their favour but are in practice unlawful, whether on account of some positive enactment, or by reason of an express or virtual contract, whereby we may be bound to relinquish one line of action in order to adopt another that is more probably correct, or safer, or absolutely safe.[28]

Henry Davis, *Moral and*
Pastoral Theology

The moral manuals teach that there are exceptions to the application of probabilism. In crisis cases Ford was willing to use probabilism selectively or to argue that its use was not appropriate. The cases of the infallibility of *Casti connubii* and of the morality of obliteration bombing demonstrate his approach to such cases.

THE CASE OF THE INFALLIBILITY OF *CASTI CONNUBII*

To favor a particular moral opinion, Ford used the strategy of emphasizing the opinion's extrinsic probability. In their book *Marriage Questions*, Ford and Kelly propose that the teaching on contraception in the encyclical *Casti connubii* had been taught infallibly. They suggest that the best way to proceed was "to study the interpretations that eminent theologians have given of Pius XI's condemnation of contraception"—in effect limiting the universe of relevant interpretations to those who agreed that the teaching was infallible. Surveying the opinions of moralists, they found five authors (Cappello, Vermeersch, Piscetta, Gennaro, and Haar) who explicitly asserted that the teaching on contraception in *Casti connubii* was an *ex cathedra* pronouncement, and three more (Creusen, Zalba, and Cartechini) who held that the teaching was infallible, not from an *ex cathedra* pronouncement but rather from an exercise of the ordinary magisterium. On the other hand, another five other authors (Hurth, Villain, Guzzetti, Bender, and Snoeck) raised the question of infallibility without giving an opinion. Josef Fuchs did not agree that the teaching in *Casti connubii* was either an *ex cathedra* definition or an infallible exercise of the ordinary magisterium. Instead he proposed that the teaching be considered as a solemn authentic declaration.[29]

Ford and Kelly explain the reason for their survey:

> Our survey of authors has not been merely a counting of heads. We wanted to see what, if anything, eminent moralists have to say about the "nota theologica" for the proposition that contraception is intrinsically and gravely immoral. Many of these authors clearly and unhesitatingly say that this proposition is already infallibly taught by the Church. And even those who avoid saying that it is taught infallibly use a form of words which make it clear that they think the doctrine is substantially unchangeable. A dogmatic note which might fairly represent a common denominator of all the authors studied, therefore, might be "at least definable doctrine."[30]

Unlike standard mode cases where Ford was willing to assess and honor the extrinsic authority of opposing moral opinions, in this case

Ford only presented the extrinsic authority that favored one side of the debate.

The Morality of Obliteration Bombing

Another strategy that Ford used in crisis cases was to choose not to apply probabilism. Ford applies this strategy to the case of obliteration bombing, arguing that an application of probabilism was not appropriate.

> I do not believe a discussion of probabilism, or of what is probably allowable in this matter of bombing, would be fruitful, once one takes the larger point of view. Probabilism is the necessary resort of those who cannot find the truth with certainty, and yet must act. In confessional practice one must rely on it in some form or other. But to approach a major moral question probabilistically would be to confess at the start that the truth is unattainable. Such a state of mind would not be likely to contribute to the science of morality.[31]

To apply probabilism to this case would be to presume at the outset that it was morally ambiguous whether the principle of noncombatant immunity should be applied to civilians during the Allied bombing of German cities. Ford did not believe that such an ambiguity existed. Writing in 1944, he found this an urgent case and directed his efforts toward generating public outrage and condemnation of obliteration bombing, with the hope that this destructive military tactic would be abandoned. In this case, where thousands of lives were at stake, there was little time to spare for discussing probable opinions.

Ford's choice not to use probabilism in the obliteration bombing case was in accord with the manualist tradition. Henry Davis, in his manual *Moral and Pastoral Theology*, describes several situations in which probabilism could not be applied. One of the situations involves "an object that must be secured beyond possibility of doubt." Another situation involves securing certain natural rights that must never be violated, where even a likely invasion of such rights would be unacceptable.[32]

Ford saw the protection of noncombatants in a time of war as "an object which must be secured beyond possibility of doubt," and the right of noncombatants to immunity from attack as a right that must never be violated. Ford's decision not to use probabilism in this case was intended to defend the right of civilians to protection from military violence.

While in standard mode cases Ford applied conventional probabilism, but in crisis mode cases he adjusted his approach, either shifting the issue to one that favored one side, or arguing that the case was not appropriate to probabilistic treatment.

Ford's Crisis Mode Approach to the Case of Contraceptives

Ford's involvement in the birth control debate before and after the publication of Humanae vitae presents a more complex group of strategies, showing more sides to his response to crisis situations. Four episodes illustrate these strategies: (a) Ford's participation in the Papal Birth Control Commission; (b) John Ford and John Lynch's debate with Richard McCormick on whether a state of practical doubt existed regarding the church's teaching on contraception; (c) Ford's work with Cardinal O'Boyle in dealing with dissenting priests in the Archdiocese of Washington, D.C.; and (d) a later article written by Ford and Germain Grisez, which argued that Humanae vitae was an infallible teaching of the ordinary magisterium. These episodes show how Ford, acting in crisis mode regarding the issue of contraception, used unconventional tactics and arguments to defend the Church's teaching authority.

JOHN FORD AND THE PAPAL BIRTH CONTROL COMMISSION

When Ford was invited to join the Pontifical Commission on Population, Family and Birth for its fourth session in the spring of 1965, he was informed that the commission would work under the authority of the Holy Office.[33] He presumed that the task of the commission was to refine and clarify the current teaching on contraception, and he did not believe that the commission was allowed to discuss radical changes to the teaching.[34] Ford expected that there would be strict papal control of the theological discussion.

Even before joining the commission, Ford had concerns about the appointment of Canon Pierre de Locht as head of the commission's theological section. These concerns were prompted by de Locht's proposed plan for the commission's theological research. Ford believed that de Locht had written the plan with the presumption that the Church could change its teaching on contraception. Ford forthrightly relays to de Locht his objections:

> It seems to me that your whole plan is written from the viewpoint of one who has already made up his mind that the Catholic Church can and should permit the various kinds of contraception as a solution to both these problems—given certain conditions and qualifications, of course.
> . . .
>
> Reading your *Projet* in the light of these positions which I take to be yours, I cannot help but see in it a tendency to prejudge the problem we are asked to solve. It seems to me (please do not take offense) a tendentious plan of research; the tendency being altogether the direction of one solution, namely that the Church can and should permit contraception. Since it is impossible for anyone to prescind from his own deep beliefs in matters of this kind, I suggest that the general plan of our studies should be worked out by several collaborators representing different points of view, including of course the teaching of the magisterium. I do not believe that we should be presented with such a one-sided plan of study.[35]

Ford also relayed to the commission's secretary general, Fr. Henri de Riedmatten, his objection to de Locht's plan of research. When his suggestion to replace de Locht with a collaborative group was not accepted by de Reidmatten, Ford considered bringing the matter to the Holy Office. He sought advice regarding the wisdom of going to Cardinal Ottaviani, head of the Holy Office, to initiate moves to replace de Locht. Ford's colleague Gerald Kelly had recently died and so he turned to another Jesuit colleague, Richard McCormick, for advice on the matter.

> Since I got no satisfaction from either him [de Locht] or de Riedmatten in answer to my letters I am thinking seriously of taking the matter up directly with the Holy Office. Our commission works under the authority and at the request of the Holy Office and I doubt whether Ottaviani realizes that a man of de Locht's views is directing the theological investigations of the commission. Should I tell him? Or should I possibly wait until after our plenary session (March 25th to 29th) meanwhile watching to see how things are going? Actually I'd rather speak up now, because I am afraid he will become entrenched and established if something is not done promptly.[36]

McCormick advised Ford that it would be better to allow de Locht to stay as head of the theological section of the commission rather than replace him. He wrote:

> Naturally I have some misgivings that a man of de Locht's view is directing the work of the theological commission. And yet when I think it over, I'm not too worried. In fact, I think it might be good to have some of his stuff come up explicitly in your Rome confrontation. The only way we can hope to exorcise from our thought those elements which are unsound in de Locht's thinking is to get them out where careful, analytic theologians like yourself, Fuchs, Zalba, de Lestapis, et al. can shoot at them. If they don't get a hearing, these guys will grumble off that they have been the victims of power plays, never got a hearing etc. and the final situation will be worse than the ferment which stimulated the study. . . .
>
> As for taking the matter up with the Holy Office, my opinion is no. My reason is that I do not see any real advantage to that and I do see several possible disadvantages. If there are a lot of fellows in Europe who share in de L's view, I would like to see it aired (not because I think it correct) but because this is the only way we'll rid ourselves of it to the extent that it is erroneous. I believe that going to Ottaviani could lead all concerned to conclude too easily that the matter was not given a hearing, that discussion was controlled by appeal to authority—and that type of thing.[37]

Against McCormick's advice, Ford reported his concerns to Cardinal Ottaviani, but the Holy See decided to retain de Locht in his position in the commission.

When Ford attended the fourth round of commission meetings in March 1965, he was disturbed to find his fellow commissioners openly discussing the possibility of changing the teaching on contraception. Believing that such discussions were not in keeping with the papal intention for the commission, Ford sought private audiences with Paul VI to warn him that the commission was proceeding in an unacceptable manner.[38] During his first private audience with Paul VI on November 22, 1965, Ford told the pope about his understanding of the scope of the discussion of the commission. "I had said to him on November 22 that in my opinion there was never any intention of reserving to the Papal Commission the right to repudiate the doctrine of *Casti Connubii* and he [Paul VI] agreed with me very heartily [underline by Ford]. He insisted

that there could not be and had not been any question of going back on
Casti Connubii."[39]

Ford also told the pope that "for him [Paul VI] to be true to his conscience and to the doctrine of the church which he must defend, he
had to intervene somehow." Ford believed that an authoritative statement from the pope would put to rest any suspicion that the teaching
on contraceptives was in doubt while the commission was still doing its
study. Ford reminded the pope that silence on his part would allow theologians to presume that the teaching was in doubt and thus they could
apply probabilism to permit the use of contraceptives. The pope agreed
with Ford, saying "silence gives consent; if the church does not forbid,
she acquiesces and the doctrine becomes probable."[40]

At his second private audience with the pope on November 23, Ford
reminded Paul VI that the Church had historically forbidden sterilizing
drugs and that Pius XII had already condemned the birth control pill.
Ford also submitted to Paul VI a "pro memoria,"[41] an outlined presentation of important points that should be included in a papal declaration
on contraception. The pope advised Ford to speak courageously in the
commission to defend the teaching on birth control.

While the birth control commission was in recess between its fourth
(March 1965) and fifth (January 1966) meetings, Ford sought to intervene in the discussions on marriage at the Second Vatican Council. In
November of 1965, the Council was preparing to finalize the chapter on
marriage of The Pastoral Constitution on the Church in the Modern World. The
initial version of the chapter had retained the traditional distinction between the primary and secondary ends of marriage and the old juridical
definition of marriage as "the right over the body for acts apt for generation of children." Later revisions replaced these concepts with a more
positive outlook on marriage, with an emphasis on a covenant model
of marriage and an affirmation of the importance of conjugal love expressed and perfected in the marital act. The fathers of the Council had
already approved the text at its second reading, with a two-thirds majority vote. Only finishing touches to the text needed to be made before
a third and final vote. A Mixed Commission composed of bishops, experts, and lay observers had the task of finalizing the language of the
whole document. Council rules stated that any additional amendments
to the text of the chapter at this point would only be considered if they
were completely in line with the text of the document and the basic in-

tention of the council majority. Specific guidelines on birth control were not included in the text in deference to the ongoing work of the birth control commission.[42]

The unfinished chapter on marriage presented Ford with an opportunity to make an intervention that would ensure that the traditional teaching on contraception would be reaffirmed by the Council and thereby negate any move by the birth control commission to reform the teaching. At his meeting with Paul VI on November 22, when Ford suggested that an intervention must be made to reaffirm the teaching of *Casti connubii*, the pope requested Ford to write amendments to be inserted into the chapter on marriage being discussed at the Council. At his second meeting with the pope the next day, Ford submitted the requested amendments, which were eventually reduced to four (one authored by Ford and three written by Carlo Cardinal Colombo of Rome, a member of the Mixed Commission).[43] These four amendments were sent to the Mixed Commission as official papal interventions.

On November 24, 1965, Cardinal Ottaviani presented a letter to the Mixed Commission from the Vatican Secretary of State with the instructions to add four *modi* (insertions) from the pope. These *modi* specified certain words and phrases to be inserted into the text of the marriage chapter which would reestablish procreation as the principal end of marriage and ban all forms of contraception.[44] The insertion authored by Ford insisted that the phrase "*artes anticonceptionales*" (contraceptive devices) be included in a list of examples of erroneous modern practices (polygamy, divorce, free love) that impair the dignity of marriage.[45]

At the next Mixed Commission meeting on November 25, the members expressed their displeasure at the way the *modi* were presented in violation of council procedures. Ford reported in his Roman Diary that the meeting was conducted with great confusion as members raised objections to the wording and manner of insertion of the *modi*. There was also disagreement over the Mixed Commission's authority to question and revise the papal insertions. That same day, a number of persons met with Paul VI to present their concerns about the *modi*.[46]

The pope sent another letter to the Mixed Commission on November 26 informing the members that although the *modi* needed to be inserted, he would allow changes in the wording and manner of insertion while reserving the right to approve the revisions. With this clarification from the pope, the members of the Commission proceeded to alter the *modi* radically to minimize their effect on the original meaning of the text. Ford's insertion of the phrase "contraceptive devices" in a list of misuses of married love was changed by the Commission to a more generic term "illicit practices against human generation." The Commission did not condemn any particular contraceptive device or practice but rather it gave the general instruction that the faithful "may not undertake methods of birth control which are found blameworthy by the teaching authority of the Church in its unfolding of the divine law" (*Gaudium et spes* 51). The demand for a specific reference to *Casti connubii* in the text of the chapter was altered to a brief mention in a footnote where it served as a reference to past teachings rather as an absolute norm for the present. More significantly, the Mixed Commission included in the same footnote a reference to the Special Birth Control Commission that was still currently studying the matter on contraception. The footnote stated that "the holy synod does not intend to propose immediately concrete solution" (*Gaudium et spes* 51n14). The altered papal insertions were presented to Paul VI who approved them without comment.[47]

Ford objected to the alterations made to the papal *modi* and he attempted to appeal to the pope. He writes in his Roman Diary:

> Ottaviani . . . had just come from (the) Holy Father to whom he had given the reworded modi. He started off by saying that he thought everything was all right. I objected in stronger and stronger terms that everything was not all right, that there were serious ambiguities. Begged him in the strongest terms to give the Holy Father my objections to the changes made . . . in rewording Mode I. I begged him. I thought he might be impressed, because he seemed so, but with the changes already gone in and everybody in a good mood to make sure the schema gets a good vote I suppose there was not really much hope. [underline by Ford][48]

The chapter on marriage was eventually finished, and on December 4, 1965, *The Pastoral Constitution on the Church in the Modern World* was approved by the Council fathers.

After the defeat of his intervention at the Mixed Commission, Ford warned Paul VI against allowing free discussions at the birth control commission that might lead to a reform of the teaching. Despite Ford's warnings, Paul VI instructed the birth control commission that its next meeting on January 1966 would include a broad discussion of natural law and birth control, with medical experts making presentations. Ford anticipated that such a wide-ranging discussion of natural law would lead to an exploration of possible alternatives to the traditional teaching on birth control. Ford perceived an inconsistency in Paul VI's stance regarding the scope of the theological discussion in the commission.

Here, I believe, there is an ambiguity or inconsistency in the Holy Father's attitude. It is not logical to insist in the strongest language that the solemn doctrine of CC [Casti Connubii] must be upheld and at the same time allow discussions to be conducted in his own commission which makes sense only in the supposition that the doctrine can be rejected. I wonder if he realizes the inconsistency of this position?[49]

While attending birth control commission meetings, Ford sent his own reports of the discussions to Cardinal Ottaviani, to inform him of procontraceptive tendencies among the members. Ford's direct reporting to the Holy Office became a source of tension between him and the commission's secretary general, Henri de Reidmatten. Ford was admonished by de Reidmatten that he acted disloyally to the papal commission by reporting its proceedings to the Holy Office and by complaining about de Locht to Cardinal Ottaviani and to the pope. De Riedmatten informed Ford that the commission was under the control of the Holy Office and the commissioners were purposely not informed about the Holy Office's supervision in order not to inhibit the freedom of the members to speak their opinions on contraception. De Riedmatten wrote Ford,

I have personally never been authorized to disclose anything about the Holy Office being highly in touch with our work. But of course it would be impertinent on my part to deny something which is stated in your letters of appointment. Perhaps you have [sic] better not talk about this since it may do [sic] some of our members being less free in their expression. But I hope it is for you a confirmation that our work is not without the most important control.[50]

Ford responded by disagreeing with the policy of not informing the commission members of the Holy Office's supervision:

As for the theologians who might feel that their liberty was infringed
if they knew the auspices under which they have been convened, I am
afraid I have little sympathy with their attitude toward Church authority
in general and in the matter under discussion. It is also difficult for me
to understand that the members of the Commission were encouraged to
express their views openly and freely as if they had nothing to fear, if in
fact they have something to fear, namely the Holy Office,—if only they
had known about it.[51]

Ford received warnings from friends that he might be dropped from
the commission; instead he continued his campaign.

I have recently been informed by very reliable friends in Rome that an attempt is now being made to have me dropped from the Papal Commission, and that Fr. de Riedmatten does not want me on the Commission
any longer, because I do not work with the Commission but go over its
head to higher authorities, and have tried to involve the Secretariat of
State more and more in its affairs. It seems to me that it is entirely possible that I am *persona non grata* on the Commission and that therefore
there may be some truth in this report.

I do not allow this threat, if it is a threat, to prevent me from doing
what I believe is right in order to help the Holy Father in the present difficult circumstances.[52]

The threat of expulsion never materialized, and Ford remained on the
commission until the publication of its final report in 1967.

Twenty-one years after the commission ended its work, Ford spoke
for the first time publicly about a crucial meeting with Paul VI that con-
firmed his commitment to defend the teaching of *Casti connubii*. Upon
receiving the Cardinal O'Boyle award from the Fellowship of Catholic
Scholars in Defense of the Faith on September 24, 1988, Ford stated:

I remain utterly convinced that that teaching will never be changed precisely because it is a truth of faith. And I would like to share with you
an experience carved in my memory, which I associate with such conviction. During an interview with Pope Paul, he and I were discussing the
positions being proposed in the Commission. The Pope was calm and
composed while we talked about these. I did have the impression that he

did not talk about the proponents of these new positions as though they were "Formati Doctores" speaking about the faith. But when I said to Pope Paul. "Are you ready to say that *Casti Connubii* can be changed?" Paul came alive and spoke with vehemence: "No!" he said. He reacted exactly as though I was calling him a traitor to his Catholic belief. I have never before told that story publicly. Perhaps you interpret his reaction the way I did and do.[53]

Ford's crisis mode approach was evident not only in his actions at the birth control commission but also in his written arguments. Ford was the main author of the minority working paper for the commission, titled "The State of the Question: The Doctrine of the Church and its Authority." It was never intended for publication and was never officially released. In this paper, Ford admits that reason was inadequate for proving the validity of the Church's prohibition against contraceptives.

If we could bring forward arguments which are clear and cogent based on reason alone, it would not be necessary for our commission to exist, nor would the present state of affairs exist in the church as it is.[54]

Ford presents a range of arguments to support his position on contraceptives. He appeals to the constancy of Christian tradition:

One can find no period in history, no document of the church, no theological school, scarcely one Catholic theologian, who ever denied that contraception was always seriously evil. The teaching of the church in this matter is absolutely constant.[55]

He questions the objectivity of those who have argued to legitimize contraceptives:

Are not these men essentially limited by the influence of their time and culture and region and by organized propaganda so that they bring to the problem only a partial, transitory and vitiated vision, one that even now is not a fair response to the mind of very many people?[56]

He also offers a slippery slope argument to further emphasize the serious consequences of a change in the teaching:

If this principle is admitted, it would seem that more serious evils can yet be expected. Perhaps the promoters of the principle do not intend this. Nevertheless, these conclusions are actually drawn by others. Thus, for example, it could be concluded that masturbation is for the good of personal equilibrium, or homosexuality good for those who are affected by abnormal inclinations and seek only friendship with the same sex for their balance. The same could be done for the use of abortives or abortion directly induced to save the life of a mother.[57]

Ford's main argument in the paper is that the Church could not change its teaching because the teaching was true. This truth claim is based on the belief that the Church could not possibly commit a grave error in its teaching on a serious matter such as contraceptives for so many centuries. The implications of acknowledging the persistence of such a grave error on the part of the Church were unacceptable.

> The church could not have erred through so many centuries, even through one century, by imposing under serious obligation very grave burdens in the name of Jesus Christ, if Jesus Christ did not actually impose these burdens. The Catholic church could not have furnished in the name of Jesus Christ to so many of the faithful everywhere in the world, through so many centuries, the occasion for formal sin and spiritual ruin, because of a false doctrine promulgated in the name of Jesus Christ.
>
> If the church erred in such a way, the authority of the ordinary magisterium in moral matters would be thrown into question. The faithful could not put their trust in the magisterium's presentation of moral teaching, especially in sexual matters. . . .
>
> For the church to have erred so gravely in its grave responsibility of leading souls would be tantamount to seriously suggesting that the assistance of the Holy Spirit was lacking to her.[58]

Ford considers this argument of inadmissible consequences as the most compelling. He admitted this in a conversation with Monsignor Josef Tomko, the Holy See's representative at the commission meetings, when they were preparing for Ford's presentation of the minority position before a group of cardinals and bishops.

> We spoke about the importance of giving the reasons for the traditional side as strongly as possible. I told my hesitation about these arguments,

and my reliance on the Magisterium, etc. I thought the best approach was to argue from inadmissible consequences.[59]

In his crisis mode response to the case of contraception, Ford made exhaustive attempts to influence the birth control commission. He actively participated in the theological debate while at the same time he engaged in behind-the-scenes interventions to ensure that his position would prevail. Ford sought to prevent a crisis of confidence in the Church's teaching authority, which he believed would be the unacceptable consequence of a change in the teaching on birth control.

JOHN FORD, JOHN LYNCH, RICHARD MCCORMICK, AND THE ISSUE OF PRACTICAL DOUBT

John Ford's crisis mode appears again in his theological disagreement with Richard McCormick about whether the Church's teaching on contraception was in a state of practical doubt during the interim period after the commission had submitted its conclusions (June 28, 1966) and before the issuance of the encyclical *Humanae vitae* (July 25, 1968).

The theological disagreement between Ford and McCormick revolved primarily around the interpretation of a papal address given by Paul VI on October 9, 1966, to the National Congress of the Italian Society of Obstetrics and Gynecology. Paul VI stated:

> We are well aware that there is expected of us a decisive word with regard to the thought of the Church on this very question. But it is clear that we cannot give it in the present circumstances.
>
> We will recall here only what We explained in Our discourse of June 23, 1964, that is: the thought and norm of the Church are not changed; they are those in effect in the traditional teaching of the Church. . . .
>
> And so the new statement which is expected of the Church on the problem of the regulation of births has not been made yet, because We ourselves, having promised it, and reserved it to Ourselves, wanted to make a careful examination of the doctrinal and pastoral aspects which have emerged with regard to this problem during these last years, studying them in the face of the data of science and experience which have been presented to Us from every field. . . .
>
> Meanwhile, as we have already declared in the abovementioned discourse, the norm taught till now by the Church, completed by the wise

instruction of the Council, calls for faithful and generous observance; nor can it be considered as not binding, as if the magisterium of the Church were now in a state of doubt, whereas it is in a state of study and reflection on whatever has been proposed as worthy of most attentive consideration.[60]

In his 1967 "Notes on Moral Theology," in *Theological Studies*, McCormick asserts that a close reading of the text of the address led him to conclude that it was not a doctrinal statement—and he adds, "only an authentic teaching statement is capable of dissipating a genuine doctrinal doubt."[61] In support of his assertion, McCormick cites the opinion of historian and jurist John Noonan: "the Pope was actually admitting a doubt as to the immutable character of the law."[62] McCormick holds that the teaching on contraceptives was in a state of practical doubt, as it had been before the 1966 papal address. He proposes that his position was an emerging probable opinion, citing Bernard Häring as one of a number of theologians who held this same position.[63]

Ford asserts that if the Church continued to delay in making an authoritative teaching on contraceptives, the probable opinions of theologians on contraception would eventually have to be applied in the confessional.

> I do not know of any theologian, probabilist or other, who ever admitted the practical probability of an opinion which contradicted the teaching of the Magisterium. But there is one point here, which is worth noting, and I am pretty sure it is the point which Dick McCormick had in mind when he said that if the Pope did not speak soon the opinion would become probable. It is this. If authors continue to propose an opinion at variance with common teaching long enough, and are not rebuked by the ecclesiastical authorities, especially if they publish with an *imprimatur*, then after a time I would have to concede this much "probability" to their opinion: I could not refuse absolution to a penitent who wanted to follow such an opinion. For if the Church by her silence permits such teaching then I cannot pass judgment on the confessional on those who follow it. Where the Church judges not, then I will judge not.[64]

Ford was concerned that probable opinions would gain currency before the magisterium gave an authoritative pronouncement on contraception. For this reason, he believed it was his duty to challenge Mc-Cormick's assertion on the state of practical doubt of the teaching on contraception.

John Ford and fellow Weston College professor John J. Lynch, SJ, counter McCormick's position through an article "Contraception: A Matter of Practical Doubt?" In this article, they argue that the 1966 papal statement clearly affirmed that the teaching on contraception is not in doubt, and that previous papal statements had already indicated the intention of the pope that the teaching on *Casti connubii* should remain the norm to be faithfully followed until new modifications are made by the pope.[65]

Ford and Lynch cite an address of Paul VI on June 23, 1964, to the college of cardinals during Vatican II, when he publicly announced for the first time that a study by a commission was being conducted on the birth control question. To avoid giving the impression that the teaching on contraception was in doubt, Paul VI added the following statement to the address:

> But meanwhile We say frankly that We do not so far see any adequate reason for considering the relevant norms of Pius XII to be superseded and therefore no longer obligatory, they should, therefore, be regarded as valid, at least as long as We do not consider Ourselves in conscience obliged to modify them.[66]

Ford and Lynch assert that this papal pronouncement on the absence of a state of doubt on the teaching on contraception was an authentic noninfallible teaching statement, which continued to be in force until such time as the pope might make an authoritative teaching statement on contraception. They also argue that Vatican II, particularly in the text of *Gaudium et spes*, prohibited any departure from the traditional teaching while the commission was still in session.

> Children of the Church are not permitted, in the regulation of procreation, to follow paths that are disapproved by the Magisterium in its explanation of divine law. (*Gaudium et spes* 51)

McCormick agreed with Ford and Lynch that the 1964 address of Paul VI, which asserted that the norms on contraception by Pius XII remained obligatory, was an authentic noninfallible teaching statement. At that point in time, when the papal commission was beginning its work, the previously held norms were not in doubt. According to McCormick, however, doubts about the certainty of existing norms emerged after 1964, precipitated by the long delay in issuing an authoritative statement.[67]

As for the text in Gaudium et spes, McCormick pointed out that the pope reserved the matter of contraception to himself, and therefore the Vatican II statement could hardly be considered final. McCormick quotes Paul VI's 1966 address:

> The new pronouncement awaited from the Church on the problem of the regulation of births is not thereby (by the Council) given, because We ourselves, having promised and having reserved the matter to ourselves, wanted to consider carefully the doctrinal and pastoral applications which have arisen regarding this problem in recent years. [68]

McCormick disagreed that the 1966 address denied the existence of practical doubt in the teaching on contraception. He quotes an address of the pope to the XIII Congress of the Italian Feminine Center:

> The magisterium of the Church cannot propose norms until it is certain of interpreting the will of God. And to reach this certainty the Church is not dispensed from research and from examining the many questions proposed for her consideration from every part of the world. This is at times a long and not an easy task.[69]

With reference to this statement, McCormick comments:

> If the magisterium cannot propose (i.e., teach) moral norms "until it is certain of interpreting the will of God," then the traditional norms reiterated by Pope Paul at that time must have represented a certain teaching of the will of God. But if this was so, why should he have delayed his decisive statement and done so precisely on the grounds that time and research was needed to achieve certainty? The obvious conclusion would seem to be that the magisterium was not certain that these norms represented God's will."[70]

Presuming that the traditional teaching was not certain, McCormick offered an interpretation of Paul VI's assertion that "the thought and norms of the Church are not changed." He proposed that the pope's words meant that the magisterium was certain only that it did not want to either modify or recall the traditional norms. This was not the same as saying that the traditional norms were certain. It expressed only the pope's state of mind while an authoritative teaching was still to be formulated.[71]

McCormick stated, "norms are not certain up to the moment of modification, then suddenly uncertain or changed with the modifying statement. To say so is to adopt a theory of 'magisterium by fiat'." A papal statement does not determine the certainty of a teaching, he contended, nor does the state of a teaching automatically hold until the pope makes a change. The judgment that a teaching is certain must depend on a reasoned evaluation of the best available evidence. McCormick warned against placing a higher value on papal authority than on the use of reason.[72]

On this issue of practical doubt, Ford depended precisely on papal pronouncements to determine the limits of a theologian's work. He did expect theologians to hold the traditional teaching as certain until the pope made a new statement. If the magisterium has already established a tradition of authoritative statements on contraception, then (in Ford's view) consideration of the existence of practical doubt by theologians will only tend to destabilize the Church's teaching authority.

Ford believed that the pope had to address the confusion "caused by the speculation of private theologians." He drafted an interim statement for the pope to read publicly. He hoped that, by this interim statement, the faithful would adhere to the traditional norms on contraception and be dissuaded from following the opinions of theologians such as McCormick. He proposed the following:

> We see clearly that no one can consider himself a true Catholic who would prefer his private judgment, based precariously on what he deems to be his private inspiration or enlightenment by the Holy Spirit, in place of the clear and authentic teaching of the Church. Nor can anyone consider himself a true Catholic who prefers the novel opinions of private theologians, no matter how eminent, learned and zealous they may be, to a teaching

which had been handed down from time immemorial, and applied to the concrete problems of modern times by our most recent predecessors, Pius XI, Pius XII, and John XXIII. Moreover, even arguments proposed by very learned theologians constitute no probability, and provide no foundation for legitimate practice, when they contradict an authentic determination of the Magisterium, even if the determination in question is not an infallible pronouncement.[73]

Paul VI never used this interim statement. The fact that Ford composed it for use as a public statement by the pope, however, reveals an insight into Ford's self-understanding as a moral theologian at the service of the magisterium. Ford's loyalty was to the papacy, not to any particular pope. Ford was concerned that Paul VI's indecision about allowing open discussions on contraception would lead to a reversal of the teachings of previous popes, and weaken the moral authority of the Church. Ford did not hesitate to correct the pope and remind him of what his conscience could or could not do. He urged Paul VI to be faithful to the tradition established by his predecessors. Ford wrote privately in his Roman Diary:

> Undoubtedly, if he [Paul VI] had been more decisive at an earlier date this unhappy dilemma would not have arisen, but when it did arise what else was there for him to do. I do not believe at all that he kept silence all along with the intention of slipping over something at the end. In fact do not believe that he was fully aware of the practical consequences of the dilemma until I pointed them out to him.[74]

During his private papal meeting on November 23, 1965, Ford wrote down snatches of his conversation with pope. The following excerpt shows Ford giving direct advice to Paul VI.

> He [Paul VI] wanted to know whether at least onanism [was] o.k. I said no. . . . Even Häring [was] against this [onanism] the last time I spoke with him. . . . [Paul VI] kept asking: But wouldn't it be right to do this or that medically with the pill. [He] gave the example of girl who takes pill to stop menstruation because she's going to take part in gymnastic exercises and doesn't want to menstruate. He pressed the medical uses of the pill. . . . I spoke of his conscience which prevents him from repudiating C.C. [Casti connubii].[75]

Ford's acts of papal intervention show that he was willing to cross the line that he himself had drawn to limit theologians acting as interpreters of papal teaching. Rather than humbly defer to the pope's silence on the matter of contraception, Ford took upon himself to urge the pope to speak out, offering his own words if necessary. In this crisis situation, Ford was ready to step in as a papal mentor.

JOHN FORD, CARDINAL O'BOYLE, AND THE PROBLEM OF DISSENT

The publication of *Humanae vitae*, which upheld the traditional prohibition on contraceptives, was greeted with a variety of responses. Some theologians reacted by assuming a stance of dissent. On July 30, 1968, the day after the release of the encyclical, theologians from the Catholic University of America released a Statement of Dissent endorsed by eighty-seven signers. Six hundred theologians from the Catholic Theological Society of America and the College Theological Society also added their signatures to the Statement.[76]

The Statement of Dissent asserts the following:

It is common teaching in the Church that Catholics may dissent from authoritative, noninfallible teachings of the magisterium when sufficient reasons for so doing exist.

Therefore, as Roman Catholic theologians, conscious of our duties and our limitations, we conclude that spouses may responsibly decide according to their conscience that artificial contraception in some circumstances is permissible and indeed necessary to preserve and foster the values and sacredness of marriage.[77]

The Archdiocese of Washington, D.C., became a focal point of dissent against *Humanae vitae*. This was not only because Catholic University lay within its jurisdiction, but also because a number of priests of the archdiocese announced to the media that they would not to apply the teaching of *Humanae vitae* in their pastoral practice.[78] Patrick Cardinal O'Boyle of Washington, a defender of the encyclical, immediately addressed the dissent. Cardinal O'Boyle and other prelates who were members of the Catholic University Board of Trustees suspended twenty professors who helped draft the Statement of Dissent. The suspensions were lifted after a year, when an inquiry board exonerated the professors.[79]

There were about fifty-four dissenting priests of the archdiocese. Cardinal O'Boyle suspended their faculties to teach, preach, and hear

confessions. Within six months, most of them had left the active ministry; nineteen remained. Those who chose to remain in active ministry
appealed to the Vatican Tribunal, the Roman Rota, to regain their faculties. Paul VI moved the case from the Rota to the jurisdiction of the
Congregation of the Clergy, which was instructed by the pope to find a
pastoral solution. In 1971, the Congregation allowed the remaining suspended priests to return to ministry without an explicit rejection of their
dissent. The only requirement requested by the Congregation was for
the priests to agree to insist that Catholics whom they counseled on the
matter of contraception be "guided by objective moral norms."[80]

In the process of dealing with dissent in his archdiocese, Cardinal
O'Boyle requested the assistance of Ford to help write a pastoral letter
to the faithful. In one of his correspondences to a colleague, Ford expresses his sympathy for O'Boyle's decision to withdraw the faculties of
dissenting priests.

> Cardinal O'Boyle's position is quite simple and, I think understandable.
> A group of his priests, publicly not to say raucously, rejected and contra-
> dicted the authentic teaching of the magisterium in the matter of birth
> control. He takes the position that he is entitled to empower the priests
> under his jurisdiction to hear confessions, preach and teach only if they
> intend to do so in accordance with the authentic teaching of the Catholic
> Church. When they publicly make it plain that they do not intend to do so,
> and persistently refuse to give him their assurance that they intend to do
> so, he believes he has no alternative but to withdraw from them the facul-
> ties to teach, preach, and hear confessions in his diocese. (The bishops
> of England and Wales have just adopted unanimously a very similar posi-
> tion. See this week's Catholic papers.)
>
> What would you feel obliged to do if you were bishop? And if you be-
> lieved the pope meant what he said in Humanae vitae? And what about re-
> spect for the Cardinal's conscience? His conscience tells him he cannot
> allow people to teach, preach and hear confessions in his diocese when
> they refuse to give any assurance that they intend to do so in accordance
> with the authentic teaching of the Catholic church.[81]

A group of Jesuits at Georgetown University had sought to act as inter-
mediaries between the suspended priests and Cardinal O' Boyle. When
their efforts to communicate with the cardinal by telephone and letters

were unsuccessful, a public letter signed by twelve Georgetown Jesuits was sent to the *Washington Post*. The cardinal's response was to summon these Jesuits to a meeting with two of his Jesuit theologians, John Ford and Pat Harran, a former professor of ethics at the College of the Holy Cross. Also included in the meeting were some suspended priests of the archdiocese and a Jesuit delegation from the Gonzaga High School Jesuit community in Washington.[82] Unfortunately, the meeting did not result in a change of position for any of the attending parties. Ford commented on the meeting:

> I just went to a parish hall at Trinity Church and met some (all?) the Georgetown signatories, and the Gonzaga delegation privately there in the hall.
>   With regard to the business of the closed mind. . . . I must say that neither at that meeting nor at any other meeting I have had with the dissidents have I seen the slightest evidence of anyone with an open mind towards the teaching of the encyclical, that is an open mind to giving the kind of assent which it demands according to the council [*Lumen gentium*, n. 25].[83]

Ford used the words "closed mind" to describe dissenting priests at the meeting, but did not see himself as having a closed mind in not entertaining the possibility of substantial change in the teaching on contraception. He was convinced that the teaching of *Humanae vitae* was true because of the inadmissibility of error in the teaching of the magisterium.

John Ford also expressed his concern that some of his fellow Jesuits were not willing to grant religious assent to *Humanae vitae* and that his religious order was being harmed by the dissent of some of its members. "My opinion is that the Society has already been permanently harmed, not only by this present controversy but by the actions of many of our fathers all over the world. I have heard Paul VI quoted as saying recently that for the first time in four hundred years the Holy See cannot count on the fidelity and support of the Jesuits."[84]

We see here an example of how Ford's position was stricter than the position of the Holy See. While Ford agreed with Cardinal O'Boyle regarding the removal of faculties of dissenting priests, Paul VI allowed the dissenters to regain their faculties without officially denying their statement of dissent. Ford's protective stance toward the authority of the magisterium led him to take a position that exceeded the reach of the pontiff.

With regard to ordinary Catholics who chose to follow the opinions of dissenting theologians rather than the teaching of Humanae vitae, Ford found it difficult to absolve these persons in the confessional. Ford had previously been willing to grant absolution to persons who insisted on using contraceptives while the birth control commission was still conducting its meetings. He acknowledged their goodwill in presuming the teaching on birth control was in doubt because of the opinions of reputable theologians. After the publication of Humanae vitae, however, Ford believed that he could no longer exercise the same pastoral approach that he had adopted before. He interpreted the encyclical as a definite teaching from the magisterium that excluded probable opinions. He was also concerned about consistency. If he wavered from a strict adherence to Humanae vitae in the confessional he would also have to be less strict on other serious moral matters.

> I still have a fundamental difficulty. It seems to me that if we can absolve Catholics who in good faith practice contraception, we should also absolve Catholics who in good faith get married outside the Church, or believe in and practice abortion, or practice premarital sex or homosexuality. Such Catholics can find Catholic theologians, in public good standing, who defend most, if not all of these, in certain circumstances. Mere good faith does not make one eligible for the sacraments of the Church. One must in addition to accept the teaching of the Church and at least sincerely try to live by it. Otherwise, won't we be as Protestants? [underline by Ford][85]

Ford's insight about moral effort became eventually the pastoral solution for Catholics who did not dissent but rather were unable to live a life of practical assent. A pastoral guideline eventually appeared in 1997 to address the difficulty of absolving penitents who are unable to follow the teaching on contraception. The Pontifical Council on the Family published The Vademecum for Confessors Concerning Some Aspects of the Morality of Conjugal Life, which advised confessors to apply the law of gradualness when dealing with persons who sincerely seek to follow the Church's teaching on contraception but who are unable to do so because of circumstances.

The pastoral "law of gradualness," not to be confused with the "gradualness of the law" which would tend to diminish the demands it places on us, consists of requiring a *decisive break* with sin together with a *progressive path* towards total union with the will of God and with his loving demands. . . .

Sacramental absolution is not to be denied to those who, repentant after having gravely sinned against conjugal chastity, demonstrate the desire to strive to abstain from sinning again, notwithstanding relapses. In accordance with the approved doctrine and practice followed by the holy Doctors and confessors with regard to habitual penitents, the confessor is to avoid demonstrating lack of trust either in the grace of God or in the dispositions of the penitent, by exacting humanly impossible absolute guarantees of an irreproachable future conduct.[86]

The *Vademecum for Confessors* incorporated Ford's concern that penitents must accept and sincerely try to live out the teaching of the Church on contraception. Absolution is not denied to penitents who did not perfectly follow the prohibition on contraception, as long as the penitents accepted the teaching of the Church and strove to grow progressively in observance of the teaching.

JOHN FORD AND GERMAIN GRISEZ ON THE INFALLIBILITY OF HUMANAE VITAE

When Ford was preparing to write the minority report for the birth control commission in May 1966, he sought the assistance of Germain Grisez, then a young professor of philosophy at Georgetown University. Grisez's views were similar to Ford's on the irreformability of *Casti connubii* and the need to defend papal teaching authority. Grisez also collaborated with Ford in writing a pastoral statement for Cardinal O'Boyle during the period of dissent in Washington, D.C., after the publication of *Humanae vitae*.[87]

In 1978, a month before the tenth anniversary of the publication of *Humanae vitae*, Ford and Grisez published "Contraception and the Infallibility of the Ordinary Magisterium" in *Theological Studies*.[88] They argue that *Humanae vitae* had been taught as an infallible teaching by the ordinary magisterium, appealing to the conditions for infallibility set by Vatican II in the *Dogmatic Constitution on the Church*:

> Although the bishops individually do not enjoy the prerogative of infal-
> libility, they nevertheless proclaim the teaching of Christ infallibly, even
> when they are dispersed throughout the world, provided that they remain
> in communion with each other and with the successor of Peter and that in
> authoritatively teaching on a matter of faith and morals they agree in one
> judgment as that to be held definitely (Lumen gentium 25).

Based on this text, Ford and Grisez enumerate four conditions for an infallible exercise of the ordinary magisterium: (a) that the bishops remain
in communion with one another and with the pope, (b) that they teach
authoritatively on faith and morals, (c) that they agree in one judgment,
and (d) that they propose this judgment as one to be held definitively.
Arguing that these conditions had been met in the case of Humanae vitae,
Ford and Grisez claimed that the dissenting opinions of some bishops,
theologians, and laypeople did not detract from the authority and universality of Humanae vitae. Their reasoning included a strategy that excluded dissenting opinions.

Ford and Grisez argued that maintaining a bond of communion between the pope and bishops was necessary and sufficient for the bishops to share in the Church's task of guarding, preaching, teaching, and
handing on the faith. This is the first condition of infallibility set forth in
Lumen gentium. Because of this, dissenting opinions held by bishops not
in communion with Rome could not detract from the unity of judgment
(the third condition) required for the bishops to teach infallibly.

Regarding the second condition, Ford and Grisez asserted that there
was nothing in past church documents that would warrant restricting
the Church's prerogative to impose specific moral norms, such as had
been done in Humanae vitae.

Concerning the fourth condition for infallibility, they claimed that
this condition had been fulfilled in the manner in which the bishops
around the world taught Humanae vitae. These bishops did not merely
demand intellectual assent from the faithful—they also insisted that the
teaching on contraception be received and acted upon as "the will of
God, which followers of Christ must live up to."[89]

In their consideration of the third condition, Ford and Grisez took
into account the very real dissent within the Church on this point. Working from the premise that the ordinary magisterium must be universal in
order to be infallible, they defined this universality as "the moral unity of

the whole body of bishops in communion with each other and the pope, not the mathematical unanimity of the bishops which could be broken by the dissenting voice of any one individual." Appealing to the example of the Arian controversy of the fourth century, they pointed out that neither before nor after the Council of Nicaea was there a mathematical unanimity among the Church's bishops regarding the divinity of Christ. They argued that if this condition of universality had been satisfied without mathematical unanimity in the past, it could not now be nullified by a lack of consensus among bishops.[90]

Ford and Grisez could not deny the reality of dissenting opinions held by some bishops. They did their best to minimize its significance.

> It is a mistake to speak of these episcopal statements as if they contributed a chorus of episcopal dissent to the dissent of some theologians, who criticized the encyclical and rejected its reaffirmation of the received teaching on contraception. None of the episcopal statements denied the competence of the magisterium to propose specific norms, norms in themselves obligatory, on the morality of contraception. Moreover, none of the episcopal statements explicitly rejects the norms restated in *Humanae vitae*. . . .
>
> The implicit contradiction in 1968 by some bishops of a teaching already infallibly proposed through many centuries takes nothing away from the objective certitude of the teaching.[91]

They also claim that there was a constant consensus of Catholic theologians in modern times, demonstrated by the manuals of the nineteenth and twentieth century. The following statement, however, reveals how this "consensus" was achieved.

> The consensus of modern theologians supports the thesis that the received teaching was universally proposed by Catholic bishops, because the works of theologians were authorized by the bishops for use in seminaries, and thus for the training of confessors who communicated Catholic moral teaching to the faithful in the confessional, in premarital instructions, in the preaching missions, and so on. As authorized agents of the bishops—during centuries in which the bishops were careful not to share their teaching authority with theologians whose views they did not accept—these approved authors teaching in their manuals exercised in

a real though mediate way the teaching authority of each and every bishop who sent his seminarians to seminaries in which these manuals were required textbooks.[92]

In other words, the "consensus" of theologians claimed by Ford and Grisez was based on a survey of those theologians whom the bishops approved for their orthodoxy. This definition neatly left out theologians who disagreed with the traditional teaching on contraception. Once more, as with the definition of "universal," Ford and Grisez made strategic use of key concepts to support their claims of infallibility.

In a similar move to exclude dissenters, Ford and Grisez employed an interpretation of *sensus fidelium* that recognized only the opinion of the faithful who followed the traditional teaching. "The opinions of Catholics who regard the use of contraceptives as morally permissible should not be considered as an expression of *sensus fidelium*," they wrote.[93]

Throughout their article, Ford and Grisez argue that the manner in which *Humanae vitae* was taught by the bishops of the world fulfilled the conditions for the teaching to be considered infallibly taught by the ordinary magisterium. They shield these claims from dialogue with contrary opinions by means of a comprehensive dismissal of dissenting voices, whether from bishops, theologians, or ordinary Catholics.

Ford's words and actions as a moral theologian in the case of contraception were in the crisis mode. From this perspective, four elements of Ford's method stand out clearly.

First, Ford gave absolute primacy to the magisterium in determining the content and limits of theological investigation. He saw the magisterium as having the prerogative to declare certain topics as off-limits to theological discussion. Theologians who dissented from church teaching placed themselves outside any discussion of moral norms for the Church.

Second, Ford's primary loyalty as a moral theologian was not to any particular pope but to the tradition of papal authority. When the moral authority of the Church to bind consciences appeared to him to be compromised by papal indecision or doubt, Ford shifted from the role of papal interpreter to the role of papal mentor. To protect the moral authority of the papacy, Ford would not hesitate to instruct and direct the pope.

Third, Ford believed that in a theological discussion, error had no rights. Ford respected the good will of erroneous consciences in situations lacking any definitive teaching, such as the case of Catholic conscientious objectors, or in situations of controversy over a church teaching, such as the period before the publication of *Humanae vitae*. When a definite teaching had been handed down by the magisterium to settle a controversy, however, the appeal to erroneous conscience can no longer be applied, except in cases of invincible ignorance. Dissenters from authoritative church teachings were simply in error; their positions no longer able to make any claim as probable opinions. Ford acted as a strict arbiter of orthodoxy, excluding all opinions he found to diverge from orthodoxy, regardless of the reputation of the theologians advancing those opinions.

Fourth, Ford appealed to his duty to follow his conscience in using the means available to him to protect the authority of the magisterium. He did not consider it improper for himself as a moral theologian to influence the outcome of papal pronouncements or to report on commission deliberations, so long as these actions were in defense of the authority and integrity of the magisterium. Ford did not apply the same respect for conscience, however, to the cases of dissenting theologians and of penitents following dissenting opinions after the publication of *Humanae vitae*.

In the crisis mode, Ford acted as if he had an urgent mission that he could not afford to fail. In the birth control case, Ford acted as a protector of the magisterium; he displayed a willingness to attempt any intervention to gain an advantage in the debate. The calm manner of his discourse, so evident in his standard mode, was replaced by the demeanor of a street fighter willing to use anything at hand to win.

Notes

1. Pius XII, "Christmas Message" (1956), 21–22.
2. Ford, Opinion (1957), 1–7.
3. Ibid., 2.
4. Ibid, 3.
5. Ibid.
6. Ibid., 4–5.

7. Ibid.

8. Ibid., 6.

9. U.S. Conference of Catholic Bishops, *Declaration on Conscientious Objection* (1971).

10. Pizzardo, "Letter to All Ordinaries" (1955).

11. Ford, handwritten notes (1955?).

12. Ford and Kelley, *Contemporary Theology, Vol. II* (1963), 213–14.

13. Ford, handwritten notes (1955?).

14. Ibid.

15. Ibid.

16. Jonsen and Toulmin, *Abuse of Casuistry* (1988), 166; Mahoney, *Making of Moral Theology* (1987), 136.

17. Jonsen and Toulmin, *Abuse of Casuistry* (1988), 164.

18. Ibid., 166.

19. Harty, "Probabilism" (2003).

20. Ford and Kelly, "Notes on Moral Theology, 1953" (1954), 97.

21. Ford, "Double Vasectomy" (1955), 533–57.

22. Ibid., 536.

23. Ibid., 548.

24. Ibid., 556–57.

25. Ford, "Notes on Moral Theology" (1943), 586–87.

26. Ibid., 587.

27. Ford, "Current Theology" (1945), 534.

28. Davis, *Moral and Pastoral Theology* (1938), 97–99.

29. Ford and Kelly, *Contemporary Moral Theology, Vol. II* (1963), 263–69.

30. Ibid., 269–70.

31. Ford, "Morality of Obliteration Bombing" (1944), 269.

32. Davis, *Moral and Pastoral Theology* (1938), 97–99.

33. Cicognani, Letter to Ford (1964).

34. Ford, "State of the Question" (1966), 556.

35. Ford, Letter to de Locht (1965).

36. Ford, Letter to de Riedmatten (1965); Ford, Letter to McCormick (1965).

37. McCormick, Letter to Ford (1965).

38. Ford, Letter to Vagnosi (1965).

39. Ford, Journal entries (1965), 6.

40. Ibid., 7.

41. Ford, Note to Paul VI (1965): Ford, "Pro Memoria" (1965).

42. McClory, *Turning Point* (1995), 80–81; Kaiser, *Politics of Sex and Religion* (1985), 153.

43. Ford, Journal entries (1965), 1.

44. McClory, *Turning Point* (1995), 83.

45. Valsecchi, *Controversy* (1968), 142.

46. Ford, Journal entries (1965), 4.

47. Valsecchi, Controversy (1968), 144–46.

48. Ford, Journal entries (1965), 13.

49. Ibid., 7.

50. de Riedmatten, Letter to Ford (1965).

51. Ford, Letter to de Riedmatten (1965).

52. Ford, Letter to Ottaviani (1966).

53. Ford, "Response" (1988), 14.

54. Ford, "State of the Question" (1968), 34.

55. Ibid., 30.

56. Ibid., 55.

57. Ibid., 59.

58. Ibid., 37–38; 60–61.

59. Ford, Journal entry (1966).

60. Paul VI, "Statement on Birth Control" (1966), 1169.

61. McCormick, "Notes on Moral Theology" (1967), 799–800.

62. Noonan, "Pope's Conscience" (1967), 559–60.

63. McCormick, "Notes on Moral Theology" (1967), 800.

64. Ford, Letter to Higgins (1966).

65. Ford and Lynch, Contraception (1968).

66. Paul VI, "Address" (1964), 564.

67. McCormick, "Notes on Moral Theology" (1966), 652.

68. Paul VI, "Statement on Birth Control" (1966), 1169.

69. Paul VI, "Address" (1966), 219.

70. McCormick, "Notes on Moral Theology" (1981), 211.

71. Ibid., 212.

72. Ibid., 214.

73. Ford, Interim statement (1966), 4.

74. Ford, Journal entries (1965), 7.

75. Ford, Notes on private audiences (1965).

76. Curran and Hunt, Dissent (1969), 6–7.

77. Ibid., 26.

78. Shaw, "Making of a Moral Theologian" (1996).

79. Kaiser, Encyclical That Never Was (1987), 256.

80. Shaw, "Making of a Moral Theologian" (1996).

81. Ford, Letter to Steve (1968).

82. Charles Currie, SJ, personal communication. Currie was one of the Jesuit participants from Georgetown University.

83. Ford, Letter to Steve (1968).

84. Ibid.

85. Ford, Christmas card to Heenan (1968).

86. Pontifical Council on the Family, Vademecum for Confessors (1997).

87. Shaw, "Making of a Moral Theologian" (1996).

88. Ford and Grisez, "Contraception" (1978).
89. Ibid., 276.
90. Ibid., 273–74.
91. Ibid., 309–11.
92. Ibid., 280–81.
93. Ibid., 300–301.

CHAPTER FOUR

THE DEVELOPMENT
OF DOCTRINE

This chapter deals with John Ford's approach to doctrinal development, particularly as his approach contrasts with that of historian John Noonan, who had proposed an alternative way of understanding the development of church teachings. The case of periodic continence will demonstrate the consistent and inconsistent aspects of Ford's approach—aspects which can best be understood in light of the history of doctrinal consistency itself.

John Ford's Approach to Doctrinal Development

Ford set continuity with tradition as a condition and a mark of authenticity for any doctrinal development. New teachings should develop gradually and organically from past teachings. Authentic doctrinal developments should take the form of a refinement or a reformulation of existing teachings, or a new application of long-standing doctrine.[1] To contradict an authoritative teaching and call it growth would be, in Ford's eyes, intellectually dishonest. "I do not consider it theologically legitimate, or even decent and honest, to contradict a doctrine and disguise it under the rubric: growth and evolution. . . . Legitimate growth and radical revision cannot live together,"[2] he wrote. "Continuity with the past is an essential element, within the Christian church, of any meaningful contribution to the future."[3]

A new teaching that breaks with tradition could give the impression that there was an error on the part of the magisterium in its previous teaching. Ford considered such a teaching unacceptable and unsuitable for theological discussion.

Ford identified two causes that could legitimately prompt the development of doctrine: the discovery of more precise scientific information about the workings of nature and the emergence of new social conditions.

In the case of temporary sterilization, for example, new physiological data could prompt the Church to reevaluate its previous teachings. "I recognize that our modern knowledge of the cycles of fertility–sterility in women make it possible and desirable to re-evaluate certain theological conclusions we have held in the past. I recognize that there is room for theological development precisely because of this scientific knowledge." He wrote, "I am not unwilling to accept developments of the theological teaching, especially when based on physiological facts that are pertinent. I think the cyclic character of female fertility–sterility is such a fact."[4]

Ford anticipated that new scientific data on the female fertility cycle and the development of various methods of fertility regulation (progestational steroids, protein diets, etc.) could open the possibility of reevaluating the teaching on direct temporary sterilization in order to allow human intervention to correct abnormal cycles.[5] "With the prospect in the not too distant future of not only detecting but of determining the exact time of ovulation, there would be grounds for hope, with Pius XII, that science will succeed in providing a sufficiently secure basis for the effective practice of periodic continence."[6]

Ford encouraged Paul VI to support further scientific and theological investigations on the regulation of the fertility cycle. "When I spoke with the Pope on June 6th about this matter of the pill, I urged him to leave this an open question for discussion by theologians and scientists. I made two principal points, first to uphold the authority of Pius XII, and secondly, to leave this question of the correction and regulation of the sterility–fertility open for discussion."[7]

Ford's interest in the development of the church's teaching on contraception led him to recommend John Noonan to the papal birth control commission as an expert on doctrinal development.

John Noonan and His Approach to Doctrinal Development

John T. Noonan, a noted jurist and church historian, wrote extensively on the historical development of the Church's teaching on a variety of subjects. In 1957, Noonan published The Scholastic Analysis of Usury, which traced the development of the Church's teaching on usury. Noonan wrote that the Church's prohibition against usury was at its most vigorous in the year 1450. Any profit on a loan was prohibited. The risk involved in lending money was not considered adequate justification to accept interest on a loan. To expect interest would violate the normal gratuitousness of the loan and would constitute mental usury. The Church regarded both actual and mental usury as mortal sins against the virtue of justice.[8]

Developments in the teaching on usury were precipitated by several factors. The increased prosperity in sixteenth-century Europe led to changes in the way credit for commerce was understood. For instance, there was a shift from a perception of money as static to a recognition of its productive character. Also, the factor of risk was gradually accepted as a legitimate reason to impose interest on a loan. Greater recognition was given to the "good intentions, honesty, and social utility" of persons involved with banking.[9]

Another significant factor in the development of the teaching on usury was the use of high casuistry by moral theologians to evaluate new forms of financial contracts as licit exemptions to the usury prohibition. Modifications by moral theologians of the natural law arguments supporting the prohibition of usury led to the development of alternative theories of profit taking. The strict universal prohibition of usury held in 1450 was eventually abandoned. The publication of the 1917 code of canon law was a final formal step, according to Noonan, of the acceptance of interest taking as allowed by civil law. The scriptural instruction to "lend and expect nothing back" (Luke 6:35) was eventually understood as a counsel of perfection rather than a strict precept. Credit transactions became the norm and the meaning of usury was restricted to the exceptional case of excessive interest-taking.[10]

Several years after the publication of his 1957 book on usury, Noonan began writing a similar work of historical research on the topic of contraception. Ford, who had been impressed by Noonan's thorough and detailed research on usury, eagerly anticipated the publication of Noonan's work on contraception.

Ford was aware of questions being raised about whether the change in the teaching on usury could also be applied to a future change in the teaching on contraception. He asserted that the teaching on contraception could not change in the same way as the teaching on usury. In a

1964 letter to Bishop John Wright of Pittsburgh, however, Ford admitted that he did not have adequate arguments to disprove a legitimate analogy between usury and contraception. "You mentioned the analogy between the Church's teaching on usury and on contraception and the necessity of pinning down this false comparison. I agree, but I'm not sure it would be an easy thing to do," he wrote.

> The reasons why I think this problem is not an easy one to pin down are these. First, it is simply a fact that the theologians' teachings on conjugal intimacy during the course of the centuries have undergone very considerable development. So it is legitimate to inquire whether further development is not possible and what direction it might take. Second, in the case of usury we say that changed economic conditions gave interest a new meaning it did not have before, or gave money a new character of fruitfulness. In the case of contraception we must remember that the doctrine of the church was formed and formulated at a time when little was known about the physiology of reproduction. The physiology has not changed but our knowledge of it has. This is one of the reasons why modern theologians have come to permit rhythm, which much of the ancients would undoubtedly have rejected, and which Augustine actually did reject, in strong terms. We now know that many, perhaps most, acts of intercourse are physically incapable of resulting in conception. The difficulties which this fact causes for natural law arguments against contraception have not been satisfactorily solved yet.—Do not conclude from this that I believe the Church can change her basic teaching on contraception or that she can retreat from the positions established authoritatively by the documents of Pius XI and Pius XII. But I do think these considerations make it difficult to pin down in any popular article the false analogy with usury, even though I think it is false.[11]

Still, Ford noted that Noonan's book on usury showed that the Church had never changed its basic position on interest-taking (i.e., a consistent condemnation of excessive and exploitative charging of interest). Ford had hoped that Noonan's book on contraception would also show the consistency of the Church's position on the topic and would provide a solid historical argument against any radical change in the teaching. With this in mind, writing to the secretary of the papal birth control commission, Ford then recommended Noonan to be the commission's expert on the history of contraception. "I have already written to you about the value to the commission of an historian of the theology of contraception and sterilization. I would like to reiterate that I think the promised work of Dr. John T. Noonan Jr., will be of great help to the group. His history of contraception will be published in the spring, and is almost ready for the press now."[12]

While *Contraception* was being prepared for publication, Noonan presented a paper to the papal birth control commission summarizing his book. Ford found some points of disagreement with Noonan over his interpretation of certain aspects of the historical development of the teaching on contraception, for instance, that some sections of the book's summary advocated a change in the teaching.[13] Noonan admitted that part of his historical work involved making hypotheses regarding collected data, and that his hypotheses were influenced by his own presuppositions.[14]

Noonan eventually published the first edition of *Contraception: A History of Its Treatment by Catholic Theologians and Canonists* in 1965. The book traced the historical development of the Church's teaching on contraception, beginning with contraceptive practices during the Roman Empire in 50 A.D. up to the most recent papal pronouncements in 1965. In his historical investigation, Noonan analyzed how the doctrine on contraception was "molded by the teachings of the Gospels on the sanctity of marriage; the Pauline condemnation of unnatural sexual behavior; the Old Testament emphasis on fertility; the desire to justify marriage while extolling virginity; and the need to assign rational purpose and limit to sexual behavior."[15]

The early formulation of the prohibition against contraceptives was shaped by the various social circumstances of the times. Noonan noted that the Church's doctrine "was formed in a society where slavery, slave concubinage, and the inferiority of women were important elements of the environment affecting sexual relations. The education of children was neither universal nor expansive. Underpopulation was a main governmental concern."[16] The teaching was also shaped as the Church used it to respond to a variety of heresies. "The doctrine condemning contraception was formulated against the Gnostics, reasserted against the Manichees, and established in canon law at the climax of the campaigns against the Cathars. Reaction to these movements hostile to procreation was not the sole reason for the doctrine, but the emphasis, sweep, and place of the doctrine issued from these mortal combats."[17]

More recent developments of the doctrine on contraception since 1850 resulted from "environmental changes." Such changes include the establishment of love as an end and means of the coital act, the emancipation of women, and the recognition of marriage based on personal decision. Noonan described the writings of such theologians as Von Hildebrand, Doms, Häring, Fuchs, Ford, and Kelly as responses to these recent changes in the understanding of marriage, love, and the role of women in society. He observed that the writings of moral theologians like Ford or Häring were very different from the writings of past theologians. "Huguccio would have marveled at the teaching of Ford and Kelly, Jerome would have been astounded at Häring."[18]

Noonan wrote that "the Church, on its pilgrim's path, has grown in grace and wisdom." It was therefore consistent with the Church's growth in knowledge to expect development in its moral teachings. He warned that "it is a perennial mistake to confuse the repetition of old formulas with the living law of the Church."[19] An attitude that treated Church teachings on contraception as eternal and unchanging lacked an appreciation of the contextual and historically conditioned development of the teaching.

Noonan enumerated examples of opinions held by past theologians regarding marriage and procreation that had been abandoned: "intercourse must be only for procreative purposes, intercourse in menstruation is a mortal sin, intercourse in pregnancy is forbidden, and intercourse has a natural position." These opinions had been formed by moralists of the past to preserve certain basic values based on the biological knowledge available during their time.[20] Just as these abandoned opinions were formulated to preserve certain basic values, the most recent teachings of the Church on contraception in 1965 were also formed to protect a number of basic values. Noonan named five propositions asserted by the Church that expressed these values: (a) procreation is good; (b) procreation of offspring reaches its completion only in their education; (c) innocent life is sacred; (d) the personal dignity of the spouse is to be respected; and (e) marital love is holy. These propositions highlighted the values of procreation, education, life, personality, and love. "About these values a wall had been built; the wall could be removed when it became a prison rather than a bulwark," declared Noonan.[21]

Future formulations of the teaching on contraception could be radically different from previous formulations, as long as the basic values of the Church continue to be promoted and protected. Previous prohibitions concerning reproduction had been abandoned in the face of new biological data and new ways of understanding love and marriage. The present prohibitions against contraception should therefore be open to new developments that remain faithful to the values of the Church.[22] Noonan expressed openness to the possibility of substantial change in the teaching on contraception as a legitimate part of the development of doctrine, a position contrary to Ford's.

While Ford appreciated and respected the historical data that Noonan had gathered, he disagreed with his interpretation of the data.

> Nobody has collected in one place so many materials on the subject. Likewise nobody anywhere ever collected so much material on the precise point of contraception. But Noonan's fundamental mistake, I think, is that he interprets the changes that have taken place in justifying intercourse for other reasons than procreation, and in giving conjugal love the place it deserves, etc., as the equivalent of a repudiation or deemphasizing of the bases on which the condemnation of contraception was built up. I believe his own book shows that this is not the case. And how he could give a list of the things the Church has always said on the subject (four or five of them at the end of the book) and leave out her condemnation of contraception is a mystery to me. The whole books shows that this is one thing she always and everywhere asserted whenever the occasion arose. He also argues to an extraordinary extent, it seems to me, from silence on this or that, and draws his own conclusions tendentiously from a silence which might have various explanations.[23]

Ford used Noonan's historical data in the birth control commission discussions to argue that the Church had an unbroken tradition of condemning contraception in its history. But he was critical of Noonan's position on development of moral doctrine: "Noonan formulates in a narrow and biased way the position that Christian morality depends on charity. His simple-minded presentation of this simply ignores all the developments of moral theory in the scholastics. In the end, Noonan hardly has room to recognize anything as contrary to charity unless it is first contrary to justice, since he himself is basically a legalistic moralist. TIME handled Noonan very kindly and so far as possible made the best of his book, which itself makes the best of a bad history for the contraceptionist cause."[24]

In an urgent letter, Ford wrote to a fellow Jesuit, Thomas F. Divine, seeking materials to dispute Noonan's work:

> I know you realize the seriousness of what is going on here, and it seems important to me to have some evidence from the other side on this usury question. John Noonan, whom I know quite well and admire, has acquired such a reputation for scholarship that everything he says is accepted as gospel and as there is nobody here to contradict him his ipse dixit carries the day. . . .
>
> I assure you, you can be of real service to me, and, I think, to the Holy Father, if you can manage to show that there are two sides to the usury analogy. For the same reason please send me a curriculum vitae of yourself, and build it up unblushingly. It's going to be one authority against another.[25]

A year after the publication of *Contraception*, Noonan wrote an article titled "Authority, Usury and Contraception." In this article, he makes a comparison between the authority that had previously supported the universal prohibition against usury in 1450 and the authority used to support the prohibition on contraception as of 1965. Presenting the different sources of authority for the prohibitions against usury and contraception (scripture texts, patristic writings, conciliar decrees, and papal statements), Noonan shows how the authority used to support the old usury prohibition had greater weight than the authority used to support the current teaching on contraception. He makes the case that if, despite more solid authority, it was possible to have radical change in the teaching on usury, it might also be possible to expect substantial change in the teaching on contraception.[26]

At the end of his article, Noonan proposes three approaches to viewing the reversal of the teaching on usury. The first approach asserts that the Church had been committed to the traditional teaching of usury based on the authoritative teaching of scripture, the Fathers, councils, popes and theologians. In order to explain the change in the teaching on usury, one would have to admit that either the Church was mistaken in having condemned usury or it had committed an error in changing the rule. To admit a grave and massive error of this scale on the part the Church would be unthinkable for traditionalist Catholics.[27]

A second approach looks at the usury prohibition in terms of its non-observance by a substantial number of people, both lenders and borrowers. This second approach places great weight on the assent and reception of the faithful of the teaching of the magisterium. This approach asserts that the magisterium was not committed to a teaching beyond what all believers assented to. Noonan points out that this approach would be problematic because it would run the risk of making the Church's moral law dependent on universal acceptance. Pushed to its logical consequences, such an approach would call into question many teachings of the Church that are not observed by any number of Catholics. This second approach would undermine the force of moral laws.[28]

The third approach, which Noonan endorses, looks at the values that the prohibition of usury was trying to protect. The Church was trying to protect justice and charity when it condemned usury. The prohibition against usury was meant to protect the poor from exploitation, to encourage the wealthy to share their resources, and to ensure the proper distribution of capital within the community. In the medieval village economy, the absolute prohibition functioned adequately to protect justice and charity. The rule against usury, however, was not exempted from reexamination and revision once economic circumstances changed. This third approach allows the possibility of significant changes in the Church's moral teaching without implying any error on the part of the Church.[29]

Noonan suggests that this third approach could be applied to the contraception debate in 1965. Using this approach, the early formulation of the prohibition against contraception can be viewed as a response to different social environments and religious movements that threatened certain goods connected with the human person and marriage. Noonan argues that "if these goods could be safeguarded without an absolute rule on contraception, then the rule might be revised if a shift in the environment made revision desirable."[30] A radical revision of a traditional teaching would not imply any error on the part of the Church. In fact it would express the consistency of the Church in seeking the best way to protect the values it held dear.

Noonan clearly expresses his support for a change in the teaching on contraception in a booklet titled *The Church and Contraception: The Issues at Stake*, published at the time when Paul VI had yet to make an authoritative pronouncement on contraception. Noonan addresses the concerns of those who feared that changing substantially the teaching on contraception would be an admission of error by the Church.

> For over nineteen hundred years Christian authority condemned contraception as evil. . . . How can the Church now abandon its norm without at the same time abandoning its authority in a confession of plain error? To some the question has seemed unanswerable, and the dilemma thereby created incurable.
>
> The question, however, in a simplistic way fails to take account of either the nature of moral rules or the nature of the Church. Moral rules have purposes; they are responses to problems. If the problem changes, but the old response continues to be given, one does not exhibit constancy but stupidity. The relevant question, then, is: does the Church today face the same problems to which the norm against contraception was a response? If it does not, the Church is free to change its rule without inconsistency. Put another way, the Church is required to be constant only to the extent the requirements of human nature are constant. Such freedom is, moreover, consistent with the nature of the Church, which the Gospel likens to a mustard seed grown into a tree. The law of life of the Church is the law of organic growth, not a mechanical repetition of molds. Only he who fails to grasp this secret of the Church's vitality will suppose that a norm once made is made to be repeated forever, however inappropriate it may have become.[31]

A pastoral question was raised: "Where would a change leave confessors who have been judging penitents guilty of sin for practicing contraception, pastors who have been preaching against it, and married couples who have formed their consciences and their lives at the Church's behest?" As a historian, Noonan responds by referring back to the Church's experience when it changed its teaching on usury.

> Where were the priests and people left who had been taught that to seek, or hope for, profit on a loan offended God and nature? They, too, were

left to the judgment of their own consciences and God's judgment as to whether they had lent money to their neighbor with conscientious respect for the norm of neighborly love determined by the spiritual community to which they gave allegiance.[32]

Noonan expressed an optimistic view that just as the Church was able to move forward without any loss in its authority or credibility when it changed its rule on usury, the Church would be able to move forward in wisdom and growth if it were to decide to change its rule on contraception to better protect basic values in the face of a new social environment.

When *Humane vitae* was promulgated, Noonan used the premise of fallibility to give the document historical context: "By all tests the new document is not an infallible statement. It is a fallible document, written by a fallible man in the fallible exercise of his office. The question may be answered from history as to what prominence and what claim on conscience is made by a fallible papal statement."[33] He cites examples of fallible papal statements in the past, which were no longer accepted in the present.

In 1302 Boniface VIII issued to the world the statement, "We declare, pronounce, define and proclaim that it is entirely necessary for salvation that every human creature be subject to the Roman Pontiff." What theologian, what bishop, what pope believes that this statement is true today? . . .

In 1832, Gregory XVI dealt with the contention that every man has a right to freedom of conscience. He described this contention as "an erroneous opinion, or rather a delirium." This view of freedom of conscience was decisively rejected by Pope Paul VI and the bishops of the Second Vatican Council in their statement on religious freedom.

It is plain that the fallible statements of earlier popes have been refuted in the course of time by the criticism and rejection of the church.[34]

Noonan appealed to Paul VI to respond to the mounting objections against the encyclical from the laity, theologians, and a number of bishops. The way *Humanae vitae* closed the door to a substantial change in the teaching on contraception was counter to the process of the development of doctrine that Noonan believed was necessary for—and demonstrably operative in—the life of the Church. Noonan urged the hierarchy to learn from the lessons of history, and to be careful in making absolute claims regarding contraception.

In his later writings, Noonan continued to assert that the Church's teaching on a number of moral issues had undergone substantial changes while basic values have been faithfully pursued and protected. In his celebrated 1993 article, "Development of Moral Doctrine," Noonan surveyed four cases of radical changes in the Church's teaching: usury, marriage, slavery, and religious freedom. In the past the Church had taught that taking interest on loans was forbidden, that the bond of marriage may under no circumstances be broken, that slavery was acceptable, and that heretics were to be ruthlessly suppressed. In the course of time, however, various factors contributed to move the Church to revise these teachings. As a result, interest-taking has become a legitimate economic activity, slavery has been rejected, religious freedom has been recognized, and exceptions have been introduced to allow the dissolution of a marriage bond. Noonan acknowledged one reason why some people in the Church resist change: the fear of intellectual inconsistency. In response to this fear, Noonan proposed that the consistency the Church should seek should not be verbal or literal but, rather, consistency with Christ.

> In the Church there can always be fresh appeal to Christ, there is always the possibility of probing new depth of insight. . . . Our world has grown through mutation, should not our morals, especially when the direction and goal are provided by the Lord? . . . Must we not, then frankly admit that change is something that plays a role in Catholic moral teaching? Must not the traditional motto *semper idem* be modified, however unsettling that might be, in the direction of *plus ça change, plus c'est la meme chose?* Yes, if the principle of change is Christ.[35]

Noonan made the case that it was possible to change substantially a teaching without any admission of error as long as the Church remained constant in the defense of basic values. Authentic doctrinal development was not a repetition of formulas but rather a creative and responsive process of fostering basic values in the face of changing environments. Noonan had hoped that the Church hierarchy would adopt this forward-looking view of doctrinal development and avoid being paralyzed by the fear of error and the loss of moral authority.

Comparing the Two Approaches

Ford agreed with Noonan that new scientific discoveries and new social environments could initiate doctrinal development, and that students of the development of doctrine needed to find the underlying historical teachings. They disagreed on how consistent a new teaching must be with the existing tradition. For Noonan, a new teaching may be reformulated to the point of reversing a strict prohibition or introducing exceptions that were not accepted previously. Ford, on the other hand, insisted that continuity with tradition was the defining mark of authentic development; therefore any proposed teaching that contradicted a previous teaching was unacceptable. Noonan, acknowledging the lessons of history, trusted that the Church was capable of moving forward with a radically new teaching without admission of error or loss of authority. Ford responded that a radical change in an authoritative teaching would bring about the collapse of the Church's moral authority.

One factor to which neither Noonan nor Ford gave sufficient consideration in their debate was the historical relevance of consistency. Noonan's position that the Church could move forward without loss of authority even if it made a substantial change in the teaching on contraception may not have adequately appreciated how much doctrinal consistency had become a primary value in the manualist tradition. Doctrinal consistency was one of the important defenses of the Church against perceived threats to its teaching authority that emerged in the nineteenth and early twentieth centuries, such as existentialism, situation ethics, and modernism. Ford, on the other hand, in seeking to refute Noonan's presentation of the change in the teaching on usury, may not have appreciated the fact that doctrinal consistency may not have been a primary value during the period when these changes were being proposed by moral theologians.

A look at the history of casuistry will help illumine the historical relevance of doctrinal consistency. The moral theologians during the high casuistry of the sixteenth and seventeenth centuries, when confronted with new moral cases that could not be handled with old norms, responded by making inductive case comparisons. Consistency to principles was not a primary consideration during this time because moralists were more concerned with looking into similarities and distinctions between hard cases and paradigm cases that could lead to new solutions to extraordinary moral situations. The twentieth-century manualist moral theologians, on the other hand, used low casuistry's deductive application of principles to resolve moral cases. The consistency of principles was more important in manualist casuistry because principles, not paradigm cases, were the standards used to measure moral cases.[36]

Ford chose to apply the approach of low casuistry to the issue of contraception, while Noonan applied the approach of high casuistry. For Noonan, the change that was possible for the teaching on usury in the sixteenth and seventeenth centuries was possible for the teaching on contraception in the twentieth century. The difference between the approaches of Noonan and Ford resulted from their different perceptions about the nature of doctrinal consistency as well as its importance. As a result, they had very different views of the possibility of change in an authoritative teaching of the Church.

Ford required that any authentic doctrinal development be consistent with tradition. But was Ford himself consistent with tradition in his treatment of the issue of birth regulation?

Case Study: The Development of the Teaching on Periodic Continence

An analysis of Ford's treatment of the case of periodic continence shows that he was not consistent with his own principles of doctrinal development, and that he actually utilized a solution that was in line with Noonan's approach to doctrinal development.

This case study will be discussed in two parts. The first part presents John Ford's account of the development of the teaching on periodic continence up to 1965. The second part of the case study investigates an inconsistency between Ford's approach to doctrinal development and his account of the development of the teaching on periodic continence.

Ford and Kelly define periodic continence as "the systematic practice of restricting intercourse to the sterile periods for the purposes of avoiding conception."[37] They consider the topic of periodic continence as an important issue in moral theology, particularly in the context of the heated debate on contraception prior to Vatican II. In *Marriage Questions*, Ford and Kelly devote a substantial section of their book to explain the history of periodic continence and to provide an updated theological and pastoral approach to the teaching.

St. Augustine made the earliest statement on the morality of periodic continence. In his debate against the Manicheans' belief that the flesh was evil and childbirth was to be avoided to prevent the entrapment of souls into flesh, Augustine condemns their practice of preventing conception by timing intercourse during what they believed to be a woman's infertile period. From the time of Augustine until the nineteenth century, the Church's opposition to the practice of periodic continence was based on the belief that procreation was the only end or purpose of marriage that avoided sin.

> To Augustine and to many theologians who followed him for centuries after, procreation was not merely the primary end of the use of marriage; it seemed to be the only entirely blameless end. . . . Augustine taught not only the essential subordination of the remedy for concupiscence to the procreation of children, but he explained this subordination as one of means to an end. The use of concupiscence was entirely without sin only because and only when it was used as a means to the procreation of children for everlasting life.[38]

A change in the teaching on periodic incontinence began in the nineteenth century. In 1853, the Sacred Penitentiary responded to a question submitted by the bishop of Amiens. The bishop had asked about what should be done regarding the matter of a couple who restrict their sexual intercourse to the woman's infertile period if they have a legitimate reason. The Sacred Penitentiary responded that the couple should not be disturbed in their practice as long as they were "doing nothing to impede conception." In 1880, the Sacred Penitentiary, responding to similar questions, reaffirmed that couples that practiced the use of the sterile period should not be disturbed in their consciences. The penitentiary did not recommend that confessors should actively promote the practice of periodic continence, but rather suggested that the confessor can "insinuate cautiously" the practice, if he is unable to convince the couple to avoid the practice of withdrawal or onanism.[39]

Moralists between 1890 and 1930 estimated that the middle of the menstrual cycle as the least probable time for conception. This estimation proved inaccurate and led to failures in the prevention of pregnancies using periodic continence. As result, until 1930, there was little controversy about periodic continence because it was not widely used.

Papal Approval of Periodic Continence

By 1930, medical findings by Hermann Knaus and Kyusako Ogino led to the development of the Ogino–Knaus method of estimating the days of a woman's fertile period. Because it was based on the rhythm of a woman's menstrual cycle, the term "rhythm method" was coined. The method was limited in its applicability because it was meant only for women with a predictable and regular menstrual cycle. Using a calendar method of tracking a woman's menstrual cycle, it required a yearlong period of abstinence in order to record twelve consecutive menstrual cycles to determine the number of days of a woman's specific cycle. Calculating from a regular twenty-eight-day menstrual cycle, the Ogino–Knaus method estimated that ovulation would occur fourteen days after menstruation and that a woman's period of fertility when intercourse should be avoided to prevent conception would be between the seventh and the eighteenth day after menstruation. Longer or shorter menstrual cycles would call for adjustments in the estimation of the fertile period. Because of many factors that can cause variations on the actual day of ovulation, such as stress, disease, age, and emotions, and because of the reality of irregular menstrual cycles in a number of women, the usefulness and reliability the rhythm method was limited.[40] Despite its limitation, however, the introduction of the rhythm method provided some hope that future medical discoveries would lead to more accurate estimation of the fertility cycle.

Pius XI refers to the rhythm method in his encyclical *Casti connubii* (1930), and he states that the use of the sterile period was not a violation of nature.

> Nor are those married couples acting against the order of nature who make use of their right in the proper, natural way, even though, through natural causes either of time or of certain defects, new life cannot hence result. For both in matrimony and in the use of the conjugal right there are secondary ends, such as mutual help, the fostering of mutual love, and the quieting of concupiscence, which the spouses are by no means

forbidden to intend, provided that the intrinsic nature of that act is preserved, and accordingly its relation to the primary end.[41]

Although *Casti connubii* recognized that the rhythm method was not contrary to nature, it did not provide any moral guidance about the systematic use of rhythm. Conflicting opinions among theologians regarding the use of rhythm led to confusion among the clergy as well as the laity. From the theological discussions on the topic, Ford and Kelly drew out three conditions that would permit the practice of systematic periodic continence: (a) both spouses willingly agreed to the practice; (b) both spouses were able to do so without either one being involved in an unjustifiable occasion of sin; and (c) there was a legitimate reason for avoiding conception. These they argued were points of agreement among most moral theologians. Moreover, they held that most moral theologians agreed that violation of the first two conditions was mortally sinful while there was disagreement regarding the violation of the third condition. A minority of theologians (e.g., Goeyvaerts, Griese, and Salsman) held that a systematic and prolonged use of rhythm without a legitimate reason was mortally sinful, while the majority held that it was at most only venially sinful. [42] Ford and Kelly concluded that this majority opinion was the more probable opinion. In terms of confessional practice, a confessor could not impose on penitents, under pain of mortal sin, the condition that there must be a legitimate reason for avoiding conception in order to engage in systematic use of periodic continence.[43]

In Ford's "Notes on Moral Theology" for 1941 and 1944, an assessment of the current medical knowledge about the fertility cycle of women had led him to conclude that there was still no unanimity on the effectiveness of the rhythm method and that pastors should be cautious in endorsing the rhythm method in order not to create confusion among different forms of birth control. Ford warns that "there is the obvious danger that the undiscriminating public, and even those who are well able to discriminate, will fail to see the moral difference between the forbidden methods of birth control and the safe period technique (rhythm)."[44]

"Do couples have an affirmative obligation to procreate?" This question is linked to the discussion of whether couples needed a legitimate reason to practice systematic periodic continence. If couples did not have an obligation to procreate then they would not need an excusing reason to practice rhythm. Ford and Kelly observe that the majority of moralists did not see any obligation for couples to procreate. "As far as we have been able to judge from the literature," they wrote, "the majority of theologians before 1951 taught that there was per se no affirmative obligation on the individual couple to procreate. Consequently on the practical level it was improper to impose this obligation on the faithful."[45]

Furthermore, Ford argued that the Church has historically accepted and even praised certain couples who have practiced perfect continence (avoiding intercourse throughout their marriage) when done for a supernatural motive and by mutual consent.[46] Notably, Ford endorses this position in his doctoral dissertation at the Pontifical Gregorian University in Rome, "The Validity of Virginal Marriage."[47]

After acknowledging the majority opinion, Ford and Kelly ask "If there is no obligation for couples to procreate, then why would a majority of theologians consider it a venial sin to use systematic periodic continence without a legitimate reason?" The two moralists declare that they were not convinced by arguments proposed by other theologians defending the requirement of a legitimate reason to practice rhythm. These arguments included the following: the danger of abuse in the use of rhythm, the possibility of selfish motivations, and the maintenance of the "ideal of fertility." Finding such arguments weak and unconvincing, Ford and Kelly assert that the more logical position was "If there is *per se* no obligation to have children, . . . it is not *per se* sinful, not even venially sinful, to practice rhythm."[48]

Significant Developments in the Teaching

A milestone in the development of the teaching on periodic continence was Pius XII's *Address to Midwives* in 1951. This papal pronouncement introduced two specific changes to the teaching. The first change concerned the prudent manner in which the message about periodic continence was to be disseminated to the public. A hundred years previously, the Sacred Penitentiary had advised that "cautious insinuation" be used by confessors when suggesting the practice of periodic continence to couples. Pius XII's address recommended that information on rhythm be made more publicly accessible to couples. The pope exhorted his audience of professional midwives that they should have accurate and up-to-date information regarding periodic continence and that they should be ready to answer questions about the practice either verbally or in publications. The fact that the pope spoke on periodic continence while publicly addressing a professional group of laywomen in the vernacular was a sign that the Church had moved forward in its manner of advocating the rhythm method. Pius XII ushered in a more direct approach to endorsing the practice of periodic continence.[49]

The second development Pius XII introduced in his *Address to Midwives* was his assertion that married couples had a duty to procreate. Ford and Kelly noted that this assertion was a surprise because it was the first time that a papal pronouncement had articulated such a duty. Because the majority opinion among moral theologians before 1951 was that there was no duty to procreate, and because Pius XI's statement regarding the duty was not enunciated in an encyclical but rather in a vernacular address to a group of laypersons, there was disagreement among theologians whether the papal address had actually established a duty to procreate. Ford and Kelly, deferring to the pope, concede that the accepted theological position was now in favor of the existence of a duty. "The papal teaching on the duty to procreate came as a surprise to many. But surprising or not, and prescinding from the degree of solemnity or authority which attaches to it, it is now the accepted theological position, and has become the object of much discussion."[50]

The *Address to Midwives* also acknowledges the existence of serious reasons capable of exempting a couple from the obligation of procreation for long periods of time. "Serious motives such as those which are frequently present in the so called 'indications'—medical, eugenic, economic, and social—can exempt from this positive, obligatory prestation for a long time, even for the entire duration of the marriage."[51]

In general, Ford and Kelly sought a benign pastoral approach for couples consulting pastors about the use of periodic continence.

> We think that the great majority of couples who take the trouble to consult the priest do have good reasons for at least a temporary practice of periodic continence. Sometimes these reasons are excellent—perhaps even compelling; and at other times they may strike the priest as somewhat insignificant or at most borderline. We believe that the priest should lean toward benevolence and away from rigorism in interpreting these

reasons; that he should accept the sincere judgment of these people who obviously want to do the right thing and then help them sanctify the practice of periodic continence.[52]

Ford was also insistent that confessors should not judge as mortally sinful the use of periodic continence without a justifying reason. In their 1953 "Notes on Moral Theology," Ford and Kelly argue that the pope did not say that use of rhythm without justifying reason was a mortal sin, even though he could have. Since theologians at that time were in disagreement about the nature of the sin involved in the unjustified use of rhythm, there was no basis to impose grave obligations in the confessional and to preach with unwarranted severity on the unjustified use of rhythm.[53]

Although periodic continence had limited applicability for many married couples, Ford hoped that future medical discoveries would make the rhythm method more accurate and dependable, thus providing a more effective alternative to other artificial means of birth control. He believed that the future development of the Church's teaching on contraception would include a refinement of the rhythm method based on new scientific data. During Ford's private audiences with Paul VI, he and the pope discussed the possibilities for development of doctrine on contraception. When Paul VI asked Ford for a solution to the Church's present difficulty with the birth control pill, Ford told the pope of the possible development of a new drug which would indicate the true time of ovulation. If such a drug would become available, its use could be considered licit. This possible new drug being developed would not suspend ovulation, like the current birth control pills, but rather it would enable couples to predict the exact time of ovulation and thus make a more accurate estimation of the days they should abstain from intercourse in order to avoid conception. Ford confidently predicted that couples might only need to abstain for a week per menstrual cycle if the drug worked effectively.

At the end of his audience, Ford told the pope that the possibility of development lay in the discovery and use of new physiological data on the fertility cycle.[54] In a letter written during the papal birth control commission sessions in 1966, Ford expresses his hope for future doctrinal development on periodic continence: "I am convinced that the legitimate development we expect in the teaching of the Church is going to be based primarily on physiological information and interpretation—because I believe that the inviolability of the sources of human life defended by the Church, like the inviolability of human life itself, is so bound up with the physiology of both, that one will depend on what is known about the other."[55]

The promised drug never materialized.

Ford's insistence on physiological data as the basis for future doctrinal development reveals a physicalist perspective that relied on nature to define moral obligation, particularly in cases involving medical and sexual ethics. We see this physicalist perspective applied in previously discussed cases. In the case of the scarred uterus, Ford changed his moral position on the issue because of new medical data on the mortality rates of women who had hysterectomies after several caesarean operations. Similarly, Ford's support for the minority opinion on the case of double vasectomy was also based on current physiological knowledge of the male reproductive system.

Taking into account the importance he gave to continuity with tradition, it seems uncharacteristic of Ford not to raise the question of continuity in his account of the development of the teaching on periodic continence. In his "Notes on Moral Theology" in 1942, Ford comments on the discrepancy between the current opinion of moralists on the use of periodic continence and the previous teaching based on Augustine's negative view of the use of the sterile period. "I have seen no thorough study which reconciles the discrepancies between what is commonly taught now, and what seems to have been more or less commonly accepted in the past."[56] Ford was at a loss to explain how the teaching on periodic continence had changed so radically and so rapidly. Despite his insistence on continuity with tradition, Ford had to recognize that the Holy See and most moralists of his time had taken a position on periodic continence that contradicted a previous tradition based on Augustine's teaching.

In a letter written to Joseph Dorsey in 1963, Ford reveals his continuing difficulty with the new developments in the teaching on rhythm. "If we are going to bring tradition into the picture, the thing that is more difficult to justify is the present attitude of the Church on rhythm. It would take too long to get into it, but the point is that the procreative purpose of sex looms so large in Christian tradition that the justification of rhythm becomes something of a problem, while the justification of contraception remains completely irreconcilable with that tradition."[57] In the same letter, Ford mentions sending the galleys of his book *Marriage Questions* to Dorsey. This fact is significant because in the final text of the book Ford did not mention any difficulty reconciling the practice of rhythm with the previous tradition forbidding such a practice. In fact, Ford readily accepted the radical changes in the teaching initiated by papal pronouncements in *Casti connubii* and the *Address to Midwives*.

Two things seemed to have been in conflict in Ford's mind while he was writing on periodic continence in *Marriage Questions*. On the one hand, Ford doubted the justification for periodic continence in the face of a long tradition that valued procreation. On the other hand, he needed to affirm the papal pronouncements on periodic continence.

It would seem that despite Ford's insistence on continuity with tradition as an essential part of any authentic doctrinal development, he was willing to revise his moral position and defer to the papal prerogative to introduce a new teaching. In the case of periodic continence, he had previously agreed with the majority opinion of moral theologians that there was no duty to procreate. But when Pius XII made the assertion in the *Address to Midwives* that there was a duty to procreate, Ford immediately conformed to the new papal position. He endorsed the papal pronouncement despite its lack of precedent in previous church documents and despite the majority opinion of moralists denying that such a duty existed.

In a letter he wrote in 1964, Ford reveals his approach of dutiful conformity to papal pronouncements. "I think the only thing we can do at the present, when there is so much ferment, and so much amateur (and bootleg) moral theology being circulated, is to stick with the Pope. In practice I am firmly convinced that Catholics are bound to follow the directives of the Holy See and that confessors must be guided by them."[58]

Ford's deference to the papal pronouncement on periodic continence is ironic when one considers his strong disagreement with John Noonan regarding the nature of authentic doctrinal development. Noonan's approach to development allowed for a radical change in church teaching if new social conditions warranted new ways of protecting and promoting basic goods that the Church valued. In the case of periodic continence, Pius XII responded to shifting social conditions and new findings on fertility by endorsing rhythm in his *Address to Midwives*. These substantial developments in the teaching introduced by Pius XII resonated more consistently with Noonan's value-based approach than with Ford's tradition-bound approach. Ford could not reconcile the difference between the traditional condemnation of the use of the sterile period since the time of Augustine and the endorsement of rhythm by theologians and the Holy See in the late nineteenth and early twentieth centuries. Noonan, however, was more open to the possibility of substantive changes in the tradition because his focus was not on the preservation of traditional formulas, but rather on the creative protection of basic values in the face of new social conditions. Ford's agreement with Pius XII's radical pronouncements on rhythm was an affirmation of Noonan's approach to doctrinal development.

James Keenan and Peter Black offer further insight into Ford's approach to consistency and continuity in moral doctrine in their article "The Evolving Self-understanding of the Moral Theologian." This article described a difference between the approach of the manualist tradition from the seventeenth century until Vatican II and that of the magisterium in the mid-twentieth century, with respect to the search for moral truth. Although the manuals had been predominantly sin-oriented and approached moral cases through a deductive application of universal principles, the manualists practiced tolerance for differences in opinion among theologians. The consistency that manualists valued in their search for moral truth was consistency with the moral tradition as it had been refined by successive generations of theologians. Their discernment of moral truth was not hampered by a need to consistently defend the Church's historical identity.[59]

On the other hand, the magisterium, by the mid-twentieth century, regarded consistency with previous papal utterances as a determinant of the truthfulness of a moral claim. The magisterium's overriding concern to defend its authority to bind consciences, and its identity as the authentic interpreter of the moral law, were reflected in an attitude that favored uniformity in moral teachings and discouraged diversity in moral opinions.[60]

The manualist stress on consistency with moral tradition and the magisterial emphasis on consistency with papal utterances are both present in Ford's two-mode moral method. In standard mode cases, Ford acted as a traditional manualist while in crisis mode cases he acted as a proxy for the magisterium. For example, in the standard mode case of the letter of the Holy Office on artificial onanism, Ford upheld the traditional manualist principle of material cooperation that favored the penitent despite the Holy Office's less lenient interpretation of the principle. Ford supported his fellow moralists at the CTSA when they issued their consensus statement on material cooperation, and he acknowledged their right to discuss the matter of material cooperation despite the Holy Office's prohibition against such discussions.

In the crisis mode case of contraceptives, Ford consistently sought to exclude from theological discussions moralists who held opinions differing from the official teaching on birth control. Instead of fostering dialogue with these moralists, Ford reported them to the Holy Office. He interpreted the papal teachings on contraceptives strictly and did not tolerate the development of probable opinion contrary to these teachings. In this crisis mode case, Ford emphasized consistency with the teaching of *Casti connubii* as the sign of doctrinal orthodoxy of a moral theologian.

One can also compare Ford's manner of dealing with two popes, Pius XII and Paul VI. In Ford's eyes, Pius XII exemplified his ideal of a pope who wielded papal authority decisively. Paul VI, however, was perceived by Ford as an indecisive and inconsistent pope. With Pius XII, Ford accepted an abrupt change in the teaching on periodic continence while with Paul VI, Ford rejected any radical change in the teaching on contraception. Ford followed Pius XII's leadership while he sought to mentor and direct Paul VI. In both cases, Ford showed his preference for a strong and decisive papacy that upheld the Church's teaching authority and controlled the direction and extent of doctrinal development in moral theology. Deference to this type of papacy had a stronger claim on Ford than the need for consistency with tradition.

Notes

1. Ford, Response to a talk by Häring (1966).
2. Ford, "State of the Question" (1966).
3. Ford, Response to a talk by Häring (1966).
4. Ford, Letter to Férin (1964), 3.
5. Ford and Kelly, *Contemporary Moral Theology*, Vol. II (1963), 360–77.
6. Ibid., 375.
7. Ford, Letter to Férin (1964), 1.

8. Noonan, *Scholastic Analysis of Usury* (1957), 56; 193.
9. Ibid., 199–200.
10. Ibid., 199–200; 393.
11. Ford, Letter to Wright (1964).
12. Ford, Letter to de Reidmatten (1964).
13. Ford, Letter to Noonan (1965).
14. Noonan, Letter to Ford (1965).
15. Noonan, *Contraception: A History* (1965), 532.
16. Ibid.
17. Ibid.
18. Ibid.
19. Ibid.
20. Ibid.
21. Ibid., 533.
22. Ibid.
23. Ford, Letter to Klubertanz (1966).
24. Ford, Letter to de Lestapis (1965).
25. Ford, Letter to Divine (1965).
26. Noonan, "Authority, Usury and Contraception" (1966), 55–79.
27. Ibid., 71.
28. Ibid., 71–72.
29. Ibid., 72–73.
30. Ibid., 74.
31. Noonan, *Church and Contraception* (1967), 6–7.
32. Ibid., 8.
33. Hoyt, "Birth Control Debate" (1968), 182.
34. Ibid., 183.
35. Noonan, "Development in Moral Doctrine" (1993), 676–77.
36. Keenan, "Return of Casuistry" (1996), 130.
37. Ford and Kelly, *Contemporary Moral Theology*, Vol. II (1963), 378.
38. Ibid., 382.
39. Ibid., 383–84.
40. Kuhn, *Rhythm* (1967), 464.
41. Pius XI, *Casti connubii* (1930).
42. Ford and Kelly, *Contemporary Moral Theology*, Vol. II (1963), 394.
43. Ibid., 387–88.
44. Ford, "Notes on Moral Theology" (1944), 509.
45. Ford and Kelly, *Contemporary Moral Theology*, Vol. II (1963), 388.
46. Ibid., 389.
47. Ford, *Validity of Virginal Marriage* (1938).
48. Ford and Kelly, *Contemporary Moral Theology*, Vol. II (1963), 393.
49. Pius XII 1951; Ford and Kelly, *Contemporary Moral Theology*, Vol. II (1963), 397.
50. Ford and Kelly, *Contemporary Moral Theology*, Vol. II (1963), 402.
51. Pius XII, *Address to Midwives* (1951), 846.

52. Ford and Kelly, *Contemporary Moral Theology*, Vol. II (1963), 447–48.
53. Ford and Kelly, "Notes on Moral Theology, 1953" (1954), 100–101.
54. Ford, Notes on private audiences (1965).
55. Ford, Letter to de Béthune (1966).
56. Ford, "Notes on Moral Theology" (1942), 598.
57. Ford, Letter to Dorsey (1963).
58. Ford, Letter to Murphy (1964).
59. Keenan and Black, "Evolving Self-Understanding" (2001), 294–303.
60. Ibid., 303–7.

PART II

MORAL OBJECTIVITY

CHAPTER FIVE

OBJECTIVE MORAL NORMS AND SITUATION ETHICS

Objective moral norms played a central role in Ford's method. This chapter illustrates his commitment to an ethics based on objective moral norms by examining his comprehensive critique of situation ethics.

Moral Norms and Obligations in Ford's Method

The manuals presented the eternal law of God as the ultimate, objective norm of morality. Since the eternal law could not be known directly by human beings, the divine law and the natural law served as the proximate, objective norms of morality that could be known by reason and revelation.[1] Ford's writings affirmed the natural law and the universal objective moral norms derived from it by human reason.

> There is a natural law known to us by the light of human reason. It is a law which independently of all human legislation and custom, forbids some things as evil and commands others as good. And by the light of reason man can find out what some of those things are—with greater or less accuracy—by looking at his own nature, the nature of the society in which he lives, his relations with his fellow-beings and his relations with God. From an investigation of all these he can conclude that some things are in accordance with his nature and therefore good; other things are repugnant to it and bad. And reason informs him with compelling insistence that he ought to do what is good,—it is an imperative ought;—and he ought not to do what is bad.[2]

Given a principle of natural law, firmly established, for example, "parricide is immoral," it is valid for all men, at all times, in all places, and if the proposition is stated with sufficient precision, in all circumstances. There are no exempt days, no exempt territory. There is no such thing as a moral holiday where natural law is concerned.[3]

Recognition of the authority of God, who created the natural order, forms the basis for the obligation to follow the objective moral norms derived from natural law.

> There is no use trying to find a natural law (according to the scholastics) which does not depend ultimately on a personal God for its meaning and efficacy . . . It is the eternal mind and will of God that establishes the essential moral order and commands that it be maintained.
>
> If you leave God out, you no longer have an adequate principle of obligation. You might, without appealing to His authority find that certain things were good and others bad, but you would not have any adequate principle of necessity which would oblige you morally to do what is good and avoid what is bad.[4]

In manualist moral theology, the obligation to obey and follow the will of God as revealed to human reason by the natural law is fulfilled through obedience to the magisterium. Since Christ commissioned the magisterium to proclaim God's revealed truth, the magisterium has the authority to act as the teacher and interpreter of the moral law. "The Catholic Church asserts that it does not make the laws of God; but it claims to be the only authentic interpreter of them. In other words, the laws mean what the Church says they mean . . . The Church has authority to teach the laws of God."[5]

Ford's Critique of Situation Ethics

Ford's commitment to an ethics based on objective moral norms found its fullest expression in his critique of situation ethics. In *Questions in Fundamental Moral Theology*, Ford and Kelly wrote a lengthy analysis of situation ethics. Tracing a succession of papal statements from 1946 to 1956, the two authors document the growing concern of the Holy See regarding the new philosophy of existentialism and the resulting emergence of a "new morality" described by names such as "ethical existentialism," "ethical actualism," "morality according to situations," and most commonly, "situation ethics."[6]

In the encyclical *Humani generis*, Pius XII criticizes existentialism for rejecting "the immutable essences of things" and focusing only on the existence of the individual. The pope expresses indignation that existentialism and similar philosophies did not give due respect to the authority of the magisterium: "It would indeed be unnecessary to deplore these aberrations from truth if all, even in the domain of philosophy, showed proper reverence for and paid attention to the magisterium of the Church which has the divinely given mission not only to guard and interpret the deposit of divinely revealed truth, but also to watch over the philosophical sciences lest erroneous theories harm Catholic dogma."[7]

In a radio message on March 23, 1952, Pius XII criticized the proponents of the new morality for removing the individual conscience from the authority of the Church, which they described as oppressive and too insistent on the rigor of the law. The advocates of the new morality proposed the law of freedom and love as the basis for morality. The pope saw this rejection of objective moral norms and the overemphasis on the freedom of the individual's conscience as the main weakness of the new morality. Commenting on the pope's message, Ford and Kelly wrote: "It was to the Church, and not to individuals, that Christ gave His revelation, 'of which moral obligations are an essential part'; and it was to the Church alone that Christ promised the divine aid required for avoiding error. The unstated conclusion of this is obvious: it is only through conformity with the teaching of the Church that the individual conscience can have security from error. The 'autonomy of the individual conscience' cannot be reconciled with the plan of Christ and can produce only 'poisonous fruits.'"[8]

Challenging the claim of situation ethics that the conscience was free to judge for itself the morality of human acts, the pope declared that there were acts that were intrinsically evil, which objective moral norms would prohibit without exceptions. He listed a sampling of twenty acts as gravely forbidden by God regardless of circumstance. The list included not only the traditionally acknowledged grievous acts such as fornication, adultery, blasphemy, and idolatry, but also acts reflecting social concerns within contemporary society, such as monopolizing vital foodstuffs, unjustifiably increasing prices, and fraudulent bankruptcy. Pius XII declared that "all this is gravely forbidden by the divine Lawmaker. No examination is necessary, no matter what the situation of the individual may be, there is no other course for him to obey."[9] The pope insisted that persons were obliged to obey prohibitions against such acts and were not, therefore, absolutely free to make their own choices as situation ethicists would claim.

Ford and Kelly noted that situation ethics was expressed in a variety of forms, ranging from a general rejection of objective norms to simply a minimization of moral prohibitions. They pointed out that the pope's statements referred at different times to various forms of situation ethics, and they identified four characteristics of situation ethics.

The first was an attitude that limited or even rejected the authority of the magisterium to impose moral norms. The authority of the magisterium was restricted to the religious sphere of human life, leaving politics, economics, science, and the arts to be governed and judged by their own laws. Ford and Kelly responded to this attitude by quoting Pius XII in *Humani generis*, who insisted on the competence of the Church to speak on the morality of every human activity.

Some carried this logic further and dismissed the magisterium's authority outright, appealing instead for a new morality governed by prudence and charity. Situation ethicists argued: "If the early Christians could serve Christ without the rules laid down later, why cannot we do the same?" Ford and Kelly insisted that the development, interpretation, and refinement of the moral law were necessary for the growth of the Church and for the ongoing formation of the consciences of the faithful.[10]

Second, they made a distinction between existentialist and Protestant situation ethics. The existential form rejected moral principles, while the Protestant form maintained a Christian view of the moral law while allowing for the higher law of love and the individual's direct relationship with God to overrule the moral law in concrete cases.[11] Ford and Kelly expressed their concern that Protestant situation ethics, which separated God's law from the moral law, had begun to influence Catholics. They praised an article by Josef Fuchs that analyzed and critiqued this form of situation ethics. Fuchs compared Protestant situation ethics to a wagon wheel:

> The spokes of the wheel are moral norms which all tend to one point, the will of God. However, the moral norms, like the spokes of the wheel, never meet, because at the center is a hole, a vacuum, in which God makes known to me here and now His inscrutable will. Consequently,

these moral norms are a general indication of God's will, but in the concrete situation, God indicates to me—as it were independently of these
norms—His present will in my regard. Since at times He may even indicate to me a course of action contrary to that prescribed in a general
norm, I must look to the actual situation to discover his will.[12]

Fuchs objected to the situationist position that an ethics based on
objective moral norms limited the absolute freedom and power of God
to command a person according to his will. He affirmed the Catholic
position that God could not give a command to an individual that contradicted natural law, because nature itself was created in the likeness
of God. If God were to command something against the natural law, he
would be contradicting himself. Fuchs also criticized the tendency of
situation ethics to view every moral situation as unique and completely
under God's mysterious will. This was contrary to the Catholic approach
of viewing each moral situation within the context of a natural order that
was sustained consistently by God. This natural order allowed persons
to discern universal moral principles that could guide decision making in future situations. Rejecting an ethics that denied objective moral
norms and imagined God's commands to be arbitrary or changeable,
Fuchs affirmed a view of ethics that was based on the order that God established in creation and communicated to human reason.[13]

Situation ethics also placed an undue emphasis on the "personal decision" that an individual must make in response to a moral situation.
This third characteristic took a variety of forms because situational ethicists differed widely on the relevance of the individual's personal decision. An extreme existentialist interpretation would view this personal
decision as completely independent of any consideration of God or
moral principles. A Protestant situation ethicist would see this personal
decision as influenced by a direct inspiration from God, which might or
might not be consistent with existing moral precepts. Here the second
and third characteristics of Protestant situation ethics reinforce one another: an individual makes a "personal decision" to follow a direct inspiration from a God who is not bound by existing moral norms.

The fourth characteristic of situation ethics identified by Ford and
Kelly was a pervasive attitude of contempt for moral minimalism.
Rather than accept mediocrity in the moral life, situationists insisted
on a moral life unencumbered by duty to moral laws and marked by

self-assertion, creativity, liberty, and spontaneity. Ford and Kelly respond by pointing out that the freedom called for by the situationists actually meant freedom from the plan of God. This form of freedom made the person the sole norm of morality. Ford and Kelly insist that freedom, as understood by the Church, "is a regulated freedom; the power of thinking and acting within a divinely-outlined pattern."[14] They also come to the defense of the so-called mediocre Christian who strived daily to avoid mortal and venial sins by dutifully following moral norms. Ford and Kelly attest to the sanctity and holiness of persons who appeared to live "negatively good lives" in the eyes of situationists.

> Any priest who has dealt intimately with consciences over a number of years comes to realize that there are many people who are capable of leading the negatively good lives criticized by the situationists, but who simply do not respond to exhortations to do more. Moreover, it is to be noted that it is not only mediocrity in the spiritual sense that the situationists (and some others) criticize. Equally subject to their censures are those large numbers of Catholics who lead good, simple lives, who do their duty as the Church through their pastors or their confessors has explained it to them. These devout persons, who will one day take their places in the ranks of the canonized saints honored on November 1, are criticized because of their "passivity," their lack of spiritual initiative, their lack of "creativeness."[15]

Near the end of their analysis of situation ethics, Ford and Kelly clarify their position on personal initiative. They were skeptical that personal initiative had any role to play regarding a moral precept. In the case of a counsel, which urges a person beyond the call of duty, they allow "room for personal initiative and for responsiveness to the voice of God (through the inspiration of grace) in the soul."[16]

We can learn several things about Ford's method from his critique of situation ethics. Although Ford acknowledged that moral principles could be discerned by human reason from divinely ordered nature, he was distrustful of the capacity of ordinary persons to recognize and grasp these moral principles correctly, apart from the help of the magisterium. In Ford's perspective, it would be irresponsible and imprudent for a Catholic to disregard the guidance of the magisterium when making moral choices. The only security that a person could have against error in moral decision making was conformity to the teaching of the Church.[17]

Ford's critique of situation ethics also reveals his strong commitment to protect the role of the magisterium as the authoritative interpreter of moral law. He saw situation ethics as a threat to the relevance of the magisterium in the moral decision making of ordinary persons. His defense of objective moral law was inseparable from his defense of the authority of the magisterium. The authoritative role of the magisterium as legislator, executor, and judge of moral norms was as essential as the existence of moral norms themselves. This view of the magisterium as the final arbiter of moral law was characteristic of mid-twentieth century manualism before the renewal of moral theology after Vatican II.[18]

Ford feared grave consequences for the Church if the authority of the magisterium were to be compromised. For instance, Ford wrote about what might befall the Church if the current norms on contraception were substantially changed and the use of contraceptives no longer condemned as intrinsically evil: "Therefore one must very cautiously inquire whether the change which is proposed would not bring along with it a definite depreciation of the teaching and the moral direction of the hierarchy of the church and whether several very grave doubts would not be opened up about the very history of Christianity."[19]

Ford's defense of the "mediocre Christian" from the criticism of situation ethicists also reveals his benign attitude toward minimalism in the moral life. The daily effort of ordinary Christians to follow moral norms and to avoid mortal sin was a praiseworthy achievement in his eyes, an achievement whose value should not be diminished by the demands of situation ethicists for a more free and spontaneous morality. The faithful observance of the objective moral norms taught by the Church was sufficient for holiness; anything "beyond the call of duty" was laudable but optional.

Ford had entrusted the formation and direction of the moral life of ordinary Christians to the magisterium. Any impression that the Church had been negligent in this duty could therefore lead to grave consequences. In this context, Ford's concern over the effects of any change in the teaching on contraception becomes intelligible. He articulates this concern in his "Statement of Position" for the final session of the papal birth control commission:

> This particular doctrine of the Church is one which has affected the in-
> timate lives of millions upon millions of Christians throughout the cen-
> turies. It has been imposed under the pain of mortal sin, and therefore
> to be observed in order to reach eternal salvation. . . . The Church could
> not have been the occasion of grave sin and even of spiritual ruin to so
> many millions through so many centuries or even one century, because of
> a substantially false doctrine promulgated authoritatively in the name of
> Jesus Christ. If the Church can have erred so egregiously, then the faithful
> can no longer believe in her teaching authority.[20]

Ford's working paper for the minority opinion in the birth control commission puts the matter in similar terms: "If contraception were declared not intrinsically evil, in honesty it would have to be acknowledged
that the Holy Spirit in 1930, in 1951, and 1958 assisted the Protestant
churches, and that for half a century Pius XI, Pius XII and a great part of
the Catholic hierarchy did not protect against a very serious error, one
most pernicious to souls; for it would thus be suggested that they condemned most imprudently, under the pain of eternal punishment, thousands upon thousands of human acts which are now approved."[21]

In summary, Ford's method of moral theology relied on a view that
creation was ordered and sustained by God and bore the imprint of
God's plan for humanity. Human reason had the capability to discern
and interpret God's mediated will in creation. Ford was distrustful,
however, of the competence of ordinary persons to grasp correctly the
moral principles that God desires to communicate through the order of
nature, because of the possibility of error and ignorance.

He had more confidence in the use of reason by the magisterium to
interpret the moral law because he believed in the unerring assistance
of the Holy Spirit to the Church. Ford was suspicious of ordinary persons relying on direct contact with the Holy Spirit in their moral decision making. He believed that it was through the magisterium that the
guidance of the Holy Spirit was relayed to ordinary persons.

Ford was committed to the manualist model of the moral life, which
was structured and shaped by objective moral norms formulated, taught,
and imposed by the magisterium. This commitment was translated into
an affirmation and defense of the magisterium as the authentic and authoritative interpreter of moral norms. In Ford's view, a moral life concerned primarily with the avoidance of evil through faithful observance

of concrete moral norms taught by the magisterium was a satisfactory goal for ordinary Christians.

Notes

1. Gallagher, *Time Past, Time Future* (1990), 86–87.
2. Ford, The Concept of Natural Law (lecture notes, 1958?), 4.
3. Ibid, 5, 11.
4. Ibid., 9–10.
5. Ford and Kelly, *Contemporary Moral Theology*, Vol. I (1958), 4.
6. Ibid., 104.
7. Pius XII, *Humani generis* (1950); Ford and Kelly, *Contemporary Moral Theology*, Vol. I (1958), 107.
8. Ibid., 110–11.
9. Ibid., 118.
10. Ibid., 130.
11. Ibid., 132.
12. Fuchs, "Situation Ethics" (1954), 25.
13. Ibid., 27–28.
14. Ford and Kelly, *Contemporary Moral Theology*, Vol. I (1958), 138.
15. Ibid., 139.
16. Ibid., 140.
17. Ibid., 121, 111.
18. Keenan and Black, "Evolving Self-Understanding" (2001), 303–7.
19. Ford, "State of the Question" (1968), 53.
20. Ford, Statement of position (typewritten manuscript, (1966).
21. Ford, "State of the Question" (1968), 53.

CHAPTER SIX

SUBJECTIVE CULPABILITY

This chapter examines Ford's nuanced approach to evaluating factors that can diminish subjective culpability of penitents. Ford presented moral presuppositions to assist moralists in judging a penitent in a manner that is neither too lenient nor too strict. He also investigated the nature of compulsions and their significance in the evaluation of moral culpability. After exploring Ford's understanding of these themes, I turn to his application of them to cases involving diminished subjective culpability viewed from the confessional context. The chapter concludes with a case study on alcoholism, illustrating Ford's nuanced consideration of the factors affecting moral culpability.

Freedom and Subjective Culpability in Ford's Method

The manualist commitment to objective moral norms was counterbalanced by its pastoral attentiveness to factors affecting subjective culpability. To assist penitents who found it difficult to follow moral norms, manualists studied the different circumstances that affect freedom and responsibility—circumstances that can lessen moral guilt. Ford contrasted the manualist approach with that of situation ethics.

> Human sympathy instinctively leads us to hope that men are not guilty of the apparently vast number of serious sins they commit; for mortal sin deprives a man of eternal life, and delivers him, if unrepentant, to eternal death. Situationists would reduce the number of mortal sins in the world by diminishing the objective binding force of the moral law; even by completely abolishing it in certain peculiarly difficult situations. Orthodox theologians know that the problem cannot be solved in this way. They are more likely to seek a solution on the subjective side, by appealing to

factors which prevent man from being fully responsible for the deeds he actually commits.[1]

In Ford's context, the introduction of Freudian psychology had influenced moral theologians to consider the effects of the unconscious on moral decision making and actions. He wrote, "The doctrines of Freud have revolutionized psychological thinking and have left a deep impress on the thought of mankind. The moralist, who by profession must be concerned with human conduct and misconduct, cannot shut his eyes to any source of information which can shed light on human motives and human responsibility. . . . We can profit by accepting, for the purposes of our discussion, the supposition that the dynamic unconscious does exist and that unconscious motivation does play a significant role in the life of conscious people."[2]

Ford was open to the insights of psychology; he was even, briefly, a lecturer on psychology at Weston College in 1933.[3] He was cautious, however, about certain schools of thought in psychology that had a deterministic view of the human person—views denying the existence of sufficient freedom for a person to be responsible for his or her actions. "The mere fact that the unconscious influences our conduct, or influences a great deal of it, or influences it to a great extent, is no direct proof that our freedom and responsibility are notably impaired, much less eliminated. We cannot immediately conclude that since there is a great deal of unconscious motivation in a given act, therefore the agent lacks the amount of freedom which is necessary to be guilty of mortal sin, or worthy of the highest merit before God."[4]

To help pastors and confessors who were confused by varying claims of psychologists about the degree of psychological freedom a person had in making moral decisions, John Ford proposed three basic theological presuppositions to guide the manualist approach to moral culpability. The first presupposition asserts that an ordinary person possesses enough psychological freedom to incur culpability. Ford quotes Pius XII's address to psychotherapists, in which he affirmed that the presumption of human culpability in grave moral acts remained true even when a person was affected by emotion, passion, or concupiscence. "Original sin did not take away from man the possibility of the obligation of directing his own actions himself through his soul. It cannot be alleged that the psychic troubles and disorders which disturb the normal functioning of the psychic being represent what usually happens. The moral struggle to remain on the right path does not prove that it is impossible to follow that path, nor does it authorize any drawing back."[5]

Ford, however, seeks to clarify the pope's statement by making a distinction between normal and abnormal situations. Pius XII refers to normal situations where persons retained a certain degree of freedom to act morally despite disturbances from emotions, temptations, and the like. Ford notes that the pope seemed to imply that a different norm of culpability was applicable to cases of mental illness. Advances in psychological research had made it possible to broaden the concept of mental illness to admit that there were cases in which some persons truly lacked the psychological freedom necessary to be guilty of mortal sin.[6]

The second presupposition is the reality of sin. Ford rejects the idea that it is almost impossible for a person to commit a mortal sin. This idea contradicts ordinary human experience as well as the teaching and practice of the Church, especially in the sacrament of confession.[7] Drawing from the experience of pastors and confessors in their ministry, Ford affirms the reality and variety of sins that ordinary persons are capable of committing with sufficient knowledge and freedom.

The third presupposition is the doctrine of grace. Ford insists that God's grace was sufficient to enable ordinary persons to avoid sin. He clarifies this, however, stating that the promise of God's grace did not mean that persons would be preserved from material mortal sin. He recognized that there were people incapable of cooperating with God's grace for various physical or psychological reasons.

> Suppose a case of a madman who goes berserk and murders his custodian. He commits a material mortal sin. Did this happen because he failed to cooperate with the grace of God? Was God's grace sufficient to keep him from being tempted above his strength if only he had accepted it, then or earlier? No one believes in any such thing, because such a person is simply incapable of any cooperation. Something similar could be true of one who is not so sick that he is incapable of a human act altogether, but is sick enough so that he is pathologically impelled to the commission of a sinful act. And so once more we see how important it is to distinguish between those who are sick and those who are well.[8]

These three presuppositions seek to guide moralists away from excessive leniency in judging the culpability of persons in matters of grave sin. As a counterbalance, Ford gives several considerations that reminded moralists not to be too strict in their judgment of penitents. These considerations are drawn from the insights of psychology on the unconscious and human freedom, and how these influence a person's actions.

To show how the findings of psychological research had been assimilated by moral theology, Ford reviewed two questions which confessors typically ask a penitent to determine moral culpability: "Did you realize fully that it is a grave sin?" and "Could you have resisted?" Previously, if a penitent had said "yes" to either of the two questions, a confessor would presume that the penitent was morally responsible for the sin confessed. With greater understanding of human psychology, however, Ford declared that even when a penitent gave an affirmative answer to one or both of these questions, it might be improper to conclude that a mortal sin had been committed and that the person was culpable.[9]

The question "Did you realize fully that it is a grave sin?" asked whether the penitent had given adequate deliberation to the grave act he or she was about to commit. Moralists, canonists, and scholastic philosophers have traditionally judged that if a person had adequate use of reason, that person also had adequate freedom to be culpable for his or her action. These moralists and canonists made this judgment based on the words of Thomas Aquinas, "To whatever extent reason remains free and not subject to passion, to that extent the movement of the will which remains does not tend with necessity toward the object to which passion inclines" (Summa theologiae, 1a 2ae, q. 10, a. 1). Ford noted that current scholastic psychologists were not willing to make a similar judgment that an intellectual recognition of the rightness or wrongness of an act directly implied that the subsequent act of will was free.[10]

Ford asserted that the traditional "advertence test" signified by the question "Did you realize fully that it is a grave sin?" was not an adequate means of judging the grave culpability of a person. He made a distinction between conceptual cognition and evaluative cognition. Conceptual cognition grasped the nature of an action, while evaluative cognition appraised the value of that action. A normal person would be able to perceive both the object and its value in the same act of cognition. There are cases, however, when a person is capable of conceptual cognition without adequate evaluative cognition. When this occurs, one could not impute full culpability to the person who performed the act. Ford explains:

In the case of ingrained habits which affect the voluntary, this evaluative cognition of the grave sinfulness of an act may be habitually present in this individual; but under the influence of habit and passion (or the unconscious) the evaluative cognition recedes into the background of consciousness. The person knows that this is a gravely sinful act (conceptual cognition) and there is actual advertence to that conceptual cognition; however, the impediments to freedom rob that knowledge of its reality and implications (evaluative cognition).[11]

The second question typically asked by confessors, "Could you have resisted?" inquires whether the penitent had sufficient consent of the will in committing the objectively sinful act, or whether there was an "irresistible impulse" affecting the will. Ford proposed two possible meanings of "irresistible impulse." The first meaning was "an impulsive movement of passion such as occurs in a sudden eruption of intense anger, or sexual outburst, also sudden and overpowering." Moralists would not assign culpability to a person committing a grave act under the influence of this first kind of irresistible impulse, because the actor lacked sufficient moral deliberation to incur grave guilt. This form of irresistible impulse has not presented a major moral problem for moralists.[12]

A second meaning for irresistible impulse was "a continuing fascination, or attraction, or temptation, which may almost obsess the mind, but which does not usually exclude all advertence to the malice of the act." A grave act committed under this type of irresistible impulse would require a more nuanced treatment by moralists. Unlike the first meaning of irresistible impulse where the will was absolutely overpowered and thus did not have full consent, the second meaning of irresistible impulse admits that freedom and consent were not totally absent in the commission of the grave act. In judging such a case of irresistible impulse, the moralist tries to find out whether the impulse was so irresistible that even though the actor's freedom was not totally destroyed, the culpability for mortal guilt was reduced or even removed. Ford proposed the term "compulsive urge" to indicate this second meaning of irresistible impulse. "Compulsive urge" implies degrees of intensity and frequency in the urges that an affected person experiences. Drawing from a variety of human experiences of compulsions, Ford presents a picture of how compulsions affect a person.

A compulsive urge in order to be compulsive need not be such in all circumstances. An urge which in some circumstances is very intense and dominating may be counteracted by other factors. It is no argument against the irresistibility of a kleptomaniac's impulse to steal that he would not have done it if there was a policeman at his elbow. The fact that a compulsive drinker stops drinking after he joins A.A. is not a proof (as we have heard said) that he was not a compulsive drinker in the first place. The fact that a masturbator does not yield to his morbid urge in the presence of other people does not prove that the urge is not compulsive when he is alone. Consequently it is impossible to say once and for all that a given urge is compulsive or not. In the same individual it may be compulsive one day and another day not compulsive. Even actions that require longer preparation or a series of preliminary steps may be compulsively performed.[13]

Ford cautions confessors against dismissing or not paying adequate consideration to the effects of compulsions on the subjective culpability of penitents.

There is a danger that some may be too mechanical in applying inadequate rules of thumb. There are such things as compulsions and uncontrollable urges. There are such things as neurotic disturbances which may fall far short of any stereotyped picture of insanity and yet have very serious effects on human acts. Any priest who has spent long hours in the confessional knows of the difficulties and weaknesses that often manifest greatly diminished culpability. We are learning more and more about the internal and emotional obstacles to the exercise of freedom. If we do not take them into account we run the risk of judging consciences too severely.[14]

Ford offers two possible explanations or analyses of how compulsive urges overcome some people. The person suffering from a compulsion may be faced with a choice between two values, but one value has a greater attraction to the person because of his compulsion towards that value. The freedom to choose remains operative, but the person is drawn to choose one value because of a "narrowing of consciousness to one all-absorbing object of desire." In this case, the person is not indifferent about the values, but rather the person, in his or her use of freedom, is predisposed to choose one value with the greater attraction of a compulsive urge. Another explanation for the failure to resist compulsive urges is the belief of the affected person that the urge is irresistible. Ford suggests that such a belief could be the result of "hopelessness induced by past experience of continual defeat or it may be born from false teaching." Such a belief convinces the person to give in to the urges in order to avoid the frustration resulting from a difficult and ultimately futile struggle against the urge. In giving in to the urge, however, the person still makes an exercise of the will.[15]

Despite the considerations that Ford presented to caution moralists against judging ordinary penitents too strictly, he refused to deny the existence of at least some degree of freedom and personal responsibility in most moral cases. Ford disagreed with the extreme position of some psychoanalysts of his time that human freedom was an illusion and that human actions were mostly directed by the unconscious. He believed that it would be in keeping with human dignity to defend the position that human beings are generally responsible for their actions and that they possess real freedom to make human choices, though their freedom may be impaired by various factors in some situations.

> It is neither a solution of the problem nor a compliment to the sinner or criminal to tell him he is irresponsible. (Furthermore it won't work, because in his heart he knows better.)
>
> When insisting on human responsibility the theologian and moralist should not be thought of as prosecuting attorneys, bent on finding men guilty of their misdeeds—while the psychiatrists are cast in the role of defense counsel. The thesis of irresponsibility may not be as comfortable as it appears on the surface. The shoe of irresponsibility fits both feet. If it excuses from sin, it also eliminates merit; if it reduces blame, it also minimizes virtue. For good actions are not imputable to a man either, unless he is free and responsible. They are not his in the moral sense. It is no compliment to human dignity to deprive man of the most human powers he possesses.[16]

In assimilating the contributions of psychology to the manualist understanding of moral responsibility, Ford consistently affirmed the existence of moral freedom.

The thing that Catholic moralists must defend (because the faith itself forces them to the conclusion) is this: that normal men and women per se have sufficient freedom in the concrete circumstances of daily life to merit great praise or great blame before God. This conclusion does not seem to us endangered by the discovery of the dynamic unconscious.[17]

Ford's General Pastoral Approach to Cases of Diminished Subjective Culpability

Ford's pastoral approach toward persons with diminished subjective culpability took a more lenient stance than the traditional manuals. "The only general rule we would recommend is this: subjective disabilities and impediments excuse the average man and woman from moral guilt much more frequently than a reading of moral theology manuals might lead one to suppose."[18]

Speaking about confessional practice, Ford recommended that confessors pay attention to the "conscious data" that a penitent provided. He objected to a revolving-door approach to confession. "A confessor or spiritual guide cannot form a prudent judgment about the state of the penitent's soul unless he takes the time and trouble to do so. If penitents are rushed in and out of the confessional they may receive valid absolution, but the confessor will fail in his office not only as a teacher, father, and physician, but, in these difficult cases, in his essential role as judge."[19] Ford insisted that confessors take the time to know their penitents in order to make appropriate judgments about the penitent's culpability and to provide honest, gentle, and effective advice.

If a confessor were to discover that the penitent suffers from a compulsion that effectively diminished culpability for a grave act, the confessor must inform the penitent not only about his diminished culpability but also about the reality of his compulsion, with the aim of urging the penitent to seek some form of help. The confessor's pastoral care for the penitent would not end with the granting of absolution but would extend to the future recovery of the penitent.

If a person is emotionally sick it is not bad tactics to tell him so, as long as you tell him at the same time that he can do something about his sickness

and you will help him do it. It is not bad tactics to tell this type of penitent, so many of whom are confused and overburdened with exaggerated,
hopeless feelings of neurotic guilt, that he is not mortally guilty when this
is the truth as you see it. It is not bad tactics to explain to him that he is
suffering from a more or less pathological obstacle to liberty, if you tell
him at the same time that he can get rid of the obstacle and that he should
get rid of it and that you will help him get rid of it.[20]

Ford reminded pastors that their consideration of subjective culpability in the confessional should be consistent with their administration of
the sacrament of the Eucharist. Using the example of a penitent with an
irresistible compulsion to masturbate, Ford appealed to the principles
of probabilism to allow communion without confession beforehand.

The confessor or spiritual father must have the courage of his convictions,
too, in accepting the logical consequences of the judgment "This penitent
is not committing formal mortal sins." When he judges prudently that in
the special circumstances of the given case future acts of self-abuse will
not involve formal mortal guilt, he must not forbid the penitent to receive
Holy Communion without confession after such material sinful acts take
place. . . . In cases where the well-informed penitent's frame of mind after such an act is this: "I have probably not committed grave sin and am
probably still in a state of grace," the penitent has the right, according to
the principles of probabilism, to receive Holy Communion after making
an act of contrition.[21]

In the case of homosexuality, Ford did not believe that the sexual behavior of the average homosexual was a problem of compulsion. He acknowledged the objection of homosexuals to being labeled as persons
suffering from a disease. He did not want to consider homosexuals as
helpless in controlling their sexual behavior just as he did not want to
consider heterosexuals as incapable of living chaste lives. Ford believed
that most homosexuals have sufficient freedom and personal responsibility to be culpable for their moral choices and actions. "I take it for
granted that as a general rule the homosexuals we deal with are not here
and now responsible for <u>being</u> homosexuals, and for having homosexual inclinations, thoughts and interests. If you wish to call this inclination 'compulsive' in the sense that they generally cannot help feeling as

they do and being as they are, I will of course agree. But then I would have to call the natural heterosexual attraction experienced by the normal population compulsive, also."[22]

Although Ford was deliberate in not judging homosexuals as compulsive persons, he was aware of the unique difficulties that homosexuals experience. He recommended that pastors and confessors adopt a compassionate pastoral approach when ministering to homosexuals. Speaking to chaplains of correctional institutes, he gave the following advice:

> We are not looking at the object of the sex attraction, the <u>direction</u> the sexual instinct has taken. . . . We are concerned with the morality of sexual <u>conduct</u>, the behavior of our clients (whether homosexual or heterosexual). And I am inclined to believe, though I could not prove it, that there is no more presumption of compulsive sex behavior in the case of homosexuals than there is in the case of heterosexuals. The direction of their sexual inclination is not within their power (at least without considerable help); their conduct generally is.
>
> It is because of their special hardships and difficulties that in our dealings with them I think we generally have to make a special effort at understanding, and take special pains to be compassionate. So often clerical advisers feel a natural aversion or repugnance towards homosexuals. As pastors we have to overcome it. All sinners deserve our understanding and sympathy; not just the ones who commit the same sins that we are inclined to.[23]

Ford recognized the difficulty of finding the exact degree of psychological freedom that was required to make a person culpable for a grave act. Two extremes were to be avoided when considering the requirement for sufficient freedom to account for moral culpability: the standard should not be set so high as to negate moral responsibility for most people, nor should it be set so low that persons with irresistible compulsions would be judged mortally responsible for their objectively grave acts. Ford believed that moral theology and pastoral practice would do well to be more lenient in judging penitents than had been done in the past. "Given the traditional conceptions of sufficient deliberation and sufficient consent, and given the psychological knowledge we now have as to emotional and instinctive obstacles to human acts, we are staying well within the bounds of the theological requirements in concluding that we should judge much more leniently than we have in the past a great many individual cases of human misconduct and frailty."[24]

A concrete application of Ford's approach to the issue of diminished culpability can be observed in his pastoral response to the problem of alcoholism.

Case Study: Subjective Culpability and Alcoholism

John Ford's interest in alcohol studies came from his own experience of alcoholism and recovery. He kept secret his story of recovery, at the urging of his superiors, in order not to diminish his effectiveness in promoting AA to Catholics. It was only during the last months of his life that Ford publicly admitted that his own interest in alcoholism issues coincided with his own recovery from alcoholism.[25]

When considering the subjective culpability of an alcoholic for acts committed while drunk, Ford's general rule was that a person was not guilty of the acts committed while drunk unless the person anticipated the possibility that these acts would happen and still deliberately decided to get drunk regardless of consequences. Otherwise the responsibility of the person for acts committed while intoxicated would depend on the amount of control and reason that the person had when he or she committed these acts.[26]

Ford described the compulsive quality of alcoholism as a peculiar way of thinking about taking an alcoholic drink that takes possession of the person's mind. When the alcoholic is caught up in this kind of obsessive thinking, he or she is not able to consider reasonably and realistically any other alternative to drinking. Alcoholics are not always under the compulsion to drink. The irresistible urge to drink may be present in some moments and may not be as strong in other times.[27]

Ford conducted extensive interviews of alcoholics, which provided him with a deeper understanding of the compulsive character of alcoholism.

> In the early stages of alcoholism it seems that the drinking becomes compulsive only after the alcoholic has had a few drinks. This is what Dr. E. M. Jellinek calls "loss of control in the drinking situation."

In the later stages there are times when the alcoholic reaches for a drink blindly and compulsively even when he has had nothing to drink for a considerable period. I was not ready to believe this at first.

But after listening to hundreds of alcoholics tell their stories, and after questioning many of them on that very point, I am convinced that not only after having had some drinks but even after a considerable period of sobriety the alcoholic at times reaches out compulsively and blindly for the first drink. This is what members of Alcoholics Anonymous mean when they say: "We are powerless over alcohol." This is the disastrous moment which they pray daily will never overtake them again.[28]

Ford expresses in vivid words the inability of alcoholics to resist this compulsion.

If you light a fire under him just before he reaches for a drink in the barroom, he will run out with the others. But he'll finish the drink first. And the chances are that even with the fire at his heels he will hang back at the last moment in the hope of taking a bottle on the way out.

The affliction and the sickness of alcoholism consists in this, that no ordinary motivation gets through to him when he is in the grip of the addiction. All the motives in the world are there to persuade him not to drink, motives that for any reasonable man would be compelling, but he cannot turn them on at will and it is difficult for anyone else to turn them on for him and make them realistic for him.

People do not go through those agonies because they want to. They do not behave so egregiously counter to their own interest, well-being and happiness out of sheer obduracy.

The late alcoholic tells the literal truth when he says, I cannot live with it and I cannot live without it." He tells the literal truth when he says, "First I drank because I wanted to, then I drank because I needed to, and finally I drank because I had to."[29]

Taking seriously the irresistible compulsion to drink experienced by alcoholics, Ford proposed a way to understand an alcoholic's moral responsibility for his or her state of alcoholism. On the one hand, Ford pointed out that there were alcoholics who had very little responsibility for their condition, either because their addiction had a physiological cause or because they were born with "addictive personalities." On the other hand, Ford also noted that there were some alcoholics who had some genuine responsibility for their condition, when it had been caused by their long-term excessive drinking. But in general, Ford believed that on the subjective level, there were few alcoholics who were "mortally guilty" for the addiction afflicting them. He viewed alcoholics as persons who suffered from a compulsion affecting their reasoning and exercise of freedom to such an extent that one could not presume that they possessed the degree of psychological freedom one would usually presume for ordinary persons.

It is difficult to judge the subjective culpability of an alcoholic's drinking behavior because so many variables are involved in every drinking episode. "There are so many kinds of alcoholics, and in each alcoholic there are so many stages of compulsion, and in each stage there are so many different circumstances in which the act of drinking takes place, that any exact, mechanical rule is impossible."[30]

Mindful of the difficulty in forming a general judgment of an alcoholic, Ford appealed to moralists and confessors to judge every alcoholic and every drinking episode according to the unique circumstances surrounding each case. He urged that "each alcoholic, each drinking episode, and even each act of drinking must be judged on its own merits."[31] He insisted that confessors and moralists should act on the side of leniency when judging the drinking episodes of alcoholics. Ford stated that, in many cases, the alcoholic was not "mortally guilty" of becoming intoxicated.

Ford offered pastoral advice to those who heard confessions of alcoholics. A confessor should not tell an alcoholic that another drink would be a mortal sin. Absolution should not be refused to an alcoholic who cannot promise never to drink again. Ford gave several reasons for his advice. First, it was difficult to judge whether a penitent who confessed excessive drinking was a true alcoholic or not. The confessor was generally not competent to make a diagnosis in the confessional.

Second, if the penitent was a true alcoholic, telling the person not to take another drink might not prevent the person from drinking. Adding the fear of mortal sin to the alcoholic's difficult state of mind might actually induce the person to drink. Unless asked by the penitent, Ford would not recommend even mentioning mortal or venial sins on the matter of drinking while hearing confession so as not to add to the emotional and psychological burdens of the penitent.

This type of drinker is often in a state of despair and frustration when he finds himself powerless to do what he wants to do. He is often the victim of pathological feelings of guilt and remorse. One of the reasons he drinks is to relieve the unbearable tension engendered by these feelings.

To put him under the additional tension of fearing that one drink means mortal sin and the loss of friendship of God may be just the touch needed to drive him to drink. Our general theological principles permit leaving him in good faith in these circumstances.[32]

Third, if the person were a true alcoholic then that person would already be under a certain compulsion to drink, and his or her freedom to make decisions regarding the next drink would already be lessened—and therefore the next drink would not be a mortal sin but perhaps only a venial sin or no sin at all. The confessor needed to keep in mind that a true alcoholic would be incapable of keeping the promise not to drink again by his or her own power, and thus it would not be right to demand such a promise from the person during confession.

In summary, Ford's approach to the issue of the subjective culpability of alcoholics took seriously the experiential data provided by alcoholics about the irresistible and compulsive character of alcohol addiction. Ford's research and experience enabled him to enter into the world of compulsive alcoholics and to understand the difficulties of living the moral life from their perspective. He perceived the alcoholic as a person with an abnormal condition preventing the full and free exercise of the ability to resist alcohol and its effects. Ford's understanding of alcoholism convinced him to presuppose a condition of diminished subjective culpability in alcoholics with respect to their drinking episodes and acts performed while intoxicated. He urged leniency in the moral judgment of alcoholics and their actions, and advocated a pastoral approach for confessors and moralists—an approach aimed at leading and encouraging the alcoholic to strive toward recovery.

Notes

1. Ford and Kelly, *Contemporary Moral Theology*, Vol. I (1958), 174.
2. Ibid., 185.
3. 1933–34 catalogue of the New England Jesuit Province.
4. Ford and Kelly, *Contemporary Moral Theology*, Vol. I (1958), 196.

5. Ibid., 214–15.
6. Ibid., 216.
7. Ibid., 216–17.
8. Ibid., 217–18.
9. Ibid., 219–20.
10. Ibid., 221–22.
11. Ibid., 223–24.
12. Ibid., 229.
13. Ibid., 229–30.
14. Ibid., 202.
15. Ibid., 231–33.
16. Ford, Pastoral Dealing with Compulsives (unpublished manuscript, 1970), 12.
17. Ford and Kelly, *Contemporary Moral Theology*, Vol. I (1958), 200.
18. Ibid., 239.
19. Ibid., 242.
20. Ibid., 244–45.
21. Ibid., 245n36.
22. Ford, Pastoral Dealing with Compulsives (1970), 21.
23. Ibid., 21–22 (underlines by Ford).
24. Ford and Kelly, *Contemporary Moral Theology*, Vol. I (1958), 247.
25. Morgan, "'Chemical Comforting'" (1999), 35.
26. Ford, *Man Takes a Drink* (1954), 75–76.
27. Ford, "Alcohol, Alcoholism" (1950), 105–6.
28. Ibid.
29. Ibid., 107–8 (underlines by Ford).
30. Ford and Kelly, *Contemporary Moral Theology*, Vol. I (1958), 292.
31. Ibid., 294.
32. Ford, "Alcohol, Alcoholism" (1950), 112–13.

CHAPTER SEVEN

JOHN FORD AND
JOSEF FUCHS

Another way to understand and appreciate John Ford's moral method as a manualist is to compare his approach with that of another leading moralist of his time, Josef Fuchs. Both Ford and Fuchs were appointed to the papal birth control commission; each wrote a report presenting a competing claim about the possibility of changing the Church's teaching on contraception. The papal birth control commission provides an important historical context for comparing the moral methods of Ford and Fuchs because Fuchs underwent an intellectual conversion during the commission meetings, which led to a shift in his approach to moral theology. Analysis of their arguments on the birth control issue illustrates the difference between Ford's approach in crisis mode and Fuchs's postconversion approach to moral discernment. Despite this difference, however, there is significant similarity between Ford's standard mode approach to moral discernment and Fuchs's postconversion approach.

Josef Fuchs was born in Germany in 1912. He received a doctorate in sacred theology from the University of Münster. After working as a parish priest for four years, Fuchs was assigned to teach moral theology at the seminary at Osnabrück in 1945. He later taught moral theology at St. George Hochschule in Frankfurt, from 1947 to 1954. In 1954 he was assigned to teach as a professor of moral theology at the Pontifical Gregorian University in Rome.[1] Fuchs taught in the manualist tradition until 1966 when he experienced his intellectual conversion during his participation in the papal birth control commission.[2]

Fuchs's Manualist Period

Before his conversion, Fuchs held manualist views similar to those of Ford. His book *Natural Law: A Theological Investigation* established him "as one of the premier moral theologians of the classical paradigm."[3] In this book, Fuchs shares with manualists the presumption that the natural order created by God was intelligible to human reason. This natural order, written as a law in creation as well as in human hearts, provides the basis for moral norms. "The nature in which reason recognizes a natural order is the work of God the Creator. Reason engaged upon the intelligibilities of nature must be seen as God's work. Only he has written the law of nature into man's heart when creating him. The voice of nature that admonishes, orders and teaches, together with the reason that scans nature and our own hearts, are the true voices of divine reason. This natural law is as certainly a manifestation of God's intellect and will as his positively revealed commandment."[4]

Fuchs believed in the human capacity to grasp intuitively the fundamental principles of natural law. He also acknowledged that obstacles can hinder the innate capacity of individuals to fully grasp the natural law, such as defective upbringing, ignorance, the influence of false teachings, addictive compulsions, etc. In response to the Protestant assertion that human reason has been objectively incapacitated by sin, however, Fuchs insisted that the fallen sinful condition of humanity left human reason intact and capable of knowing the basic principles of natural law. "Reason remains one of man's faculties and truly belongs to his nature, even though this nature is fallen. In accordance with its inner structure, reason is directed towards the knowledge of reality. No special grounds could be adduced for excluding the knowledge of the natural law from the capabilities of the human intellect. . . . There are habits, inclinations, and dispositions in every man that hinder him from acquiring insight into reality. These have the same effect as blinkers; they obscure the field of vision without necessarily injuring one's eyes or destroying one's sight."[5]

Fuchs distinguished between the objective capacity of human reason to grasp the fundamental principles of natural law and the impaired capacity of individuals to attain a full knowledge of natural law caused by subjective impediments.

[Pius XII] states that the voice of nature teaches "even the uneducated and what is more, those who do not yet enjoy the cultural values of mankind, what is just and unjust, permitted and forbidden." To understand this, at least the main principles of the natural law must be known easily by all whereas we notice that the more difficult and more detailed moral norms are in fact often unknown. There is consequently, a domain of the natural law that is easily and correctly known by everyone, even in the state of original sin. Nonetheless, the exercise of the intellectual faculty is impeded in other ways to a greater or lesser extent.[6]

With these difficulties in mind, Fuchs asserted the importance of the magisterium as the authoritative interpreter of natural law. Like John Ford, Fuchs believed in the Holy Spirit's assistance to the magisterium, enabling the Church to be a reliable guide in the moral life.

Many statements contained either in the ordinary teaching or even in the papal encyclicals and allocutions and in the decrees of the Roman Congregations do not have that character of infallibility that gives ultimate security. Consequently they cannot be the object to our irrevocable faith. They are, all the same, the work of that teaching office to which the assistance of the Holy Ghost was promised, although that does not mean that the Holy Ghost will supplement or effectively make up every human deficiency when no ultimate issue is at stake. Where the silence of the Holy Ghost is not evident, the presumption is first of all in favour of the word of the Church and against a personal conviction standing in opposition to this word. Thus the Christian can see in the word of the Church a real aid to the knowledge of the truth in matters bearing upon his moral behavior, and he ought to accept it as such with joy.[7]

Fuchs's deference to the magisterium was not determined by the ecclesiological concerns that were so apparent in Ford's method.[8] Fuchs believed that the Holy Spirit enabled the magisterium to achieve deep insight into natural law. In his perspective, the magisterium's claim to obedience stemmed not from its competency in moral matters but because its teachings were consistent with the natural law.[9] Moral rightness or wrongness was not determined by the legislative power of the magisterium. Moral objectivity was derived from the moral demands that human reason grasps from reality. "In what does moral objectivity consist?" Fuchs wrote. Not "in the fact that these laws are externally proposed to us, for example, by the theologians or by the Church. . . . [Moral] objectivity is in this, that this order is grounded in (human) being and consequently can be known from (human) being.[10]

Ford shared with Fuchs the same belief that the magisterium was given special enlightenment by the Holy Spirit to faithfully interpret God's will in nature. Ford, however, focused on defending the authority of the magisterium as the authentic interpreter of natural law. Although he had admitted some unresolved difficulties about consistency in church teachings (e.g., the case of periodic continence), in general Ford remained confident about the competency of the church to interpret moral norms. He asserted, "the [moral] laws mean what the Church says they mean."[11] For Ford, a moral norm taught by the Church was valid because the Church said so, and could never be wrong because the Church is guided by the Holy Spirit. For Fuchs, a moral norm taught by the Church was valid primarily because it corresponded with reality.

The Papal Birth Control Commission and Josef Fuchs's Intellectual Conversion

Josef Fuchs was one among the first theologians (along with Bernard Häring, Pierre de Locht, Jan Visser, and Marcelino Zalba) appointed to the Papal Commission on Population, Family, and Birth at its second meeting in April 1964. He was chosen because of his expertise in sexual morality and his classical view of moral theology.[12] Ford was appointed to the commission only in 1965, and was only able to attend the fourth (March 1965) and fifth (April to June 1966) rounds of meetings.

During the commission's second meeting, Fuchs disagreed with the nontraditional views of fellow commission member Bernard Häring. In his presentation to the commission, Häring had expressed his objection to the Church's teaching that the primary end of intercourse was procreation. He argued that since most acts of intercourse occurred during periods when the union of egg and sperm was not possible, it was not important that every act of intercourse of a married couple be open to procreation. What was more important was that the marriage in its totality should be procreative and that mutual love between spouses be given greater importance in the Church's understanding of marriage. Using the principle of totality, he contended that the use of the contraceptive pill was an intrinsic evil that must be forbidden in every circumstance. Häring also stated that the task of a Christian was to "discern the will of God regarding parenthood within existing conditions and in an environment of love."[13]

In response to Häring, Fuchs insisted on the traditional teaching of the Church on procreation. McClory reported: "Since an 'ordination to procreation' is inherent in each sexual union (even though physiologically speaking procreation may be impossible), Fuchs said, 'the integrity of the act itself' is destroyed when contraceptive measures are taken. Furthermore, said Fuchs, this new emphasis on love, however well-intentioned, seems to distort the time-honored Christian doctrine. After all, he noted, the essence of marital consent is the mutual 'exchange by man and woman of their rights to sexual activities apt for procreation.'"[14]

Although Fuchs had initially expressed objection to Häring's ideas, he gradually began to reconsider his position. The commission reconvened for its third meeting on June 14, 1964. The members were informed that the pope intended to make a public announcement of the existence of the commission on June 24 and he would like to have answers to three questions: "What is the relationship of the primary and secondary ends of marriage? What are the major responsibilities of married couples? How do rhythm and the pill relate to responsible parenthood?"[15] At the end of their meeting, the commission members were not able to provide clear answers to the pope's questions. The group unanimously gave approval to rhythm as a legitimate means of birth control for couples, but they lacked agreement on how to approach the matter of the birth control pill.

At this point, Häring and fellow commission member Pierre de Locht urged that the group should raise fundamental theological questions about the Church's understanding of marriage and the use of contraception within marriage. This crucial suggestion provided a turning point for the commission. Until their third meeting, the members of the commission saw themselves "as court advisers to the Holy See, operating more or less strictly within the limits of the relevant encyclicals and traditional theology."[16] At this point, however, some commission members began to realize that the traditional teaching on marriage needed to be reexamined.

This shift in the direction of the commission's discussions was made possible by certain factors. When the birth control commission was formed during the papacy of John XXIII, one of the immediate tasks given to it was to assist the pope in addressing the population policies of the United Nations and of various countries. Since this task was related to international diplomacy, the commission was placed under the jurisdiction of the office of the Vatican Secretary of State, headed by Amleto Cardinal Cicognani. After the death of Pope John XXIII in 1963, his successor Paul VI kept the same arrangement for the commission. Cardinal Cicognani, who had authority over the commission, was tolerant of open theological discussions and decision making through vote.[17] The Holy Office monitored the work of the commission but it could not set limits to the theological discussion. Although the appointment letter of the commission members stated that the commission worked under the general authority of the Holy Office, the rules of protocol prevented the Holy Office from directly intervening in the commission's work.[18] This setup made it possible for the commission to gradually come to a decision to reexamine the Church's position on contraception.

In preparation for the commission's fourth meeting, Häring and de Locht proposed to Paul VI that an expansion of the commission was necessary in order that a diversity of views be heard. Significantly, they also suggested that married couples, who were most affected by the current teaching, should be allowed to participate and be heard in the commission sessions. Thus, for the next meeting of the commission in the spring of 1965, the membership of the commission was expanded to fifty-eight members, which included three married couples. John Ford was also among the new members appointed to this expanded commission. It was shortly before his attendance at this fourth meeting that Ford consulted Richard McCormick about reporting Pierre de Locht to the Holy Office about having him replaced as head of the commission's theological section. It was also during this time that Ford recommended John Noonan to present a summary of his book on the development of the teaching on contraception. And it was during and after this meeting that Ford began his reporting to the pope and the Holy Office about commission members with procontraceptive views.

During the fourth meeting of the papal birth control commission in March 1965, the commissioners were divided into working groups to facilitate focused discussions on specific topics. The theologians' group had to respond to a basic question: "Was the teaching on contraceptives reformable?" John Ford argued strongly that the teaching was not—but on the contrary, it was practically infallible. He quoted the words of *Casti connubii* to prove his point: "'This prescription [against contraception]

is in full force now as it was before, and so it will be tomorrow and for-
ever, because it is not a mere human enactment but the expression of a
natural and divine law.' If this isn't infallible language, what is?"[19] Other
commissioners such as Marcelino Zalba, Stanislas de Lestapis, and
Archbishop Leo Binz supported Ford's position. On the other hand, a
number of commissioners believed that the teaching was reformable.
Philippe Delhaye, a moral theologian from France, argued that documents such as *Casti connubii* should not be regarded as unchanging and
infallible but rather should be seen as open for modification when circumstances change. Häring argued that infallibility pertained only to
matters of divine revelation and not to moral interpretations of natural law. Michel Labourdette, a Dominican from France, reminded the
group that Pius XII himself had reformed the teaching on contraception
through his approval of periodic continence in his *Address to Midwives*.[20]

   Henri de Reidmatten, the secretary general of the commission, called
for a vote to see where the working group stood on the issue of reformability. The group voted twelve to seven in favor of the reformability of
the teaching on contraception. Josef Fuchs surprised the commission
by stating his position that the teaching on contraception was reformable. However, he cautioned the commission against moving too fast
on making changes to the teaching: "Declaring these statements reformable does not make them uncertain. Theologians cannot simply
abandon them until they have good reason to do so."[21] Although Fuchs
acknowledged that the teaching on contraception was not infallible and
thus could be reformed, he was not yet convinced that there were adequate reasons to initiate a change in the teaching.[22]

   Despite his caution about moving too precipitously to change the
teaching on contraception, Fuchs already felt a growing dissatisfaction
with the current teaching. Mark Graham describes the beginnings of
Fuchs's intellectual conversion.

> In Fuchs' mind, the church's position on contraception was still valid and
> obligatory; but unbeknownst to the other commission members, Fuchs
> was privately struggling with the contraception issue. As he would reveal
> later, he had already begun to question the church's teaching on contra-
> ception, and his growing doubt would not only cause him to stop teaching
> at the Gregorian University during the 1965–66 academic year because he
> refused to teach a doctrine about which he was ambivalent, but it would

prompt him in 1965 to request that his manual in sexuality, which upheld received teaching on contraception, not be reprinted.[23]

Fuchs's initial support for rhythm as the sole acceptable means of birth control for Catholics was gradually eroded by crucial information provided by other commission members. Fuchs received practical and concrete information about the use of rhythm from John Marshall, a physician and medical researcher who explained that "the rhythm method proved to be unsatisfactory for some married couples either because of medical conditions that might be physically debilitating or perhaps even life-threatening if pregnancy occurred, or because abstinence during the fertile period was difficult and caused tension between spouses."[24]

Fuchs was also influenced by the presentation made by Patrick and Patricia Crowley, founders of the Christian Family Movement (CFM). The Crowleys presented the results of an extensive survey of CFM couples who had been trying to live out the Church's teaching on contraception. The survey revealed that despite the great sincerity and effort of these couples to adhere to the Church's teaching, most expressed a desire for a change in the teaching.

> We have gathered hundreds of statements from many parts of the United States and Canada and have been overwhelmed by the strong consensus in favor of change. Most expressed a hope that the positive values in love and marriage need to be stressed and that an expanded theology of marriage needed to be developed. Most say they think there must be a change in the teaching on birth control. . . .
>
> Most expressed dissatisfaction over the rhythm method for a variety of reasons, running from the fact that it was ineffective, hard to follow; and some had psychological and physiological objections.[25]

The Crowleys appealed to the commission to listen to the experience of people most affected by the Church's teaching on contraception. They noted that when the Church reconsidered its teaching on usury, the concerns of businessmen and merchants were taken into consideration.[26] Before the close of the fourth meeting, the Crowleys were asked by the commission to conduct a more extensive and more scientific survey of CFM couples all over the world regarding their experience of using the rhythm method. The results of this survey would be presented at the fifth and final meeting of the commission in 1966.

It was during this interim period between the fourth and fifth meeting that Ford had met privately with Paul VI to warn the pope about the dangers of reforming the teaching on contraception and to report commission members, such as Häring and de Locht, who had proreform views. It was also during this time that Ford convinced the pope to intervene in the processes of writing the Vatican II document *Gaudium et spes* in order to assert the traditional teaching on contraception.

At the fifth meeting in April–June 1966, the theologians debated once more the possibility of reforming the teaching on contraception. By this time John Ford and Josef Fuchs had begun to hold directly opposing positions.

> John Ford insisted doubt shouldn't even be discussed because on the matter of birth control there is no doubt. The magisterium has spoken; obedience is the only appropriate response. . . .
>
> Fuchs disagreed, contending that such a literal line of thought would take everyone down a blind alley: "Continuity of a teaching doesn't consist in repeating what has been said before in other circumstances but in continuing to see if these earlier pronouncements actually took permanent values into account. We are not talking about fidelity or infidelity to prior teachings; we are trying to see if there are some truly new perspectives which would require new responses."[27]

Fuchs took the same position as John Noonan who argued that authentic doctrinal development should be properly understood as the consistent defense of values in a manner that is responsive to new social situations.

The commission sought to have a better sense of the mind of the faithful by giving the lay members a more prominent voice in the proceedings. The Crowleys presented the new survey on rhythm that the commission requested. The respondents were three thousand CFM couples in eighteen countries. The results showed a great dissatisfaction with rhythm among a majority of the respondents.[28]

The most moving testimony offered by the laity during the meeting occurred when the four married women on the commission were asked to speak to the whole group and share their views on sex, rhythm, abstinence, and conception. The women, who came from Canada, India, the United States, and France, all spoke about the important role of sex in their marriage. They spoke about the great difficulty that they and other women like them experienced in attempting to use rhythm to regulate family size. Patricia Crowley shared that, although the Church considered rhythm to be "natural," women found rhythm unnatural because it hindered the natural rhythm of a married couple's cycle of sexual desire and their natural inclination to express marital love spontaneously. The CFM survey showed that married couples experienced tensions in their marital relationship because of their difficulty and frustration with the rhythm method.[29]

Patricia Crowley made a strong appeal to the commission: "We think it is time that this Commission recommend that the sacredness of conjugal love not be violated by thermometers and calendars. . . . We sincerely hope and do respectfully recommend that this Commission redefine the moral imperatives of fertility regulation with a view toward bringing them into conformity with our new and improved understanding of men and women in today's world."[30]

Colette Potvin gave the most personal witness by describing to the group what lovemaking meant for her and her husband. "'Marvelous moments' she said, 'when each of us accepts the other, forgives the other and can give the best of ourselves to the other.' The morning after such a communion with her husband, she said, she felt more serene, more patient with her children, more loving to everyone. Nothing contributed more to her family's equilibrium. . . ."[31]

The women's testimony had a significant impact on the theologians' group. A new vote among the theologians on whether *Casti connubii* was reformable resulted in a fifteen-to-four vote in favor of changing the teaching on contraception. Josef Fuchs, who had previously cautioned the theologians during the fourth meeting against changing the teaching without a good reason, found sufficient evidence from the testimony of the married women that changing the teaching on contraception was necessary and justified.

When the time came to write the final document of the commission that would be presented to the pope, the commission secretary general appointed a group of theologians to write a working paper that would express the recommendations of the majority of the commission. Josef Fuchs was chosen as the primary author of this working paper. The resulting document was titled "Schema for a Document on Responsible Parenthood," and was intended to be the official final report of the commission. This document was commonly referred to as the "Majority Report."

The minority group of the commission, who dissented against any proposed change in the teaching of *Casti connubii*, made their own plans to write a document that defended the traditional teaching on contraception. John Ford, with the help of Germian Grisez, who was flown in by Ford to Rome to assist in writing the document,[32] wrote the document titled "State of the Question: The Doctrine of the Church and its Authority." This document, commonly referred to as the "Minority Report," was intended by Ford to give voice to the minority opinion and to show that the commission was not unanimous in approving a change in the teaching.

Ford was the first to submit his working paper to the commission's secretary general, Henri de Reidmatten, on May 23, 1966. Three days later, on May 26, Fuchs submitted the working paper representing the majority opinion of the commission. The Majority Report, after some adjustments and after approval from a committee of bishops, was submitted to the pope as the definitive final report of the commission. In order to address the issues raised by Ford in his Minority Report, de Reidmatten requested that Fuchs and other theologians write a response. This response, titled "Summary Document on the Morality of Birth Control," was submitted on May 28, 1966.[33] This response is commonly referred to as the "Rebuttal Report."

The arguments contained in these three documents show clearly the differences between the manualist thinking of John Ford and the postconversion thinking of Josef Fuchs.

Ford's Crisis Mode Approach and Fuchs's Postconversion Approach

Ford's approach (in crisis mode) and Fuchs's contrasting approach (after his conversion) are well represented in the documents they authored for the papal birth control commission. In his Minority Report, Ford argued in crisis mode for the retention of the prohibition on contraceptives. The Majority Report and Majority Rebuttal contain

Fuchs's arguments for a revision of the teaching to allow for married couples to make prudent decisions regarding the means of regulating birth, citing magisterial authority, natural law, and moral discernment.

Ford and the Minority Report

Ford wrote the Minority Report in the crisis mode. He believed that the authority of the magisterium to teach on moral matters would be seriously compromised if the teaching on contraception, expressed in the encyclical *Casti connubii*, were substantially changed. Using a casuistic method of argumentation similar to the one he employed in the case of obliteration bombing and the scarred uterus case, Ford presented an array of arguments creating an "accumulation of reasons" and presenting his position in the best possible light. He built a protective wall around the value that he perceived as threatened: the teaching authority of the magisterium.

Ford admitted that arguments from natural law were insufficient to defend the traditional teaching. Despite this admission he presented one natural law argument: that the sacredness of life has endowed the integrity of the "generative processes" with a sacredness that must not be violated by human intervention. He also invoked the slippery slope argument to warn against sexual abuses that could result from a change in the teaching on contraception.[34]

Ford also offered the argument that "conjugal love is above all spiritual (and the love is genuine) and it requires no specific carnal gesture, much less its repetition in some determined frequency." He reasoned that since the intimate love between brother and sister or father and daughter did not require sexual expression, married couples could be presumed to have the capability to sustain their conjugal love without the necessity of frequent sexual acts.[35] This view of the minimal role that regular sexual intercourse played in the well-being of a marriage was already present early in his intellectual formation, as we saw in his doctoral dissertation *The Validity of Virginal Marriage*. There he used the marriage of Mary and Joseph to argue that marriages could be considered valid even when the parties involved vowed themselves to perpetual virginity.[36]

Behind all these arguments was Ford's fear regarding the consequences to the magisterium's credibility as a moral authority. Any argument that would cast doubt on the teaching on contraception was viewed by Ford as a direct threat to the magisterium. "In dealing with this question," he reasoned, "to dispute in a subtle way whether the teaching is technically 'infallible by judgment of the magisterium' is empty-headed. For if this doctrine is not substantially true, the magisterium itself will seem to be empty and useless in any moral matter."[37]

Fuchs, the Majority Report, and the Majority Rebuttal

Fuchs's moral reasoning in the Majority Report and in the Majority Rebuttal did not evidence any overriding concern to centralize authority in the magisterium. For Fuchs, the debate was not about the authority of the magisterium.

On Magisterial Authority

In the Majority Rebuttal, Fuchs wrote that *Casti connubii* was not a defined doctrine: it was neither an apostolic tradition nor an attestation of faith but rather an expression of a tradition that has been expressed in diverse ways in the Church's history.[38] In contrast to Ford, who did not agree that the current state of affairs in the 1960s justified a serious revision of the teaching on contraception, Fuchs believed that various circumstances pointed toward the legitimacy of a reconsideration of the traditional teaching in the present context. In the Majority Report, Fuchs lists some of these circumstances:

> Social changes in matrimony and family, especially in the role of the woman; lowering of the infant mortality rate; new bodies of knowledge in biology, psychology, sexuality and demography; a changed estimation of the value and meaning of human sexuality and of conjugal relations; most of all, a better grasp of the duty of man to humanize and to bring to greater perfection for the life of man what is given in nature. Then must be considered the sense of the faithful: according to it, condemnation of a couple to a long and often heroic abstinence as the means to regulate conception, cannot be founded on the truth.[39]

This different emphasis notwithstanding, however, Fuchs directly addressed Ford's concern that a change in the teaching would harm the credibility of the magisterium. He gave the assurance that the emergence of doubts based on adequate reasons and the subsequent revision of church teachings were part of the process of growth and development of the Church. A change in the teaching should be viewed constructively as "a step toward a more mature comprehension of the whole doctrine of the church."[40] Fuchs's ability to envision a Church that acknowledges its fallibility without any substantial loss to its teaching authority enabled him to speak fearlessly about changing the teaching on contraception.

On Natural Law

Mark Graham observed that there was a significant difference between Fuchs's understanding before his conversion of nature and of human nature, and his understanding after it. Before his conversion, Fuchs and Ford shared the same understanding of nature as a source of moral norms. Fuchs did not make any distinction between nature and human nature with respect to their function in revealing God's will to human reason. "Both [nature and human nature] were considered proximate sources of natural law, conduits untarnished by original sin through which the divine essence and will were known, and the standards by which the liceity of all actions were judged."[41]

After his conversion, Fuchs developed a different understanding of nature and human nature. He no longer gave nature the normative status it had in the classical tradition. Nature no longer automatically expressed God's will; rather, he saw it as "raw material that must be shaped and perfected by humankind's intentional activity and intervention."[42] In his Majority Report and Majority Rebuttal, Fuchs emphasized the active role that rational human beings must play in the task of working with the raw material of nature in order to attain the perfection God desires for humanity and for all of creation. "It is proper to man, created to the image of God, to use what is given in physical nature in a way that he may develop it to its full significance with a view of the good of the whole person."[43] He also wrote, "In the course of his life man must attain his perfection in difficult and adverse conditions, he must accept the consequences of his responsibility, etc. Therefore the dominion of God is exercised through man, who can use nature for his own perfection according to the dictates of right reason."[44]

In Fuchs's early postconversion writings, he gradually shifts his identification of the proximate source of moral norms from human nature to human reason. In his later postconversion writings, Fuchs refers less frequently to human nature and begins to equate natural law more with reason.[45]

Fuchs's turn to human reason as a source of norms was evident in his two commission documents. In the Majority Report, Fuchs urges the magisterium to respect the capacity of married couples to use their formed consciences in making prudent decisions about family size and birth regulation. "Let couples form a judgment which is objectively founded," he wrote, "with all the criteria considered. This they may do without major difficulty, and with peace of mind, if they take common and prudent counsel before God. . . . Well instructed, and prudently educated as Christians, they will prudently and serenely decide what is truly for the good of the couple and of the children, and does not neglect their own personal Christian perfection, and is, therefore, what God revealing himself through natural law and Christian revelation, sets before them to do."[46]

In the Majority Rebuttal, Fuchs argues that married couples were divinely mandated to use their reason responsibly to shape nature and formulate norms applicable to marital relations. While agreeing with Ford that the sources of life should be valued and respected as life itself, Fuchs asserts that the sources of life were not the sexual organs but rather the human persons involved in the conjugal act. To value the sources of life was to value the good of the married couple. An important part of promoting the good of the couple was to respect and value their full exercise of reason, in keeping with their dignity as rational human beings.[47]

A fundamental part of the vocation of a married couple is responsible parenthood, which involves careful consideration of the best way to promote the good of their children. They are the ones who make the decisions regarding the number of children they will raise and educate, using objective moral criteria and in consideration of the unique circumstances that surround and affect their family situation. Referring to the section on marriage in *Gaudium et spes* (#51), Fuchs explains that the meaning of sexuality in marriage and the meaning of mutual giving should guide married couples in their discernment about intervention in conception.

Addressing the meaning of sexuality in marriage, Fuchs acknowledges that marriages have a procreative end. However this procreative end need not be fulfilled in every act of intercourse. Married couples can responsibly choose to exclude conception in specific marital acts in order to better provide adequate resources for the raising and education of present and/or future children.

> This procreative end does not have to be realized by a fertile act when, for instance, parents already have children to educate or they are not prepared to have a child. *This obligation of conscience* for not generating springs from the rights of the already existing child or the rights of a future child. A *child has a right* to a "community of life and unity" so that it can be formed and educated. Therefore the procreative end is substantially and really preserved even when here and now a fertile act is excluded; for infecundity is ordered to a new life as well and humanly possessed. Man is the administrator of life and consequently of his own fecundity.[48]

Explaining the meaning of mutual self-giving in marriage, Fuchs also argues that there were times when the mutual self-giving of married love would need to be expressed in sexual intercourse for the good of the spouses and for the strengthening of their relationship. These sexual expressions of marital love need not be procreative in order to contribute substantially to the overall good of the couple's married life.[49]

This shift in Fuchs's understanding of nature allowed him to look beyond the physical processes of reproduction as the sole standard for moral norms on sexual relations of married couples. Unlike Ford, who maintained that the order of nature was the blueprint of God's will for the moral life, the postconversion Fuchs gave primacy to the right use of reason as the means to attain the perfection that God desired for human persons. Rather than treat nature like a book of morals, persons were called to cooperate and discern with God in the ways in which nature may be shaped in order to achieve the greatest good for all.

The preconversion Fuchs shared with Ford a distrust of the capacity of ordinary Catholics to use their power of reason to grasp the concrete moral demands of natural law. This distrust was based on the presumption that there were many objective and subjective factors that could impair the ordinary person's use of reason. It was this presumption, in turn, that had made the authoritative moral guidance of the magisterium seem so necessary. In this view, moral theologians served as the interpreters of magisterial teachings, providing norms for the concrete application of general papal pronouncements. The task of the individual was simply to receive the moral norms as interpreted by moral theologians from magisterial teachings, and apply them concretely in his or her life.

The postconversion Fuchs questions this classicist view of the moral competency of individuals and the inerrancy of the magisterium. Fuchs expresses doubt about the Church's capacity to predict what the Holy Spirit would allow or forbid in every possible circumstance. He points out that there have been occasions when the Church had been mistaken in its moral teaching.[50] Moving away from the manualist deference to the authority of the magisterium, Fuchs began giving greater attention to the individual person as an active moral agent capable of making the concrete application of general norms to his or her concrete situation. James Keenan, in his article "Josef Fuchs and the Question of Moral Objectivity," wrote:

> If one understands the tradition of Catholic moral teaching well enough, one recognizes that Fuchs has not only changed the locus of moral rightness but also democratized the process of determining the morally right. . . . Historically, the judgment of the moral theologian advanced moral argument: the locus of specific moral truth was actually in the human judgment of approved moral theologians.
>
> In contrast, Fuchs no longer leaves the moral theologian to mediate a judgment as to the correct determination of moral rightness. Instead the individual agent is understood to be more competent to judge specifically about the course of moral action to be taken. This competency is based on the agent's familiarity with the details of the task: to know one's own self, to grasp the situation, to understand the significance of particular circumstances, and to appreciate the way actions redound to the person of the agent and to those for whom the agent is responsible. These factors make the agent the most competent person for determining moral action.[51]

Fuchs's recognition of the moral competency of the individual and his "democratization" of the interpretation of moral laws broke away from the classical view that supported a hierarchical process of passing on moral teaching in the Church from the pope to the faithful. This is clearly seen in the difference in positions held by Ford and by Fuchs in the commission documents.

In the Minority Report, Ford upholds the competence of the magisterium as an authoritative moral guide and he expresses his negative view of the moral competence of individuals. "This view [that the natural law remains uncertain] does not do justice or protect either the competence which the church has so many times vindicated for herself for the interpretation of the natural law, nor the church's effective capacity of discerning the moral order established by God, which is so often obscure to fallen man."[52] The "democratization" of moral discernment that Fuchs proposed in his Majority Report was viewed by Ford as a threat to the Church's hierarchical structure. "The *authenticity of the magisterium* seems to be substantially violated, he wrote, "*by taking away from the magisterium the authority* to discern the requirements of the natural law and to teach authoritatively when a large part of the faithful are in doubt. In this they approach the mentality of other Christian churches and offend against the genuine hierarchical structure of the church of Christ."[53]

Fuchs, on the other hand, expresses confidence that married couples, aided by grace, were capable of developing well-formed consciences that would enable them to make appropriate moral decisions on birth regulation to provide the best possible good for their family, their future children, and their larger community.

> Responsible parenthood—that is, generous and prudent parenthood—is a fundamental requirement of a married couple's true mission. Illumined by faith, the spouses understand the scope of their whole task; helped by divine grace, they try to fulfill it as true service, carried out in the name of God and Christ, oriented to the temporal and eternal good of men. To save, protect and promote the good of the offspring, and thus of the family community and of human society, the married couple will take care to consider all values and seek to realize them harmoniously in the best way they can, with proper reverence toward each other as persons and according to the concrete circumstances of their life.[54]

Fuchs envisioned a revised role for the moral theologian based on his new emphasis on the moral competency of individuals. As Graham writes,

Before his conversion, Fuchs presented the moral theologian as an intermediary between the magisterium and the individual moral agent whose functions were hermeneutic, adjudicatory, and constructive: hermeneutic, by interpreting the meaning and content of received teaching; adjudicatory, by determining whether certain ambiguous situations or actions should be regulated by preestablished norms, and by rendering concrete moral judgments about particular individual cases; and constructive, by probing, testing, scrutinizing, revising, and expanding moral concepts and norms in order more accurately and more cogently to render natural law's content intelligible to the faithful.

In the two commission documents, however, the adjudicatory role was transferred from the moral theologian to the married couple in the concrete situation (at least on the issue of contraception); the spouses themselves considered the "objective criteria" in their circumstances and determined what natural law forbade or permitted in their particular case.[55]

In all of his postconversion writings, Fuchs remained faithful to this revised role of the moral theologian. He continued to interpret received teaching and investigated moral concepts, but he no longer offered concrete directives. Practical decision making became the responsibility of the concerned moral agent. In the case of contraception, Fuchs simply offered objective criteria to guide married couples in their decision to use birth control. They should choose methods that were convenient, more fitting and connatural to the perfection of nature, conformed to the marital expression of love, respectful of the dignity of the partner, and effective.[56]

Fuchs emphasized the need for continuing education, formation, and renewal of couples in order that they may be able to decide and act prudently. He also addressed the fears expressed by Ford about possible abuses that might occur if couples were allowed to make decisions regarding conjugal relations in view of the totality of their marriage rather than on individual conjugal acts. Ford had raised the slippery slope argument that illicit sexual activity such as extramarital relationships, oral and anal copulation, and masturbation may find justification if couples no longer adhered to the strict maintenance of the natural integrity of every conjugal act. In the Majority Rebuttal, Fuchs argued that the right reasoning that was demanded of couples would not allow acts that were self-centered, destructive of innocent life, demeaning to human dignity, or harmful to individual and marital chastity.[57]

Commentators have pointed out that Fuchs's intellectual conversion was decisively influenced by the testimony of the married couples in the birth control commission, who shared with the group the real-life struggles of marital life.[58] The fact that Fuchs responded to the testimony of the married couples in the commission by advocating a change in the teaching on contraception did not mean, however, that Ford was unaffected or unsympathetic to the plight of married persons. While insisting on the traditional teaching, Ford's writing provides evidence of his efforts to respond to the plight of married penitents struggling with the Church's teaching on contraception. Previous to the publication of *Humanae vitae*, Ford was willing to allow absolution of penitents who insisted on following the probable opinion of reputable theologians regarding the legitimate use of contraceptives, recognizing the penitents' good faith and the confusion that the birth control debate has caused the faithful.[59] He was insistent on not condemning material cooperation in the case of withdrawal despite instructions from the Holy Office to the contrary.[60] Ford denied that conservative theologians who were against contraceptives were unconcerned about the plight of married couples. "Catholics should realize, too, that not only those theologians who tend to enlarge the legitimate scope of the pill, but those who tend to restrict it, are equally concerned over the trying problems married people face today."[61]

Ford did not respond to the testimony of the laity in the commission by recommending a change in the teaching on contraception because he believed that a great evil—namely, the loss of the magisterium's moral authority—would befall the Church. Ford believed that despite the difficulties of rhythm, future scientific developments might make it more effective and easier for couples to use. One is reminded again of the expectation Ford expressed to Paul VI that a pill may soon be developed that could make ovulation more regular and predictable.[62] Rather than give couples the responsibility to make their own moral choices regarding birth regulation, as Fuchs did, Ford insisted on the objective norms of *Casti connubii* in order to preserve the authority of the magisterium; and he sought instead to find subjective excuses for married couples who fail despite their best efforts.

In the birth control case, the postconversion Fuchs was able to envision and develop a new way of looking at natural law, a new way of doing moral theology, and a new way of looking at the roles of the magisterium, moral theologians, and individual moral agents in the life of the Church. Ford chose to proceed according to the manualist approach, maintaining the view of nature as a divine blueprint and preserving the hierarchical relationship between the magisterium, moralists, and the faithful.

Nevertheless, when Ford operated in the standard mode, the solutions he proposed to a number of other moral cases resonated with the new approach of the postconversion Fuchs.

Ford's Standard Mode Approach and Fuchs's Postconversion Approach

Ford's support for the primacy of the magisterium over the individual discernment of married couples in the birth control case reflected his crisis mode response to a perceived threat to the moral authority of the magisterium. There is evidence, however, to support the claim that Ford's treatment of some standard mode cases displayed similarities with the approach of the postconversion Fuchs, with regard to the competency of individuals to make moral decisions in moral cases where the church's teaching is inadequate. An analogy can be drawn between Ford's moral solutions in three particular cases (alcoholism, chemical comforting, and the scarred uterus case) and Fuchs's postconversion approach.

The Case of Alcoholism

The similarity between Ford's standard mode approach and Fuchs's postconversion approach is best demonstrated in Ford's treatment of alcoholism. Both Ford and Fuchs had been moved to rethink their moral method after listening to personal testimony by persons most affected by a moral problem. In the case of Fuchs, the testimony of the married couples in the commission convinced him that they were the most competent persons to make decisions for the planning of their families because they understood intimately all the unique and numerous factors that affect the economic, social, psychological, physical, and spiritual dimensions of their family.

In the case of Ford, his deep interest in alcoholism studies prompted by his own personal experience of recovery moved him to gain as much personal knowledge as possible about the spiritual, psychological, and physical struggles of alcoholics. Hearing the stories of alcoholics he encountered in interviews, at AA meetings, and in counseling sessions and confessions, Ford was influenced to alter some of his presuppositions about alcoholics. He became convinced that alcoholism was not merely a moral problem but a psychological and physical problem as well. His eyes were opened to the reality of alcoholic compulsion and the powerlessness of alcoholics to resist such compulsions on their own strength.[63]

In the same way that Fuchs recognized married couples as the best persons to decide the appropriate means of birth regulation for their family, Ford also recognized the individual conscience as the best judge on whether a person was subjectively culpable for his or her alcoholism. Ford admitted that while the alcoholic continued drinking, he or she was a poor judge about his or her drinking behavior. However, Ford believed that once an alcoholic was able to attain sobriety and was enlightened about his or her condition (e.g., through recovery programs like Alcoholics Anonymous), that person would be able to offer a credible assessment of his or her personal responsibility for his or her alcoholism. Ford wrote that "a great many alcoholics who have come back to normal and have been properly instructed about themselves and their alcoholism have learned to look at themselves honestly and objectively. The honest and enlightened testimony of their own consciences is often the best criterion we have of the degree of their responsibility."[64]

In the contraceptives case, Fuchs moved the "locus of moral competency" from the magisterium and moral theologians to married couples. In the case of alcoholism, Ford moved the locus of judging moral responsibility from moralists to the conscience of recovering alcoholics.

Ford treated the individual's conscience in the case of alcoholism differently from the case of contraception because of his perception that the case of alcoholism was an abnormal case in which the proper use of reason was impaired by compulsion. Since there was no tradition of authoritative magisterial teaching on alcoholism to guide moralists, Ford was willing to allow the alcoholic's conscience to serve as the judge of his or her responsibility for becoming an alcoholic.

Ironically, in the case of contraception, where the severe impairment of reason was not the main issue, Ford was less willing to allow the individual conscience to serve as the final arbiter in assessing personal responsibility for the use of contraception. This was because there was already a body of authoritative teaching on contraception that required religious assent from the faithful. In the contraception case, Ford insisted that it was the magisterium that sets the criterion for judging the morality of the use of contraception. For individual cases of contraception, Ford refused to allow couples to make their own conscientious decision regarding contraceptive use. Yet he still saw the pastoral possibility of considering factors that might limit the subjective culpability of contraceptive use in some cases.[65]

The Case of Chemical Comforters

Another case where Ford respected the prudential judgment of affected individuals was the case of the use of chemical comforters. Ford had proposed a new virtue, *pharmacosophrosyne*, to help persons find the proper balance in using drugs that lessened pain as well as altered mood and disposition. Although Ford was aware of the dangers of addiction and adverse physical effects that could result from the abusive use of chemical comforters, Ford believed that the ordinary person was capable of making reasonable and prudent decisions in the use of these comforters. He left it to individuals to make responsible use of these potentially addictive and dangerous substances. "This is a highly personalized exercise of judgment," he wrote. "A man must use his own reason to settle his own case. He must study the scientific facts, look around him, compare and evaluate, select and reject, in this matter as in any other if he wants to find the permissible course, the wiser course, the more perfect course for himself. No one can do it for him. He cannot even do it for himself without the enlightenment of God's grace."[66]

In this case, Ford exercised his role as a moral theologian in a manner much like that of the postconversion Fuchs in the Majority Report. Rather than give concrete directives about what drugs to avoid or what specific drug intakes were allowable, Ford simply gave a general criterion to guide persons in their choice and use of chemical comforters.

In the use of such substances, where there was a wide range of options between what was considered safe usage and what was considered harmful, Ford did not want to impose rigid universal norms to prevent persons from developing addictions. Knowing that different persons respond differently to the same substance, Ford allowed the person involved to make the prudential judgment about the appropriate use of chemical comforters. "In matters of this kind one must be careful about imposing strict moral obligations on the whole community and on each individual within it on the basis of the statistically calculated danger of what may take place in the far distant future."[67]

Similarly, Ford also did not want to impose on persons any strict norm regarding how they should avoid chemical comforters for the sake of mortification and growth in holiness. "That is why we leave so much to the liberty of the individual in his choice of appropriate objects of mortification. It does not help people grow in holiness to insist on uniform measures of renunciation which are too heroic for them."[68]

The difference between Ford's trust in individual moral discernment in the case of chemical comforters and his insistence on strict adherence to established norms in the contraceptives case is not based on a difference in Ford's perception of the moral competence of two different groups of people. It is not the case that Ford saw drug users and recovering alcoholics to be more responsible and trustworthy moral agents than faithful and well-formed married couples. The difference between Ford's positions in the cases of chemical comforters and contraceptives is rooted in Ford's view of the moral nature of two different acts. Ford saw the use of chemical comforters as morally neutral and not strictly regulated by church law while he considered every act of artificial contraception as a violation of natural law condemned by the Church as intrinsically evil. He could therefore allow the use of comforting substances within the boundaries of moderation, while he would adhere to the Church's prohibition of contraception.

The Case of the Scarred Uterus

Another point of similarity between the standard mode Ford and the postconversion Fuchs involves the right of the Church to demand heroic efforts from moral agents. In the Majority Report, Fuchs argued against

imposing rhythm as the only legitimate means of birth regulation available for married couples. The long periods of abstinence required by the
method, combined with the heightened sexual desire that accompanied
these periods, made it extremely trying for couples to faithfully apply the
rhythm method without straining their marital life. Moved by the testimony of the women in the commission regarding the difficulties inherent to the rhythm method, Fuchs appealed for a serious consideration
of the sense of the faithful. He stated that "condemnation of a couple to
a long and often heroic abstinence as the means to regulate conception
cannot be founded on the truth."[69] Fuchs believed that the Church had
no right to demand such heroic abstinence from married couples.

Although John Ford did not agree with Fuchs's recommendations
because of ecclesiological concerns, Ford was also not willing to impose
the burden of "heroic abstinence" on married persons. An example of
this can be found in his treatment of the scarred uterus case. Ford criticized the position of some moralists who recommended that a woman
with a weakened uterus should simply abstain from intercourse in order
to avoid a dangerous pregnancy. Such a demand for abstinence on the
part of the couple, in Ford's view, was unacceptable. "To say that she can
avoid this danger by imposing perpetual abstinence on herself and her
husband is to require a degree of heroism to which our moral principles
do not oblige her."[70] Ford used his casuistic skills to argue for a preemp-
tive hysterectomy in order to preserve the life of the woman and to prevent a heavy burden of abstinence to be imposed on a married couple.

A similar refusal to impose an unreasonable demand for heroic efforts could be seen in Ford's advice to confessors not to impose immediate abstinence on alcoholic penitents under the pain of mortal sin.[71]
Ford recognized that an alcoholic would find it impossible to fulfill such
a demand. His extensive knowledge of the dynamics of alcoholic compulsion impelled Ford to give serious consideration of the experience
of alcoholics and adjusted his pastoral approach to accommodate their
unique situation. Similarly, Ford also gave serious consideration to the
situation of persons who suffered from compulsive masturbation. He
urged pastors not to deny them communion due to their condition.[72]
Just as he did not expect alcoholics to be able to exercise immediate
long-term abstinence from alcohol, Ford did not expect the same capability for abstinence from those suffering from compulsive self-abuse.

As we have seen, the moral method of John Ford in standard mode bears striking similarities to some aspects of Josef Fuchs's postconversion approach to moral theology. In particular, Ford's serious consideration of the lived moral situation of alcoholics and other persons suffering from compulsions is analogous to the attentiveness that Josef Fuchs gave to the lived experience of married couples. Ford was willing to recognize the moral competency of individuals in making personal moral decisions on matters that were not strictly regulated by church norms. He was unwilling to impose heavy demands on individuals to abstain from certain actions which their personal circumstances made it extremely difficult for them to avoid. In the standard mode, Ford encouraged individual moral decision making even when the subject matter involved potentially dangerous substances or situations. He advised pastors to exercise pastoral leniency toward people with compulsions, and he urged confessors to pay attention to the self-evaluation of penitents regarding their culpability for compulsive acts.

Ford showed himself to be well rooted in the manualist tradition, but he was also capable of moving this tradition forward by introducing new ways of thinking and new pastoral approaches in response to the struggles of moral agents dealing with issues in particular areas of the Church's life. Like Fuchs, Ford contributed to a revision of moral theology. In Ford's case, however, the revision he initiated was not a replacement of manualism but rather a development of manualism that would give greater recognition to the moral competency of individuals and encourage a more sophisticated understanding of compulsions and other factors that affect subjective culpability.

Notes

1. Fuchs, *Natural Law* (1965), back cover.
2. Graham, *Fuchs on Natural Law* (2002), 83; Kaiser, *Encyclical That Never Was* (1987), 172–73; McClory, *Turning Point* (1995), 70–71.
3. Keenan, "Josef Fuchs" (1998), 253.
4. Fuchs, *Natural Law* (1965), 9.
5. Ibid., 145–46.
6. Ibid., 151.
7. Ibid., 158–59.
8. Graham, *Fuchs on Natural Law* (2002), 49.
9. Ibid., 50.

10. Fuchs, *General Moral Theology*, Pt. I (1963), 32; Graham, *Fuchs on Natural Law* (2002), 49.
11. Ford and Kelly, *Contemporary Moral Theology*, Vol. I (1958), 4.
12. Graham, *Fuchs on Natural Law* (2002), 87–88.
13. McClory, *Turning Point* (1995), 49.
14. Ibid., 49.
15. Graham, *Fuchs on Natural Law* (2002), 89.
16. McClory, *Turning Point* (1995), 53.
17. Ibid., 41; 77.
18. Cicognani, Letter to Ford (1964).
19. Kaiser, *Politics of Sex* (1985), 88–90.
20. McClory, *Turning Point* (1995), 70.
21. Kaiser, *Encyclical That Never Was* (1987), 126.
22. Graham, *Fuchs on Natural Law* (2002), 90.
23. Ibid.
24. Ibid., 92.
25. McClory, *Turning Point* (1995), 72.
26. Ibid.
27. Ibid., 99.
28. Graham, *Fuchs on Natural Law* (2002), 93.
29. McClory, *Turning Point* (1995), 103–4.
30. Ibid., 105.
31. Kaiser, *Encyclical That Never Was* (1987), 184.
32. McClory, *Turning Point* (1995), 110.
33. Ibid., 109–10; Graham, *Josef Fuchs on Natural Law* (2002), 94–95.
34. Ford, "State of the Question" (1968), 34–36; 55.
35. Ibid., 54–55.
36. Ford, *Validity of Virginal Marriage* (1938), 131–32.
37. Ford, "Contraception" (1968), 39.
38. Fuchs, "Liberals Reply" (1968), 64.
39. Fuchs, "Responsible Parenthood" (1995), 178–79.
40. Fuchs, "Liberals Reply" (1968), 68.
41. Graham, *Fuchs on Natural Law* (2002), 95.
42. Ibid., 96.
43. Fuchs, "Responsible Parenthood" (1995), 177.
44. Fuchs, "Liberals Reply" (1968), 68–69.
45. Graham, *Fuchs on Natural Law* (2002), 96–97.
46. Fuchs, "Responsible Parenthood" (1995), 182.
47. Fuchs, "Liberals Reply" (1968), 70–71.
48. Ibid., 74; italics by Fuchs.
49. Ibid., 74–75.
50. Ibid., 67.
51. Keenan, "Question of Moral Objectivity" 1998, 255–56.
52. Ford, "State of the Question" (1968), 50.
53. Ibid., 52.

54. Fuchs, "Responsible Parenthood" (1995), 175.
55. Graham, *Fuchs on Natural Law* (2002), 103–4.
56. Fuchs, "Liberals Reply" (1968), 75.
57. Ibid., 75–77.
58. Graham, *Fuchs on Natural Law* (2002), 103; Keenan 1998, 254.
59. Ford, Letter to Higgins (1966).
60. Ford, Handwritten notes (1955?).
61. Ford, *Morality and the Pill* (1964?).
62. Ford, Notes on private audiences (1965).
63. Ford, "Alcohol, Alcoholism" (1950), 105–6.
64. Ford and Kelly, *Contemporary Moral Theology, Vol. I* (1958), 295.
65. Ford and Grisez, "Contraception" (1978), 312.
66. Ford, "Chemical Comfort and Christian Virtue" (1959), 378.
67. Ibid., 372.
68. Ibid., 377.
69. Fuchs, "Responsible Parenthood" (1995), 178–79.
70. Ford and Kelly, *Contemporary Moral Theology, Vol. I* (1958), 335–36.
71. Ford, "Alcohol, Alcoholism" (1950), 112–13.
72. Ford and Kelly, *Contemporary Moral Theology, Vol. I* (1958), 245n19.

PART III

MORALITY AND LAW

CHAPTER EIGHT

OPPOSING TOTALITARIANISM AND PROTECTING THE VULNERABLE

We have seen how Ford encountered Noonan and Fuchs, and we have seen how different his moral method was from the contemporary mindset with regard to development of doctrine and moral objectivity. At the same time, we have seen throughout his writings and case treatments Ford's sensitivity to the plight of vulnerable persons. In this chapter I show how Ford used his skills as a manualist to defend the rights of vulnerable persons in society from current or potential abuses of power by persons in authority. Ford's critique of the totalitarian character of the legal philosophy of Oliver Wendell Holmes sets the stage for this discussion. A variety of cases follow, illustrating his use of moral and pastoral theology to assist and protect vulnerable individuals and groups.

Totalitarianism and Oliver Wendell Holmes Jr.

During World War II, Ford wrote a series of articles on law and morality with a particular emphasis on the danger of separating God's moral law from human law. He warned that "law without God leads to law without justice. The tyranny of totalitarianism is the end result."[1]

In a book review of *My Philosophy of Law: Credo of Sixteen American Scholars*, Ford criticizes the realist view of law expressed by a number of legal scholars. He warns that a philosophy of law separated from God can lead to a situation where law would be equated with brute force. If this realist view is adopted as the philosophy of American jurisprudence, a reversal of democratic ideals will result. "What a long way we shall have come, from a theory of democracy in which the power of the majority was powerless to touch these sacred rights of minorities to a theory in which the power of the majority makes the only rights there are! It is the whole road from democracy to totalitarianism."[2]

At the traditional Red Mass for judges and lawyers of Boston in 1942, Ford spoke of the irony of having American soldiers in battlefields in Europe fighting in the name of justice and law while in their own country, law and justice were being endangered by realists and pragmatists. Using a rhetorical approach reserved for crisis mode cases, Ford emphasized his point:

> How tragic it would be, if when the war for justice is won, these heroes who sacrificed so much to win it were to return home and find that the old ideals, the sacred ideals of law and justice had been driven from their shrine. How tragic for them and for all of us, if, after the horrors and heroism of total war, they were to come back only to find that the law and justice envisioned by the Founding Fathers of this Republic—which they have fought to preserve—had perished here at home. Worst of all, how tragic if they found that it was the legal profession itself, the official protectors of law and justice, who had been their betrayers.[3]

Ford appealed to the traditional unity of the "three-fold law": the law of God, the law of the conscience, and the law of the land. The unity of these three laws had come under attack by some jurists who have emphasized human law while dismissing fundamental morality as merely the product of personal preferences.[4] Ford warned that eliminating the link between a nation's laws and the laws of God and conscience would lead to dire consequences.

> To divorce the law of the land from the law of God and of conscience inevitably degrades it to the position of a mere physical force. . . . From that point on, the mere might of the stronger group makes the only right there is.
>
> What will become of the law of the land if it is cut from its moorings? It will drift into the fatal vortex of lawless theories—into Communistic no-law or the Nazi philosophy of force.[5]

Ford particularly criticized the philosophy of law expounded by Oliver Wendell Holmes Jr. (1841–1935), a highly respected jurist who greatly influenced the development of constitutional law in America. Holmes had taught law at Harvard, sat on the Massachusetts Supreme Court for twenty years, and served as a justice of the Supreme Court of the United States for thirty years. He was called "The Great Dissenter" for the originality and persuasiveness of his dissenting opinions in major cases.

Although Holmes's parents were descended from Puritans and his grandfather was an orthodox Calvinist pastor, Holmes himself was an agnostic. Ford emphasizes this fact as important context for understanding Holmes's philosophy.

> [Holmes] was simply not a Christian at all. By no stretching of terms could he be called a Christian believer. Though he grew up in a civilization still largely devoted to orthodox Christian beliefs, he did not share them. It is important to recognize this fact—which is also true of so many other intellectuals of the past few generations—because otherwise one is not prepared for the shock of discovering that Holmes's views of law and life were thoroughly totalitarian in many important respects.[6]

Holmes had many admirers among legal scholars and practitioners. Ford acknowledges Holmes's positive qualities as a judge that earned him the respect of his colleagues: "He was a great judge, the champion of free speech and social reform legislation. After all he was a human character who inspired the deepest esteem and respect of those who came in contact with him. After all he was an incredibly well read scholar, a hard consistent thinker, and a sincerely honest man."[7] Ford was nevertheless concerned that many of Holmes's admirers were either ignorant of the consequences of his philosophy of law, or indifferent to them. He warned against the dangerous consequences of Holmes's ideas on American jurisprudence.

Ford described Holmes's philosophy of law as totalitarian. Holmes wrote that force was the essence of law, and that legal rights and duties were not based on objective criteria of right or wrong but rather were based on predictions of punishments imposed on those who would violate the law.

> Law is merely "a statement of the circumstances in which the public force will be brought to bear upon men through the courts."[8]
>
> Just so far as the aid of the public force is given a man he has a legal right, and this right is the same whether his claim is founded on righteousness or iniquity.[9]

In his writings, Holmes consistently defended the separation of law and morality. For example, he wrote, "For my part, I often doubt whether it would not be a gain if every word of moral significance could be banished from the law altogether and other words adopted which should convey legal ideas uncolored by anything outside the law. We should lose the fossil records of a good deal of history, and the majesty got from ethical associations, but by ridding ourselves of an unnecessary confusion we should gain very much in clearness of thought."[10]

He rejected the concept of natural law. "The jurists who believe in natural law seem to me in that naïve state of mind that accepts what has been familiar and accepted by them and their neighbors, as something to be accepted by all men everywhere."[11] He also rejected the idea of absolute natural rights and moral obligations. What people claimed to be rights and duties were dismissed by Holmes as simply conventions drawn from the preferences of the majority of the community. These conventions are enforced by the majority through legislation and through the imposition of punishments on violators.

Holmes believed that the chief duty of a judge making a judicial decision was the weighing of social advantages. Whatever would be to the advantage of the majority of the community should prevail in law. Ultimately, it was the majority's use of power that determined what was lawful. In Holmes words, "A dog will fight for his bone."[12]

The existence of absolute values was rejected by Holmes. Speaking in the context of World War I, Holmes expresses his negative opinion of the idea that the human person has intrinsic value.

> I don't believe that it is an absolute principle or even a human ultimate that man always is an end in himself—that his dignity must be respected, etc. We march up a conscript with bayonets behind to die for a cause he does not believe in. And I feel no scruples about it. Our morality seems to me only a check on the ultimate domination of force, just as our politeness is a check on the impulse of every pig to put his feet in the trough. When the Germans in the late war disregarded what we called the rules of the game, I don't see there was anything to be said except: we don't like it and shall kill you if we can.[13]

Ford cited two court rulings by Holmes as examples of how Holmes's philosophy of law diminished the rights of the human person in society. In the case of *Dietrich v. Northampton* 138 Mass. 14 (1884), Holmes wrote a court ruling, as a justice of the Massachusetts Supreme Court, denying the rights of a child to sue after birth for injuries received while still in the womb. Ford argued that this ruling disregarded the human personality of the unborn child as the subject of rights in common law.[14]

In the case of *Buck v. Bell* 274 U.S. 200 (1927), the United States Supreme Court upheld a statute of the State of Virginia that enforced compulsary sterilization for the mentally retarded for the good of society. Holmes wrote the ruling on this case. A young woman, Carrie Bell, a patient in a mental institution in Virginia, had a mental age of nine and her mother had a mental age of eight. Carrie had three children with no clear knowledge of their fathers. The Board of Directors of Carrie's mental institution petitioned for her compulsory sterilization, in accordance with a Virginia statute passed in 1924 that allowed for compulsory sterilization for eugenic purposes. In Holmes's ruling, he places the welfare of society above any individual rights.

> We have seen more than once that the public welfare may call upon the best citizens for their lives. It would be strange if it could not call upon those who already sap the strength of the State for these lesser sacrifices, often not felt to be such by those concerned, in order to prevent our being swamped with incompetence. It is better for all the world, if instead of waiting to execute degenerate offspring for crime, or to let them starve for their imbecility, society can prevent those who are manifestly unfit from continuing their kind. The principle that sustains compulsory vaccination is broad enough to cover cutting the Fallopian tubes.[15]

Holmes concludes his ruling with the phrase: "Three generations of imbeciles are enough."

Ford emphasized that Holmes did not use his position as judge to actively promote the totalitarian use of force. In general, Holmes followed the rules of law strictly and objectively.

> It was part of his philosophy . . . to consider the law as absolutely divorced from morality. But however one abhors that philosophy one can be glad that at least Holmes believed in sticking to objective standards of decision. The rules were there. They meant something. He knew what they meant and he decoded accordingly. . . . He knew his place as judge. He did not confuse himself with the legislature. He was not addicted to the reading of his own views into the law.[16]

Ford recognized the power of ideas, however, and that the philosophy of law Holmes expressed in his rulings would eventually influence the direction of future court rulings. For example, the case of *Korematsu v. United States*, 323 U.S. 214 (1944), which validated the internment of Japanese Americans and Japanese nationals in the United States during World War II, is traceable to prior court decisions written by Holmes. Supreme Court decisions in two other cases, *United States v. Dotterweich*, 320 U.S. 277 (1943) and *Application of Yamashita*, 327 U.S. 1 (1946), applied Holmes's theory of jurisprudence and resulted in the weakening of the protection of a person against arbitrary government action.[17]

Ford admitted that Holmes was considered a "god of lawyers and legislators" and that law schools "worship at his shrine." To call attention to the objectionable aspects of Holmes's legal philosophy, Ford composed a summary:

> The essence of law is physical force. Might makes legal right. The law is to be divorced from all morality. There is no such thing as a moral *ought*—it is a mere fiction. Ultimately there is only the physical necessity of behaving or being killed. There is no absolute truth. Man is a cosmic ganglion. His ideas probably have no more cosmic value than his bowels. He himself has no more cosmic significance than a baboon or a grain of sand. To the state man is a means to be sacrificed if necessary to the interest of the state. The ultimate arbiter of life is physical force. The ultimate *ratio decidendi* when men disagree is this, in Holmes's words: 'We don't like it and shall kill you if we can.'"[18]

Ford's commitment to maintaining a strong unity between law and morality is in direct opposition to Holmes's realist philosophy. The manualist approach used by Ford, which treated every human activity as the proper object of moral evaluation, is itself in disagreement with Holmes's dismissal of moral language from the field of law. Their approaches were in particular conflict over the use of power. The essence of law in Holmes's philosophy was public force: the more powerful majority can arbitrarily define and impose what was lawful according to its preferences, regardless of any detrimental effects on the welfare of individuals or minority groups. In such a legal paradigm, the intrinsic value of the life and dignity of the individual person was denied or disregarded. In contrast to Holmes's philosophy, Ford insisted that the exercise of authority and power must be guided by objective moral norms.

A good illustration of the contrast between the approaches of Ford and Holmes is the issue of the primacy of conscience in time of war. Holmes wrote that he would not have any scruples to force conscripts to fight in a war they did not believe in. Ford, on the other hand, defended the right of Catholic conscientious objectors to claim exemption from a military draft. While Ford sought to protect the primacy of conscience, Holmes supported the right of the majority to impose laws by force even in violation of the conscience of the minority.

Holmes and Ford also disagreed over the value of the individual. Holmes wrote: "It seems to me clear that the *ultima ratio* not only *regum* but of private persons, is force, and that at the bottom of all private relations, however tempered by sympathy and social feelings, is a justifiable self-preference. If a man is on a plank in the deep sea which will only float one, and a stranger lays hold of it, he will thrust him off if he can. When the state finds itself in a similar position it does the same thing."[19] While Holmes was ready to sacrifice the individual for the greater good of the state, Ford strongly objects to the treatment of persons as disposable objects, or as means to an end. In his treatment of the case of obliteration bombing, Ford appeals to objective moral principles and the intrinsic values of persons to argue for the protection for civilians against the indiscriminate use of force in pursuit of wartime objectives.

Ford's objections to the totalitarian tendencies he saw in Holmes's philosophy of law reveal Ford's profound concern about the potentially abusive uses of power—uses endangering the safety, integrity, or dignity of the individual person, whether in peacetime or in war. Protecting vulnerable persons was an underlying theme in Ford's treatment of a number of moral cases, as we shall see.

Protecting the Vulnerable

As a moral theologian, Ford argued for the protection of persons he perceived to be marginalized by society or threatened by the abusive use of power.

Protecting Persons Affected by War

In a 1942 journal article "Patriotic Obedience in a Time of War,"[20] Ford discussed the virtue of patriotism during wartime. He viewed the

entry of the United States into World War II as an act of justified defense against an aggressor, and he urged his fellow citizens to support
the government in its wartime efforts. He stated that national unity was
"absolutely indispensable" for a country at war. The ordinary obedience
that citizens rendered to their government during peacetime would not
be adequate to move the population to bear the sacrifices necessary to
win a war. Obedience to the government needed to be directed by the
virtue of patriotism in order to more effectively unite citizens with their
leaders for concerted wartime action. Ford asserted, however, that patriotism according to Catholic tradition was a well-ordered love for one's
country.

> The moral pronouncements of the modern Popes on the virtue of pa-
> triotism have steered a middle course. That excessive patriotism which
> degenerates into nationalism or racism is condemned. But condemned
> likewise is the opposite error, that a preferential love of one's own coun-
> try is incompatible with international peace . . .
>
> True patriotism does not mean flag waving. It does not include ha-
> tred of other nations, whether enemies or allies. Nor does it necessarily
> include love of the administration. Administrations come and go. The fa-
> therland endures.[21]

Ford's support for America's involvement in World War II did not
prevent him from considering other opinions regarding the war. In his
"Notes on Moral Theology" in 1941, Ford reviewed pacifist writings that
had been published at the beginning of World War II. Although there
were "practical inconsistencies which were unavoidable in the pacifist
position," Ford did not discount the possibility for a Catholic to be a
conscientious objector.[22] He proposed that there was a middle ground
of Catholic opinion that allowed for selective conscientious objection,
which holds that "in some circumstances conscientious objection is justifiable, in others not."[23] Using probabilism, Ford argued for the protection of the Catholic conscientious objector even in the absence of an
authoritative teaching from the magisterium.

> When the infallible Church has not spoken and will not speak on the jus-
> tice of a given war, and when the Church Hierarchies of opposing enemy
> nations do speak on it and give opposite answers, and when moralists
> and theologians are still in the process of forming their opinions, the very

least we can say is that, as far as confessional practice is concerned, the sincere conscientious objector is entitled to freedom of conscience. The fact that he is a Catholic does not make it wrong for him to be a conscientious objector, too.[24]

In the 1950s, Ford extended his protection of the Catholic conscientious objector beyond the confessional. He advised bishops not to assist the U.S. State Department in prosecuting Catholic conscientious objectors.[25] He also made personal interventions to aid individuals struggling with their conscience regarding the military draft.

In one letter, dated 1951, a man sought Ford's advice on how to answer his questionnaire from the draft board. Although the man did not believe that war was generally immoral, he believed that the saturation bombing conducted by the Allies in World War II was morally unacceptable and he did not want to be involved in any similar military action. Using the principle of cooperation, Ford explained to the man that he could avoid going to jail while at the same time avoiding direct involvement with possible future saturation bombings by joining the medical corps or by requesting to serve among the ground personnel if he entered the Air Force. Ford assured the man that even if his work with the medical corps or the ground crew of the Air Force were linked to an instance of saturation bombing (e.g., he helped service a bomber plane or he released another person in the medical corps to became a bomber pilot), his cooperation would have been a remote and material cooperation.[26]

In another letter, dated 1957, Ford was asked by a fellow Jesuit, Edmund Hogan, for advice regarding a Fairfield University alumnus who claimed exemption from the military draft on the grounds of conscientious objection. An agent of the FBI had gone to Fairfield University to ask Hogan for a statement regarding the church teaching on conscientious objection in order to clarify the alumnus's claim for exemption. Ford responds with this advice:

> I would not consider it appropriate to give an FBI man a theological dissertation or a detailed theological statement of the Catholic position on conscientious objection. If I would not advise the Bishops to make such a statement to the Justice Department, *a fortiori* I would not advise a priest to make a statement to an FBI man.

> Personally, I do not see why a Catholic conscientious objector should
> not receive the benefit of the law. . . . I do not think the matter is so clear
> that he has to be refused absolution if he claims honestly that his con-
> science absolutely requires of him that he should not take up arms in a
> given concrete situation. . . .
>
> Let the Justice Department fight their own legal battles; and let them
> respect the rights of the Catholic erroneous conscience also, as well as
> that of other religions.[27]

Ford did not deny the government's right to intervene if the actions
of a person following an erroneous conscience would cause harm to
himself or to others. However, he made the argument that the government should respect an individual's conscientious decision to avoid an
activity perceived to be immoral according to the individual's religious
beliefs, even if that perception were erroneous. Just as the government
respects the status of conscientious objectors whose religions do forbid the use of or participation in violence, a person who erroneously believes that his religion forbids participation in war should also receive
the same respect.

In a third letter, dated 1964, Ford made his most direct intervention
to assist a conscientious objector. The Catholic Peace Fellowship (whose
stationery listed Daniel Berrigan, Dorothy Day, and Thomas Merton as
among its sponsors) requested Ford to assist Stephen, a twenty-five-year-
old employee at a Wall Street brokerage firm, who sought exemption
from the military draft as a conscientious objector. Stephen's case had
already been denied by both local and state draft boards. The Fellowship
sought to bring the case up to a presidential review, and asked Ford to
write a brief statement on the Catholic position regarding conscientious
objection to be included in Stephen's draft file. If a presidential review
were not granted, the case could go to court and a statement from Ford
could be used as evidence to support Stephen's claim. Setting aside his
previous hesitancy to provide written statements to government authorities regarding conscientious objection, Ford sent a response to support
Stephen's exemption claim. He argued that a Catholic could claim exemption from military induction as a selective conscientious objector
because of the nature of modern warfare.

> A Roman Catholic may in all sincerity be conscientiously convinced
> because of his religious training and belief that any modern war is

immoral—at the very least to the extent that such a war will inevitably be
waged by immoral means. In particular the use of massive nuclear attacks
against whole cities has been condemned by various Catholic theologians
as intrinsically immoral. . . .

I feel sure that the Roman Catholic hierarchy of the United States
would agree with the proposition that even in a just defensive war a Roman Catholic could and should refuse, in all good faith, to take part in
military procedures which according to the teaching of Catholic theology
he judges are opposed to the law of God.

As for refusing not only to take part in such procedures but even to
be inducted to the armed services at all, it is also entirely possible, in my
opinion, for a Roman Catholic to be honestly convinced, because of his
Catholic religious training and belief, that he must so refuse. The question is not whether Catholic theology teaches him that he has such an
obligation. The question is whether he sincerely, even if erroneously, believes, on the basis of his Catholic religious principles and their application to modern war, that God demands of him that he refuse induction.[28]

Ford's pastoral concern was not limited to those who were seeking
to avoid the military draft; he was also concerned for those already in
military service. For example, he condemned the practice of using live
machine-gun fire to train soldiers to crawl under enemy fire. He asserted
that even military training for war must follow the standards of justice
and should respect innocent life.[29]

This pastoral care for persons in military service can also be seen in
Ford's confessional approach toward the troubled consciences of military personnel commanded to carry out morally objectionable military
actions. Acknowledging the difficulty of applying general moral principles to concrete wartime situations, Ford offered some advice on confessional practice:

The application of our moral principles to modern war leaves so much
to be desired that we are not in a position to impose obligations on the
consciences of the individual, whether he be a soldier with a bayonet, or a
conscientious objector, *except in cases where violation of natural law is clear.*[30]

Ford applied such a pastoral approach in the case of bomber pilots
involved in saturation bombing: "I believe the confessor is justified in

absolving the bombardier who feels forced to carry out orders to take part in obliteration bombing, unless the penitent himself is convinced (as I am) of the immorality of the practice," he wrote.[31]

Ford's condemnation of obliteration bombing by Allied forces of German cities during World War II was his most critical intervention to protect persons threatened by war. He deplored the violation of the just war principle of noncombatant immunity, and criticized the misuse of the principle of double effect to justify the bombing of factory workers' homes to paralyze war material production and to degrade the enemy's morale.[32] Ford countered the tendency to demonize war opponents by presenting civilians in Germany as being no different from civilians of Allied countries. He illustrated the effects of obliteration bombings on Germans by presenting a hypothetical scenario of an obliteration bombing attack on Boston and its surrounding metropolitan area, using the same criteria used by the Allied military leaders for bombing industrialized areas in Germany.

> If Boston were subject to obliteration attack, not all the area would be a target. But the principal, more densely populated parts of it would, e.g., North End, South End, West End, East Boston, South Boston, Dorchester, Charlestown, Everett, Chelsea, Brighton, parts of Brookline, Cambridge, Hingham, Quincy, etc. Perhaps the number of munitions workers and "warlike" workers in these districts forms a higher percentage. It is impossible to find out. (Nor would the Germans bother to find out if they could take up obliteration bombing against us, as we have against them.) In any event, to say that two-thirds of the civil population liable to this kind of bombing is innocent is to make a conservative estimate.[33]

There was an undeniable difference between those directly involved in war such as military leaders and soldiers, and those who were only remotely involved with warfare. Ford argued that it was one thing to seek to assassinate the Führer at night while he is unarmed in bed, and it was a different matter to seek the death of "a sixteen-year-old German girl who spends ten hours a day in a munitions factory testing the timing devices on bombs."[34]

Ford consistently strove to give a human face to every potential victim of war, whether it was a soldier, a conscientious objector, or a noncombatant. By appealing to the human capacity to see others as fellow human beings, he sought to reverse the dehumanizing effects of war. His contribution to the protection of vulnerable persons in wartime was an imaginative and assertive use of moral theology that upheld human dignity, the right to life, and freedom of conscience.

Protecting the Privacy of Religious Subjects

John Ford addressed a group of serious problems involving the governance of religious orders. Writing primarily in the context of male religious orders, Ford observed that there was a growing erosion of the filial confidence of members of religious congregations for their superiors. These problems could be traced to the ignorance or erroneous ideas of some religious superiors regarding the difference between their roles as a father and as a judge in relation to the members of their religious community.[35] The introduction of psychiatric care into the communities compounded these confusions because the therapeutic relationship involved making much private psychic matter known to the psychiatrist, who also properly owed some kind of report to the superior to enable the superior to make wise decisions for the community.

THE PATERNAL FORUM AND THE JUDICIAL FORUM

Rules governed the use of information received by a superior from a religious subject, and these rules differed depending on whether the superior communicated with the subject as a father (in the paternal forum) or as a judge (in the judicial forum). An action of a religious superior regarding a religious subject could be a paternal or a judicial procedure depending on the purpose of the action. The difference depended on whether the superior acted principally for the good of the individual subject or for the good of the congregation.

> If he is acting *principally* for the good of the delinquent, in order to have him amend his fault, then he is acting as a father, even though as a means to this end some penance is imposed (*of a private nature*), or some remedy is used which is repugnant to the subject, for example, a change of appointment. But if he acts *principally* for the good of the congregation, the common good, and seeks to inflict punishment as a vindication of religious discipline which has been violated, especially if the punishment is public, or if the idea is to make an example of someone, and most of

all if the punishment in question is expulsion—in such cases he is acting as a judge.[36]

There was a boundary separating the paternal forum from the judicial forum, which the religious superior was required to respect. No information a religious subject shared with his superior in the paternal forum could ever be used judicially. If the superior, acting as a father, found it necessary to impose a form of punishment on the subject, it could only be a private punishment that would not diminish the subject's public reputation in the community. If the superior were to act in a manner that confused his roles as a father and as a judge—that is, if he were to use information from the paternal forum to make judicial decisions—his religious subjects would naturally become distrustful about sharing any information with him in the paternal forum. His effectiveness as a religious superior would be compromised once his subjects lost confidence in his trustworthiness to protect the sanctity of the paternal forum.[37]

Ford's writings on religious governance, particularly on the prudent use of personal information by religious superiors, gained him respect among religious superiors not only within the Society of Jesus but also in other religious orders and congregations. Religious superiors consulted him on matters involving the proper treatment of information received in various circumstances such as spiritual direction and private consultation.

In one letter, Ford advised a religious superior against acting judicially on information reported in the paternal forum by a religious subject against a fellow religious.

> I believe that when a subject goes to the superior and reveals the fault of a fellow religious to him in the paternal forum the matter is automatically restricted in the paternal forum from the nature of the case. The classical authors (Lugo, Suarez) made some exceptions where the superior could transfer or might have to transfer the matter to the external forum, but as I read them, these cases would be distinctly exceptional. I think these matters remain in the paternal forum whether they are known to the delator through a secret or not.[38]

In the same letter, Ford also firmly advised against superiors using the paternal forum to extract incriminating information from a subject against another subject for the purpose of punishment. Even in the judicial forum, a superior may not interrogate a subject simply based on a suspicion of wrongdoing. A religious subject must be made aware beforehand whether the information being sought by his superior will be used paternally or judicially.

Ford also asserted the right of a religious subject to seek advice confidentially from fellow religious without being reported to the superior.

> I think it is extremely important that people who are in trouble can confide in someone, even if not a priest, in order to get advice, or help, or even the consolation of that non-directive counseling which may come from pouring out the story to a good listener. If one scholastic goes to another scholastic in these circumstances, making it clear that he wants to talk confidentially to him, and revealing himself only because he believes that the other will consider it a strict confidence, I consider this a committed secret. This is the only way some matters of this kind are ever effectively dealt with. The troubled person opens up to a friend, only because he can trust him, and the friend sees to it that he gets help—by getting him to go to the spiritual father or even to the superior with his problem.[39]

In another letter, Ford gave concrete advice to a novice master dealing with sensitive information received in the paternal forum. He firmly advised the novice master against using such information judicially without the religious subject's permission. This permission may not be coerced or presumed. This excerpt of Ford's letter reveals his protective stance toward religious subjects vulnerable to accusation made against them in the paternal forum.

> With regard to A, it appears to me that although you have suspicions concerning him, you do not, in your own mind, feel you have sufficient grounds for advising him to go, apart from what X has told you. If this is the case, then I do not see how you can advise him to leave without making use of X's information. And I do not see how you can make use of this without X's permission.
>
>   It would be unjust, it seems to me, to advise A to go on the basis of an accusation which is not made known to him and against which he has no opportunity to defend himself. There is an added reason for hesitancy, seeing that the original accuser of A (i.e., D) has now retracted his

story, although he has done so under very suspicious circumstances. On the other hand, to use X's information without his permission in order to dismiss the culprits, seems to me not only to endanger X, but to be a judicial use of information intended to be used in the paternal forum. When such information is used to dismiss, the proceedings, in my opinion, are no longer paternal but judicial. I admire very much your wisdom in respecting this distinction, because I think it will mean a great deal to these young men later on, in fostering a spirit of filial confidence in superiors.

Consequently I would consider it wiser, and better for the common good in the long run, to do nothing about A, serious as the matter seems, rather than act without X's permission. . . .

Considering the terrible aversion of American boys have for "squealing," remembering certain cases . . . where a man's reputation with his companions continued to suffer seriously for many years because of his sincere efforts to keep the rule on fraternal correction, I do not believe it would be justifiable to oblige X under pain of serious sin to give permission that the information be used for the dismissal of A and D.[40]

Ford asserted that information received in the context of spiritual direction or private consultation must not be relayed to a religious superior except in the extreme case when the common good of the community is endangered. He was also strongly against keeping files of personal information on religious subjects obtained in the paternal forum for use by future superiors. Such a practice would compromise the sanctity of the paternal forum.

No material received either in the forum of direction or the forum of personal consultation should be included in the report to Major Superiors.

If the material has been received as an entrusted secret it should not be given to the Major Superiors and a fortiori should not be kept on file where other masters of novices may have access to it. Even if the matter contained in these reports is only that which is legitimately communicated to the Major Superior for the purpose of enabling him to judge about admitting the candidate to vows, etc., in my opinion it should not be kept on file for future masters of novices to use. I believe that this would be an imprudent way to use the material, to say the least.[41]

Ford also wrote on the sanctity of "manifestation of conscience," a Jesuit practice where a religious subject reveals the state of his or her

conscience in order that the superior may help the subject grow in perfection as a religious.

> In the manifestation itself, . . . the strictest secrecy is to be observed. I
> have found no author who will permit the revelation of the secret, i.e.,
> the thing revealed and the identity of the person revealing it to anyone
> for any reason without express permission. In this it is like the secret of
> confession.
>
> As to the use of information received in manifestation: if the subject
> makes no objection a certain limited use can be made, (*salvo semper secreto,
> et salva fama subjecti*) for the good of the subject and the good of the Soci-
> ety, because these are among the purposes for which manifestation was
> instituted. But the information cannot be used to the harm the subject,
> or to punish him,—least of all to dismiss him from the Society. And if
> his self-revelation involves an accomplice the superior cannot make use
> of this knowledge in any way that would get the person revealing it into
> trouble.[42]

PSYCHIATRISTS AND THE PRIVACY OF RELIGIOUS SUBJECTS

In his book, *Religious Superiors, Subjects, and Psychiatrists*,[43] Ford observes
that the relationship between the religious superior and his subjects was
made complicated by the introduction of a third party, the psychiatrist,
who gains access to confidential information on religious subjects who
come to him for treatment.

The religious subject considering psychiatric treatment is often aware
that such treatment may entail a significant amount of self-revelation
that could include material that belongs to the confidential encounters
of confession, spiritual direction, and manifestation of conscience. It
may even include revelation of "unconscious psychic materials, the hidden depths of personality which the patient himself may not even sus-
pect."[44] Ford describes the dilemma of the religious subject in need of
psychiatric treatment:

> He cannot get the care he needs without revealing many of the secrets of
> his interior life. But he will not reveal these secrets if he thinks the psy-
> chiatrist is free to communicate them to his superior, especially if the
> superior is free to use them for his government. He recognizes his depen-
> dence on his superior, but even in the paternal forum this dependence is

not so complete that he is obliged to yield up to the superior, through a psychiatric report, the secrets of his conscience.[45]

A religious superior needs to have a report from the psychiatrist treating his subject in order to be able to make appropriate decisions for the welfare of his subject. However, the report may include self-revelatory information from the subject that was drawn out by a psychiatrist without the subject being fully aware of the nature or the extent of his self-revelation. Since canon law at that time (1917 Code of Canon Law # 530) forbade a superior from demanding a manifestation of conscience from his subjects, a superior may not use a subject's psychiatric treatment as a means to obtain information about his subject. Any information unintentionally revealed by a subject to a psychiatrist and included in his psychiatric report may not be used by the superior outside the paternal forum.[46]

On the matter of psychological tests on religious subjects, Ford maintained two principles: the subject's right to psychic privacy and the necessity of informed consent.[47] Sometimes a religious subject is asked to reveal parts of his or her inner life, such as in sacramental confession, the manifestation of conscience, or in the application process for admission to religious life. In these instances, the seal of strict confidentiality protects the self-revelation volunteered by the person. The confessional secret is inviolable and the secret of a person's inner life obtained in nonconfessional circumstances may not be used for administrative purposes without the person's consent.

Regarding a religious subject's self-revelation in the context of psychological testing, Ford quoted Pius XII to emphasize the importance of a person's consent regarding the scientific probing of his inner life: "it is immoral to penetrate into the conscience of anyone; but this act becomes moral if the interested party gives his valid consent."[48] In order for a subject to be able to give valid consent to psychological testing, the subject must be informed of the purpose of the test or interview and he should be given a clear idea of what kind of information about himself he might reveal. "The subject should know whether the test is a measure of intelligence, or of aptitude, or of interest, and that the latter may reveal personality traits too. He should know that, if it is a personality test, it will reveal hidden traits of character, including perhaps embarrassing matters, and matters which, being in his unconscious, are not even known to himself."[49]

While a religious candidate usually allows substantial self-revelation in psychological testing for the purpose of application to religious life, the candidate should be informed whether the results of such tests would be used for other purposes after his admission to religious life (e.g., for the purpose of evaluation for vows or ordination, future assignments, etc.). The subject's consent must be obtained for other uses of the results of his or her psychological tests. The subject should be informed about the persons who will have access to the psychological reports and he or she should be allowed to withdraw consent for extraneous uses of these psychological test results.

In order that the subject could give a valid consent to psychological testing, Ford recommended that those who administer the tests should provide the subject with some samples of psychological test results and reports.

> One way of making sure that the client's consent to testing, evaluation, and treatment is valid, would be to let him see some samples of psychologists' and psychiatrists' reports, including a very favorable one, a very unfavorable one, one indicating serious mental illness, and some average ones. If he has this kind of concrete information, and furthermore knows what use is going to be made of the reports, his consent will be valid. Without such adequate briefing, he may well have good grounds for the complaint being heard that he has been tricked into revealing the depths of his soul, and that his consent was not valid.[50]

Ford believed that providing full and adequate knowledge of the purpose and implications of psychological testing and treatment, and securing the subjects' informed and valid consent to any psychological test would help address the concerns that have been raised regarding the use of psychiatry and psychological testing in religious communities.[51]

Ford objected to obligatory personality testing of members of religious communities. Such required testing aimed at obtaining private information about religious subjects' personality for administrative purposes are violations of the religious subjects' right to privacy and informed consent.

By ordering subjects to undergo testing or evaluation for administrative purposes, the superior, it seems to me, can rather easily go counter to the policy, if not the law, of the Church, and even violate a natural law right to psychic privacy. Even apart from canon 530 he is not entitled to invade this privacy for administrative purposes, using the instrumentality of the psychiatrist's evaluation or the psychologist's test. I do not believe any religious is obliged to reveal the secrets of his conscience to psychiatrists and psychologists for the administrative use of his superiors in governing him externally.[52]

Ford objected to the practice of some superiors who required entire groups of religious subjects to take personality tests for the purpose of evaluating their suitability for vows, entry into theology studies, or ordination. This practice adds to the confusion between the internal forum of the conscience and the external forum of administration. To assist religious subjects to protect their right to psychic privacy, Ford composed a statement of position that may be used by religious subjects to assert their refusal to participate in obligatory personality testing. He argued that it should not be held against religious subjects if they refuse to participate in obligatory personality tests. Superiors are not to coerce subjects to take personality tests by making them a condition for reception of vows or orders. Adequate data for evaluation of subjects are available from other sources (e.g., observations of external behavior in community and ministry, feedback from fellow religious, etc.) without relying on obligatory personality testing.[53]

Ford's commitment to protect the privacy of religious subjects was concretely expressed in his crisis mode response to a case of obligatory personality testing. The major superior of the New England Province of the Society of Jesus, to which John Ford belonged as a religious, had sent out a questionnaire to all members of the province. The questionnaire was intended to produce a general personal profile of the individual subject to whom it was sent. The personal profiles would be kept on file at the provincial office in order to help the major superior make appropriate decisions regarding the administration of the province and for making decisions regarding individual subjects. Ford sent back the form that he received, with a strongly worded letter objecting to the wholesale gathering of personal information for the purpose of administration. He believed that the information that would be revealed through the questionnaire was matter proper to the manifestation of conscience. Ford also strongly objected to the idea that such a substantial amount of sensitive personal information would be kept indefinitely in provincial files. An unknown number of persons would have access to such files and there was no provision for individual subjects to control or monitor access to their personal files. There was the possibility that such personal information, obtained through subtle psychological questions, would be used to the prejudice of the religious subject.

> This type of psychological questionnaire involves self-revelation of material which theologians consider as belonging properly to the domain of manifestation of conscience as the latter has been traditionally practiced in religious life and as it is understood in Canon Law. . . .
>
> The purpose of the questions in the present questionnaire is not at all clear, but among the possible uses to which they could be put by some future Provincial, even if you have no such intention, especially the questions of Part II, would be to discover whether individuals should be considered "conservative" or "liberal", or to discover how groups or individuals are affected toward Superiors, or toward the then current Province planning and Province planners.
>
> Respondents to questionnaires like this one have no way of knowing the kind of information they may be revealing about themselves, or the kind of conclusions the questioners may draw. The questions are purposely unrevealing and even deceptive. . . .
>
> I protest against the whole project of this questionnaire as a departure from the form of religious government called for by our Constitutions, as a debasement of the Jesuit idea of manifestation of conscience, and as an illegitimate invasion of the psychic privacy of the members of the Province. And I ask you, because of the urgency of the matter, to put an immediate stop to the collection and examination of this material. I also request an early answer to this letter of mine, because if nothing is done immediately I intend to present my objections to Roman authorities.
>
> I am sorry to have to speak in such imperative tones, but I consider the matter to be of vital, urgent concern for the Province.[54]

Ford's major superior responded by assuring him that the questionnaire was voluntary and that it was not meant for evaluative purposes but rather it was "aimed at producing a personal profile on an attitudinal scale." The superior pointed out that Ford's objections were not shared by other members of the Province, as proven by the rapid return of completed forms to the superior's office. The superior urged Ford to greater faith in his superior's commitment to respect confidentiality.[55]

Ford responded to his superior's assurances by insisting once more on his objection to the whole project. "Despite what you say, the questionnaire is 'a type of personality test' as I said in my letter; it does call for manifestation material, and it is clearly intended to use the results of the questionnaire administratively."[56]

There was no evidence to suggest that Ford referred the matter to Rome. In the absence of a copy of the actual survey form, there is no way to judge objectively whether Ford's reaction to the survey form was appropriate or extreme. However, his readiness to confront his major superior regarding a possibly grave violation of the privacy of his fellow religious and his willingness to raise the matter to higher ecclesiastical authorities indicate a strong commitment on Ford's part to protect vulnerable religious subjects from violation of their privacy.

Assisting Persons with Addictions and Compulsions

As mentioned in previous chapters, Ford addressed the difficult situation of persons suffering from addictions and compulsion at several levels.

At the sacramental level, Ford formulated pastoral guidelines for confessors to guide them on how to appropriately minister to alcoholics, addicts, and sufferers of compulsions. He argued for providing unhindered reception of sacraments, particularly confession and the Eucharist, to persons who were still suffering from addictions or compulsions.[57]

At the level of moral responsibility, Ford sought to understand the physical, spiritual, and psychological dynamics involved in compulsions and addictions. Taking into consideration the diminished subjective culpability of persons affected by addictions and compulsions, Ford developed a lenient pastoral approach toward the moral evaluation of the actions these persons.

At the level of preventive strategies, Ford introduced approaches that contributed to the prevention of addictions. He used virtue ethics to address the problem of drug addiction and he campaigned for alcohol education for both the clergy and laity. He wrote articles and pamphlets that addressed the misconceptions and myths about alcoholism in order to educate persons in responsible use of alcohol.[58] He recommended that seminary programs should include a course on alcohol education in order to teach seminarians about facts regarding alcoholism and he urged his students who graduated from Weston College to go to AA meetings in order to learn about their recovery program.[59] Ford was a cofounder of the National Clergy Council on Alcoholism, a Catholic advocacy and public information association aimed at providing clergy and laity with the information necessary to address alcoholism in personal life and in ministry.[60]

At the level of providing assistance for recovery, Ford used his stature as a reputable moral theologian to endorse Alcoholics Anonymous to clergy and laity. Catholic acceptance of Alcoholics Anonymous was an important goal for Ford. Oliver Morgan describes Ford as "an ambassador and interpreter between AA and the Catholic community."[61]

On the personal level, Ford dedicated many hours to assisting individual alcoholics through the sacrament of confession and through personal counseling. He had a long association with Alcoholism Information Referral, Inc. (AIR), a telephone counseling service located at Lemuel Shattuck Hospital in Jamaica Plain, Massachusetts. He had been involved with this counseling service in various capacities as counselor, trustee, and treasurer.[62] Ford engaged in alcoholism counseling for more than thirty years and he served as counselor for the AIR Hotline until the age of eighty-six, shortly before his death in 1989.[63]

Ford's multilevel approach helped affirm the dignity of persons suffering from addictions and compulsions, especially alcoholics. He believed that "responsibility is the most distinguishing characteristic of a human being. It is the most human thing about a human being."[64] His efforts to provide addicts and alcoholics with a variety of means to aid their recovery (education, pastoral guidelines, the sacraments, AA programs, personal counseling, and public policy initiatives) helped affirm the humanity and dignity of alcoholics and addicts by giving them ultimate responsibility for their recovery. This humanizing approach is perhaps one of the most significant contributions of Ford to the field of addiction prevention and treatment.

Assisting Persons with Serious Medical Conditions

Ford also dealt with medical cases where access to urgent, life-saving medical treatment may be impeded by certain interpretations of the moral or civil law.

BLOOD TRANSFUSIONS FOR JEHOVAH'S WITNESSES

In his article "Refusal of Blood Transfusions by Jehovah Witnesses," Ford investigates the complex moral and legal issues involved in the religiously motivated refusal of Jehovah's Witnesses to accept blood transfusions for themselves or for their children. He looks at the moral obligations of all parties involved in the case, the legal liabilities that affect physicians and hospitals treating Witnesses, and the possible public policies that could address the problem. Ford argues for the protection of the consciences of adults from coercion by the State while at the same time he also insists on the protection of the children of Witnesses from being endangered by the religious beliefs of their parents.

The question was raised whether a blood transfusion was an ordinary or an extraordinary means of preserving life. From the point of view of most physicians and most moralists, blood transfusion was ordinary means. However, Ford also took into consideration subjective factors that affected patients who might consider certain ordinary medical procedures as so objectionable that they choose to omit such procedures from their medical treatment. The religious belief of Jehovah's Witnesses is one such subjective factor. "With a sincere Jehovah's Witness who is firmly convinced that a transfusion offends God, we are dealing with a case where his conscience absolutely forbids him to allow the procedure. In this mistaken frame of mind he would actually commit sin if he went against his conscience and took the transfusion. I see no inconsistency in admitting that this frame of mind is a circumstance which makes the transfusion for him an *extraordinary* means of preserving life."[65] Thus, Ford argues for the protection of the sincere conscience of the Jehovah's Witness. The physician and the hospital treating the Witness were not under any obligation to give the blood transfusion if the Witness objected to it.

Ford made a crucial distinction between a decision based in an erroneous conscience to act in a way harmful to one's self, and a similarly based decision to omit an action that could avoid harm or even save one's life. There was general agreement that one should prevent a person from acting on an erroneous belief to endanger self or others—e.g., one should prevent acts such as suicide or human sacrifice irrespective of their motivation. But in the case of a conscientious choice, however erroneous, to forego a procedure that might preserve his or her life, Ford could only counsel persuasion to change the person's mind. One might not coerce a person to accept a positive medical procedure to which the person objects.[66]

In the case of blood transfusions for the children of Jehovah's Witnesses, however, Ford took a protective stance. He favored saving the lives of these children—even if it meant violating the conscience and religious beliefs of their parents. There was a difference, he argued, between allowing an adult with an erroneous conscience to omit life-saving medical procedures for himself, and allowing such an adult to make choices that would be detrimental to the health of others, and especially to a child without the capacity to make his or her own decisions. In the situation involving children, the natural right of children to ordinary care should prevail over the rights of a parent with an erroneous conscience.

> It is clear that a child has an objective right to ordinary care, no matter what the parents' mistaken beliefs may be. Consequently, when a blood transfusion is a necessary part of this ordinary care, the parents have an objective moral obligation to supply it, and if they fail to do so others who have undertaken the care of the child, such as physician and hospital authorities, have *per se* a moral obligation to see that the child gets it. . . .

> When serious bodily harm to the child, or even its life is at stake, no one will concede that the parents' erroneous religious beliefs must be respected; they have no right to inflict them on their children. . . .

> There are limits to the power of disposal which parents have over the bodies of their children. They cannot do them bodily injury and they cannot refuse them ordinary medical care.[67]

While physicians had the moral obligation to provide ordinary medical care to the child of Jehovah's Witnesses even against the religious beliefs of the parents, the same physicians might nevertheless face obstacles that could prevent them from proceeding with a blood transfusion without parental consent. The parents might request that a doctor who disagreed with them be removed from their child's case; they might choose to transfer the child to another hospital. If the physician insisted on proceeding with the medical procedure and unexpected complications arise, the physician might face criminal or civil liability. Ford acknowledged that a physician considering giving a blood transfusion to a child of Jehovah's Witnesses would face conflicting legal obligations.

> He is obliged not to undertake a surgical procedure, even if he judges it necessary, without the parents' consent. . . . On the other hand, is he not obliged to give a blood transfusion which is desperately needed, when the parents who refuse to provide it are guilty of criminal neglect? But then, in doing so, he is really taking it upon himself to decide two questions which in a given case, or in a given jurisdiction, might be open to dispute: the question of facts: "Is this transfusion absolutely necessary?,", and the question of law: "Is this transfusion part of the reasonable medical care which the law requires parents (and others) to provide?" And finally, . . . he would be violating the well-established rule that to operate without consent is to be guilty of assault and battery.[68]

In Ford's view, the sole legal protection that a physician could use when considering a blood transfusion for a child without parental consent would be a court order that could empower the physician to proceed with the transfusion. In an urgent case, however, when there was no time to obtain a court order, Ford believed that a physician need not fear legal liability if he or she chose to give the necessary life-giving transfusion to the child.

Ford offered a caution to lawmakers and moralists considering how public policy could respond to such cases. He saw two extremes that should be avoided in formulating laws. The first extreme would be to give the state exaggerated powers to impose policies in violation of the individual liberty of minority groups. Ford was vehemently opposed to reducing public policy to the will of the majority.

> Democracy does not mean that the majority is *right*. Majority rule is a practical way of making a republic work. If it were true that mere force of numbers made the difference between right and wrong, good and bad,

then mere force would be controlling. Might would make right. But if anything is clear in the fundamental political thought of our country, it is the idea that minorities have a right to exist and to propagate their ideas. It was a minority that thought slavery was wrong and finally abolished it. Right and wrong are not determined by a show of hands. They are determined by a show of minds.[69]

Ford believed that the freedom of minority groups like Jehovah's Witnesses to profess and practice their religion should be protected by law, as long as the common good and the rights of others were also protected. On the other hand, Ford cautioned against the opposite extreme of tolerating every religious practice, regardless of its danger to others, out of respect for sincere religious beliefs. The state had the right to prevent certain dangerous practices that might be considered by some groups as part of their religious belief.

> The State can and ought to prevent the Hindu widow from casting herself on her husband's funeral pyre; or the Japanese officer from committing hara-kiri; or anyone at all from committing suicide; or the Mormon from practicing polygamy; or the evangelical fanatic from exposing others to snakebite; or the Christian Scientist from neglecting ordinary medical care for a dangerously sick child; or a Hindu from going about unvaccinated in an epidemic because he has religious scruples about using cows to produce vaccine; or a Christian congregation from conducting services when quarantine has been imposed to the safeguard public health.[70]

Ford was not, however, advocating a government that would regulate all religious practices. He favored a government that exercised minimal intervention, and only in cases where there are "strong, clear reasons of the common good or the clear necessity of protecting the rights of others, especially defenseless children."[71]

The case of blood transfusions for Jehovah's Witnesses highlighted several conflicting rights that Ford desired to protect: the right to omit extraordinary means of preserving one's life, the right of a child to ordinary medical care, the right to practice religion (within limits) without government interference, and the right of the state to protect the welfare of its citizens from dangerous religious practices. In discussing these conflicting rights, Ford focused primarily on vulnerable persons who might be threatened by the exercise of the rights of others. In the complicated legal and moral discussions about the case, it was still the care and protection of the individual human person that claimed Ford's attention and care.

ADVISING RADICAL SURGERY

In an article cowritten with J. E. Drew, "Advising Radical Surgery: A Problem in Medical Morality," Ford discusses the moral dilemma of physicians advising seriously ill patients to consider an experimental medical procedure that might prolong life but would proceed at the cost of extensive mutilation of body organs.

> When mutilation and/or permanent incapacitation with excessive strain on family and finances can result from a therapeutic procedure, the surgeon frequently asks himself (or is asked) if such measures are morally defensible. . . .
>
> Every year new surgical techniques are developed and physicians are confronted with the question, "Shall I advise my patient to undergo this surgery?" or, in closer reality, "How shall I present the case to the patient?"; for, as all physicians know, the manner of presentation is frequently one of the, or even the, deciding influence as to whether the patient has the procedure carried out.[72]

A physician's presentation of a new medical procedure could significantly influence a patient's decision to agree to the procedure or not. Two different physicians could present the same procedure and give the same medical facts, but might emphasize either the positive or the negative aspects of the procedure.

> For example, the physician can stress the fact that the procedure is still somewhat in the experimental stage (and therefore new and relatively untried); that it is mutilating; that it is risky; that it is costly not only in money but also in human stress; that the ultimate chance of complete success is statistically small; and, in short, that the price is very great. On the other hand, the physician could make it very difficult for the patient not to accept the program by stressing the desperate nature of the patient's present condition; the fact that this program appears to the best and probably

the only means that offers any hope for a satisfactory outcome; and that, in spite of a considerable price, the possible great gains are worth it.[73]

The particular medical procedure that had prompted Ford's consideration of the morality of advising radical surgery was the procedure known as pelvic exenteration, a radical attempt to treat cancer of the bladder which could not be treated by other means such as radiation therapy or a simple cystectomy (where the urinary bladder is removed). Pelvic exenteration would require the removal of all organs in the pelvis, leaving only bilateral openings on the skin to allow for waste disposal. At the time of the writing of the article, Ford claims that there were not enough data to evaluate the procedure's overall effectiveness.[74]

Ford presents a hard case of pelvic exenteration in order to illustrate the physician's problem of speaking about experimental radical surgery to seriously ill patients.

> This whole problem was brought to sharp relief in the case of a 7-month-old girl with a heretofore fatal type of sarcoma of the bladder. In such cases, simple cystectomy had been tried, but local recurrence in the pelvis had been the outcome. At the present state of knowledge, pelvic exenteration would seem to be the most likely procedure to rid the infant of cancer, although it had not actually been carried out before on an infant with this disease. Could one morally undertake pelvic exenteration on a child of this age? And if it was morally permissible, how should one present in all fairness the case to the parents? It might be strongly pointed out to the family that this demanding procedure would be the child's only chance for survival. Or might it be presented to the family as a hopeless situation in which an experimental, untried, and mutilating procedure might be carried out if they, realizing the chance for success was at best quite small, wished. In the first instance, it would be difficult for the family to turn down the operation, but, in the second instance, they could have done so very easily.[75]

Ford admits that "hard cases make bad laws" and that those formulating guidelines for physicians should not let their attention be monopolized by one particular aspect of a hard case.[76] The overall picture of the case must be considered. Among the many factors, the patient's personal good must be given primary consideration. Ford warns physicians against placing their scientific interests ahead of the patient's welfare, particularly in cases when new scientific data could be gained through an experimental medical procedure. The physician must view the patient primarily as a human being in need of care, rather than as a subject in a medical experiment.

> The patient comes to the physician in the faith that the physician will do the best that he can for him. Accordingly, decisions must be made primarily from the patient's standpoint. Other persons and other values have a distinct secondary role. In this doctor–patient relationship, the physician's responsibility to the family, to the patient's employer, to science generally, to the hospital, and to society are secondary. These secondary responsibilities are real, and they deserve to be considered in their proper sphere, but they must not be allowed to outweigh the primary consideration, which is the good of the patient himself. Even in modern times, the spectacle of medical men considering themselves as mere technicians, forgetting the reverence due to the individual, and putting their scientific skills at the service of inhuman experimentation has been witnessed. The tradition of the medical profession holds that the individual human life is precious. Indeed it is this tradition that allows the patients to put their very lives in the hands of the profession. The physician who undertakes the care of a patient is first a healer who uses science and his techniques for the good of the patient; never the other way around.[77]

Focusing on the physician's role as counselor to the patient, Ford proposes a set of factors arranged in order of importance, for the physician–counselor to consider in order to prudently advise the patient about a radical medical procedure. The spiritual welfare of the patient is the first consideration that a physician must weigh. The physician must ask the questions "Is he prepared to die?" and "Is there a chance that he would be prepared, or better prepared, if his life were prolonged?" The other considerations, in descending order of importance are: the patient's own desire to continue his life by radical, extraordinary measures; the expected length of survival and degree of comfort; the effect of the patient's survival on his associates; and—last on the list—the advancement of science. The factor of the advancement of science should only be considered if the patient himself expressed a desire to contribute to medical research. This consideration for scientific advancement must not come into conflict in any way with the interests of the patient.[78]

Ford insists, in this article, on a physician's approach that would reverence the individual patient. Every patient must be treated as a unique human being surrounded by a distinct set of circumstances. The physician should not only consider the physical state of the patient but also give attention to the patient's psychological and spiritual state. Ford was keenly aware of the vulnerability of seriously ill patients who might easily be swayed by professional medical advice to consent to radical experimental surgery. Some unethical physicians interested in medical research might use their powers of persuasion to convince patients to undergo experimental treatment, even if that is not in the patients' best interest. Ford sought to protect seriously ill patients from unwittingly becoming subjects of research.

Ford viewed the physician as a person who had a vocation for healing, and who was responsible for his ailing fellow human being. The physician was not simply a medical technician but a healer and counselor; as such, he or she should be interested in the good of the patient above all other considerations. Ford appealed to the common humanity shared by physician and patient as the link that would ensure that the interest of the patient would be protected.

> When a rule is sought by which the doctor can fulfill his obligation to the welfare of this patient, no better one has ever been found than the Golden Rule. "Do unto others as you would have others do unto to you." However, as good as it is, this general rule does not solve all the problems. One cannot say what he would do if he were in another man's shoes because he can never really be in those shoes. Striving for this ideal will, however, avoid many of the pitfalls that self-interest prepares for everyone. And so, in the moral consideration of advising radical surgery, the best personal interests of the patient are foremost. When the physician is at the bedside of the patient he is not a mere technician or practitioner of objective medicine; he is a healer who has become a counselor to the patient and even to the patient's family. In this dual role of healer–counselor the Golden Rule is the fundamental guide.[79]

Ford makes the emphatic assertion that "the physician–counselor at the bedside must answer 'yes' to the question 'Am I my brother's keeper?'"[80] By appealing to the common bond of humanity shared by the physician and the patient, Ford aims to protect vulnerable patients from ill-advised experimental surgical procedures.

Summary

In the cases presented in this chapter, Ford consistently affirmed the basic and inviolable humanity of the individual person. He sought to give a human face to individuals threatened by the abuse of power. By seeking to present the potential victim as a human being who was no different from those who wielded power, Ford appealed to the human capacity for compassion toward one's fellow human being. He refrained from demonizing those who may have caused or are tempted to cause harm. The key to protecting the weak was not to vilify their oppressors, but rather to create an atmosphere of mutual respect and care that would lead the powerful to protect rather than harm the weak. Through a variety of moral arguments and rhetorical pleas, Ford consistently expressed the message that a person remains a member of the human family regardless of his or her situation, and every person deserves protection from any form of discrimination, rejection, abuse, violation, or threat.

Ford's creative and uncompromising defense of vulnerable persons, whether they were enemy noncombatants, conscientious objectors, alcoholics, religious subjects, Jehovah's Witnesses, or seriously ill patients, provides an instructive illustration of how moral theology could make a significant difference in the lives of others. Ford showed that moral theology can be a practical and effective means to defend persons from present or future harm, and to contribute to the common good through the building of relationships between persons of unequal status based on justice, compassion, and mutual responsibility.

Notes

1. Ford, "Law Without God" (1942), 207
2. Ibid., 206
3. Ford, "Unity of the Threefold Law" (1942), 2
4. Ibid., 3
5. Ibid., 5

6. Ford, "Totalitarian Justice Holmes" (1944), 114–15.

7. Ford, "Fundamentals" (1941), 72

8. Holmes, *Justice Oliver Wendell Holmes* (1936), 157

9. Ford, "Totalitarian Justice Holmes" (1944), 118

10. Holmes, *Collected Legal Papers* (1920), 179

11. Ibid., 312

12. Ibid., 314

13. Holmes, *Justice Oliver Wendell Holmes* (1936), 187

14. Ford, "Totalitarian Justice Holmes" (1944), 117

15. *Buck v. Bell*, 274 U.S. 200 (1927)

16. Ford, "Totalitarian Justice Holmes" (1944), 116

17. Witherspoon, "Holmes, Oliver Wendell" (1967).

18. Ford, "Fundamentals" (1941), 77

19. Holmes, *Common Law* (1938), 43

20. Ford, "Patriotic Obedience" (1942), 301–5.

21. Ibid., 302–3.

22. Ford, "Current Moral Theology" (1941), 547–48.

23. Ibid., 550.

24. Ibid., 551–52.

25. Ford, Opinion (1957), 1–6.

26. Ford, Letter to William (1951).

27. Ford, Letter to Hogan (1957).

28. Ford, Draft Statement of Catholic Conscientious Objection (1965).

29. Ford, "Notes on Moral Theology" (1943), 587.

30. Ford, "Current Moral Theology" (1941), 556.

31. Ford, "Morality of Obliteration Bombing" (1944), 269.

32. Ibid., 289–302.

33. Ibid., 287.

34. Ford, "Notes on Moral Theology" (1943), 586.

35. Ford, "Paternal Governance" (1943), 149.

36. Ibid., 152.

37. Ibid., 153.

38. Ford, Letter to Cloran (1962).

39. Ibid.

40. Ford, Letter to Wernert (1957).

41. Ford, Letter to Matthew (1962).

42. Ford, Fragment of a manuscript (n.d.).

43. Ford, *Religious Superiors* (1963).

44. Ibid., 29.

45. Ibid., 29–30.

46. Ibid., 30–31.

47. Ibid., 32–33.

48. Pius XII, *Si diligis* (1958), 276.

49. Ford, *Religious Superiors* (1963), 43.

50. Ibid., 48.

51. Ibid., 49.
52. Ibid., 71.
53. Ibid., 72–73.
54. Ford, Letter to Guindon (1970).
55. Guindon, Letter to Ford (1970).
56. Ford, Letter to Guindon (1970).
57. Ford and Kelly, *Contemporary Moral Theology*, Vol. I (1958), 245n36.
58. Ford, *Alcoholism: Education for Sobriety* (1950); Ford, "Alcoholism: Society's Taint" (1951); Ford, "Depth Psychology" (1951); Ford, *Man Takes a Drink* (1954).
59. Ford, "Alcohol, Alcoholism" (1950), 125.
60. Morgan, "'Chemical Comforting'" (1999), 34–35.
61. Ibid., 35.
62. Ibid.
63. Ford, Letter to George L. (1978).
64. Ford, "Pastoral Dealing with Compulsives" (1970), 4.
65. Ford, "Refusal of Blood Transfusions" (1964), 215.
66. Ibid., 216.
67. Ibid., 216–17.
68. Ibid., 219.
69. Ibid., 224.
70. Ibid.
71. Ibid.
72. Ford and Drew, "Advising Radical Surgery" (1953), 711.
73. Ibid.
74. Ibid., 712.
75. Ibid.
76. Ibid, 713.
77. Ibid.
78. Ibid., 715.
79. Ibid., 713.
80. Ibid., 715.

CHAPTER NINE

JOHN FORD AND HIS LEGACY

John Ford's legacy includes both the advance of an approach to moral theology that was falling out of favor even as he refined it, and profound human and pastoral insights that have borne fruit in the theological world and in actual human lives.

Lights and Shadows

Ford was an extraordinary manualist. His moral method was animated by dynamic tensions, and his commitment to defend objective moral norms was complemented by a pastoral stance that accommodated circumstances diminishing subjective culpability. His respect for ecclesiastical and civil authority allowed for critical challenges, especially when vulnerable persons were affected. He could shift between the role of interpreter of papal pronouncements and that of self-appointed guardian of orthodoxy.

Adept at using the rich resources of the whole Catholic moral tradition, Ford was able to use both principle-based manualist casuistry and case-based high casuistry in resolving hard moral cases. His skill in interpreting the nuances of ecclesiastical pronouncements when the magisterium spoke was matched by his ability to evaluate and propose probable opinions when the magisterium was silent.

Ford actively sought new solutions to old moral problems. His pastoral solutions to the problems of alcoholism, addiction, and compulsions involved sensitive innovation. He even proposed norms and guidelines in anticipation of new moral problems. His article on obliteration bombing, for example, anticipated the future use of weapons of mass destruction. Increasing use of chemical comforters led him to propose a new virtue to regulate drug use. Advances in medical research led him to propose norms for advising seriously ill patients regarding experimental medical procedures. As psychology came into increasing use in religious communities, he proposed guidelines to prevent violations of the privacy of religious subjects.

Ford contributed to the development of twentieth-century manualism, even though it would soon be replaced by the renewal of moral theology after Vatican II. In a limited way, he applied Fuchs's innovative approach toward the moral competency of the laity. Reluctant to apply this approach to moral cases where there was already a tradition of authoritative church teaching, Ford nevertheless gave primacy to the judgment of moral agents in cases where there was no body of authoritative teaching, particularly those involving alcoholism, chemical comforting, and the scarred uterus. He recognized that the individuals directly affected by these difficult moral situations were in the best position to make prudent personal decisions. Ford's recognition of the moral competency of persons, while limited to standard mode cases, was an important shift from the traditional manualist approach that had placed the interpretation of the moral law primarily in the hands of the magisterium and moral theologians.

Ford also extended the concerns of manualist moral theology beyond the analysis of sins. In the cases of alcoholism and other addictions, the confessional was not only a place for the remission of sins and the formation of conscience—it also became a starting point for the substance abuser's journey of recovery.

There were limits to Ford's method. His reliance on enlightened moral professors to address minimalism in seminary formation was insufficient to reverse manualism's orientation toward sin and legalism. His deference toward papal pronouncements led to inconsistency in his approach to the development of doctrine, exemplified by the case of periodic continence. His protective stance toward the magisterium limited his capacity to listen to dissenting voices within the Church.

John Ford's Humanity and His Moral Method

Many aspects of Ford's method were influenced by the type of person he was. His personality and subjectivity shaped and directed both his moral method and the way he approached individual cases. Ford's leg-

acy carries a lesson for moralists today: moral theology is a deeply human activity, one that engages and amplifies both the strengths and the
weaknesses of the moral theologian—along with his or her preferences
and concerns, and hopes and fears. How one does moral theology re-
flects who one is.

Although Ford insisted on the objectivity of moral norms, he was
highly subjective in many of his moral judgments. His decision to approach a case in standard mode or in crisis mode depended on his perception of the urgency and seriousness of the threat to the values or
persons involved.

Ford's life experiences influenced his responses to particular moral
cases. For example, his reaction to the destruction caused by obliteration bombing in World War II led him to reject of the use of weapons
of mass destruction in modern warfare. It also influenced his staunch
defense of Catholic conscientious objectors. His personal history of alcoholism and recovery, along with his personal contact with other alcoholics, encouraged him to seek a comprehensive and constructive
pastoral response to persons affected by addictions and compulsions.
Ford's experience of religious life provided him with the insights and
motivation to address the need to protect the privacy of other religious.
His audiences with Paul VI were foundational moments that defined for
him the papal intention regarding contraception, which he committed
himself to defending.

Ford's appeal to the dictates of his conscience as justification for his
actions at the papal birth control commission reveals how much his
moral practice was shaped by what he sincerely believed was the right
thing to do. During the debates on population and birth regulation in
Rome, for example, Ford deliberately engaged in behind-the-scenes activity to ensure that traditional teaching on contraception would prevail
in theological debates. His conscience would not be at peace unless he
accomplished what he thought was the right response to a moral situation. Despite being admonished for these actions, Ford insisted that he
had acted correctly because he was acting according to his conscience.

Ford's moral imagination was a significant element in his method.
He was able to imagine himself as the alcoholic, the German civilian,
the conscientious objector, and the woman with the scarred uterus.
He presented to his readers a vivid picture of the difficult moral situations these individuals faced, and made dramatic appeals for immediate

assistance for them. His imagination was limited by his commitment to defend papal authority, however. Unlike John Noonan or Josef Fuchs, Ford could not imagine that the Church could change substantively an authoritative teaching without significant loss of moral authority. He could not imagine an authentic development of doctrine that involved a radical change in papal teaching, even if the cases of usury and periodic continence proved this was possible. He could not imagine a theological discussion that included dialogue partners who dissented from the magisterium. He could not imagine that Paul VI would substantially reverse the authoritative teaching of a previous pope and risk the perception of error on the part of the magisterium. His moral imagination could not go beyond what he believed was possible and acceptable.

The end of Ford's teaching career as a moral theologian at Weston College in 1969 illustrates his acceptance of the limits of his views on moral theology. In his letter to his major superior, Ford expressed several reasons why he chose to resign from teaching moral theology. Along with advancing age and declining health, Ford mentioned two personal reasons. First, he realized that the renewal of moral theology then underway had made his manualist approach unappealing to Jesuits in formation. If he were to continue teaching, he stated, the new system of optional classes would have him "talking to empty benches." Second, he disagreed with the plan of Weston College to move to Cambridge, Massachusetts, and to allow Jesuits in training to cross-register in non-Catholic theological schools such as Harvard Divinity School and Episcopal Theological School. Ford believed that such a move would compromise the formation of future Jesuits priests in the Catholic tradition. Ford saw the revision of moral theology and the relocation of Weston College as post–Vatican II developments that were incompatible with his personal convictions. He admitted, "It is too late for me to change my fundamental ways of thinking about these matters, even if I wanted to, which I don't."[1]

Ford expressed both his humanity and his sincere convictions in his method and practice of moral theology. He had immense goodwill and concern for penitents and vulnerable persons, accompanied by courage and the intellectual and rhetorical skills to defend values and persons he perceived as threatened. At the same time some aspects of his method expressed the frailties of his humanity. He could be inconsistent, stubborn, aggressive, and intolerant of dissenting opinions on certain matters.

Ford believed that he did his best in his work as a moral theologian; he viewed his work in moral theology with great pride and without regrets. A year before he died, Ford publicly declared "It has been my privilege to have devoted my life to working for the Roman Catholic Church and it fills me with pride to be able to say that."[2] John Ford lived out the premise that, for a moral theologian, the practice of moral theology is inseparable from the theologian's unique personality and personal journey as a follower of Christ.

Notes

1. Ford, Letter to Guindon (1969).
2. Ford, "Response" (1988), 14.

TIME LINE OF THE LIFE AND CAREER OF JOHN C. FORD, SJ

1937–45: Professor of Moral Theology at Weston College, MA
  (1939) Cofounded the journal *Theological Studies*
  (1941) Wrote "Current Moral Theology and Canon Law" in *Theological Studies*
  (1941) Published *The Fundamentals of Holmes' Juristic Philosophy*
  (1942) Wrote "Notes in Moral Theology" in *Theological Studies*
  (1943) Wrote "Notes in Moral Theology" in *Theological Studies*
  (1943) Wrote "Paternal Governance and Filial Confidence in Superiors" in *Review for Religious*
  (1944) Wrote "Notes in Moral Theology" in *Theological Studies*
  (1944) Wrote "Morality of Obliteration Bombing" in *Theological Studies*
  (1944) Wrote "Totalitarian Justice Holmes" in *Catholic World*
  (1945) Wrote "Notes in Moral Theology" in *Theological Studies*

1945–47: Professor of Moral Theology at Gregorian University, Rome
  (1947) First encounter with Alcoholics Anonymous

1947–48: Professor of Moral Theology at Weston College, MA
  (1948) Attended the Yale Summer School for of Alcohol Studies and became a regular lecturer

1948–50: Professor of Moral Theology at Weston College, MA, and Professor of Ethics at Boston College, MA
  (1950) Published *Alcoholism: Education for Sobriety*

1950–59: Professor of Moral Theology at Weston College, MA
  (1951) Published *Depth Psychology, Morality, and Psychology*
  (1953) Edited *Twelve Steps and Twelve Traditions* for Alcoholics Anonymous
  (1954) Published *Man Takes a Drink*
  (1954) Cowrote with Gerald Kelly "Notes on Moral Theology" in *Theological Studies*
  (1956) Advised U.S. Bishops on Catholic Conscientious Objection
  (1956) Received the Cardinal Spellman Award from the Catholic Theological Society of America

(1957) Edited *Alcoholics Anonymous Comes of Age* for Alcoholics Anonymous

(1957) Wrote "Hydrogen Bombing of Cities" in *Theological Digest*

(1958) Published *Questions in Contemporary Moral Theology Vol. I* with Gerald Kelly

(1959) Wrote "Chemical Comforting and Christian Virtue" in *American Ecclesiastical Review*

1959–66: Professor of Moral Theology at Catholic University of America, Washington, D.C.

(1961) Published *What About Your Drinking?*

(1963) Published *Questions in Contemporary Moral Theology Vol. II* with Gerald Kelly

(1963) Published *Religious Superiors, Subjects, and Psychiatrists*

(October 1964) Appointed to the expanded Papal Birth Control Commission

(March 1965) Joined the fourth meeting of the Papal Birth Control Commission

(November 22–23, 1965) Private meetings with Paul VI during the Papal Birth Control Commission sessions; instructed by Paul to make an intervention at the discussions on the Vatican II text on marriage.

(November 25–26, 1965) Debate in the Mixed Commission on the papal insertions to the Vatican II text on marriage

1966–68: Professor of Moral Theology at Weston College, MA

(May–June 1966) Participation in the fifth and final meeting of the Papal Birth Control Commission

(May 23, 1966) Submitted the Minority Report to the Papal Birth Control Commission

(1967–68) Debate with Richard McCormick over the existence of practical doubt regarding the current teaching on contraception [before the publication of *Humanae vitae* on July 30, 1968].

(October 1968) Assisted Cardinal O'Boyle in Washington, D.C., in writing pastoral letter on *Humanae vitae* and address the situation of public dissent

1969–89: Professor Emeritus at Weston College, MA

(January 6, 1969) Tendered resignation as professor at Weston College

(March 1970) Debate with his major superior regarding psychological survey of religious subjects

(1978) Cowrote with Germaine Grisez "Contraception and the Infallibility of the Magisterium" in *Theological Studies*

(1988) Received the Cardinal O'Boyle Award for the Defense of the Faith

REFERENCES

Works and Unpublished Material by John Ford
Much of the unpublished material in this list is from the John Ford collection, housed in the Archives of the New England Province of the Society of Jesus, Dinand Library, College of the Holy Cross, in Worcester, Massachusetts. This collection is cited here as the Ford Collection.

1938
The Validity of Virginal Marriage. Worcester, MA: Harrigan Press.

1941
"Current Moral Theology and Canon Law." *Theological Studies* 2:527–77.
"On Cheating in Examinations: A Letter to a High School Principal." *Theological Studies* 2:252–56.
"The Fundamentals of Holmes' Juristic Philosophy." In *Phases of American Culture: Proceedings of the Jesuit Philosophical Association Eighteenth Annual Convention in Georgetown University September 2–4, 1941.* Worcester, MA: Holy Cross College Press.

1942
"Law without God." *Thought* 17:204–7.
"Patriotic Obedience in Time of War." *Review for Religious* 1 no. 5:301–5.
"Unity of the Threefold Law." *Catholic Mind* 40:1–9.

1943
"Notes on Moral Theology." *Theological Studies* 4:561–600.
"Paternal Governance and Filial Confidence in Superiors." *Review for Religious* 2:146–55.

1944
"Notes on Moral Theology." *Theological Studies* 5:495–538.
"The Morality of Obliteration Bombing." *Theological Studies* 5:261–309.
"Totalitarian Justice Holmes." *Catholic World* 159:114–22.

1945
"Current Theology." *Theological Studies* 6:530–40.

1947
Letter to the editor of *American Journal of Obstetrics and Gynecology,* September 15.

1950
"Alcohol, Alcoholism and Moral Responsibility: When a Skinful Is Sinful." In *Blue Book II: Proceedings of the Second National Clergy Congress on Alcoholism, in St. Joseph*

College, Rensselaer, Indiana, August 22–24, 1950, 89–116. Tulsa, OK: National Clergy
     Council on Alcoholism.
Alcoholism: Education for Sobriety. New York: America Press.

1951
"Alcoholism: Society's Taint." Catholic Mind 49:730–34.
"Depth Psychology, Morality, and Alcoholism." Theological Digest: 46–52.
Letter to William, May 25, 1951. Box 46, File 6, Ford Collection.

1953
with J. E. Drew. "Advising Radical Surgery: A Problem in Medical Morality." Journal of
     the American Medical Association 151 (9): 711–14.

1954
Man Takes a Drink. New York: P. J. Kenedy & Sons.
"Notes on Moral Theology." Theological Studies 15:52–102.
with Gerald Kelly. 1954. "Notes on Moral Theology, 1953." Theological Studies 15:52–102.

1955
"Double Vasectomy and the Impediment of Impotence." Theological Studies 16:533–57.
Handwritten notes, n.d. [1955?]. Box 28, File 3,Ford Collection.

1957
"Hydrogen Bombing of Cities." Theology Digest 5:6–9.
Letter to Bernard J. Wernert, 13 May, 1957. Box 10, File 7, Ford Collection.
Letter to Edmund Hogan, March 7, 1957. Box 46, File 6, Ford Collection.
Typewritten manuscript, opinion by John Ford on the letter of T. Oscar Smith of the
     U.S. Department of Justice to Archbishop Patrick O'Boyle concerning the Pope's
     Annual Christmas Message (1956) and Catholic conscientious objection. Box 46,
     File 6, Ford Collection.

1958
"The Concept of Natural Law." Typewritten notes for a lecture given at Western Re-
     serve University, Cleveland, Ohio. Ford Collection (no reference number).
with Gerald Kelly. 1958. Contemporary Moral Theology, Vol. I: Questions in Fundamental
     Moral Theology. Maryland: Newman Press.

1959
"Chemical Comfort and Christian Virtue." American Ecclesiastical Review 141:361–79.
Letter to Brendan Forsyth, April 20, 1959. Box 31, File 21, Ford Collection.
"The Clergy's Role in Alcohol Problems." In Blue Book XI: Proceedings of the Eleventh
     National Clergy Congress on Alcoholics, Notre Dame University, March 31–April 2, 1959,
     35–55. Tulsa, OK: National Clergy Council on Alcoholism.

1961

What About Your Drinking? Glen Rock, NJ: Paulist Press.

1962

Letter to Armand Matthew, 8 April, 1962. Box 10, File 7, Ford Collection.
Letter to O. M. Cloran, December 3, 1962. Box 10, File 9, Ford Collection.

1963

Letter to Joseph Dorsey, September 28, 1963. Box 22, File 2, Ford Collection.
Religious Superiors, Subjects, and Psychiatrists. Westminster, MD: Newman Press.
with Gerald Kelly. *Contemporary Moral Theology, Vol. II: Marriage Questions.* Westminster, MD: Newman Press.

1964

Morality and the Pill. n.d. [1964?] Pamphlet. Washington, D.C.: Family Life Bureau.
Letter to Paul Murphy, March 8, 1964. Box 32, File 6, Ford Collection.
Journal notes from May 19 to June 7, 1964. Box 31, File 7, Ford Collection.
Letter to Bishop John Wright, July 23, 1964. Box 32, File 6, Ford Collection.
Letter to Henry Cosgrove, August 28, 1964. Box 32, File 4, Ford Collection.
Letter to J. Férin, November 13, 1964. Box 31, File 3, Ford Collection.
Letter to Francis Furlong, November 21, 1964. Box 30, File 1, Ford Collection.
Letter to Henri de Reidmatten, November 21, 1964. Box 23, File 8, Ford Collection.
"Refusal of Blood Transfusions by Jehovah's Witnesses." *Catholic Lawyer* 10:212–26.

1965

Journal entries, Rome, November 24–26, 1965, typewritten. Box 23, File 3, Ford Collection.
Letter to Bishop Egidio Vagnosi, November 6, 1965. Box 25, File 3, Ford Collection.
Letter to Henri de Riedmatten, January 4, 1965. Box 23, File 8, Ford Collection.
Letter to Henri de Riedmatten, July 1, 1965. Box 23, File 8, Ford Collection.
Letter to John Noonan, April 19, 1965. Box 21, File 5, Ford Collection.
Letter to Pierre de Locht, January 3, 1965. Box 23, File 8, Ford Collection.
Letter to Richard McCormick, February 20, 1965. Box 23, File 8, Ford Collection.
Letter to Stanislaus de Lestapis, July 26, 1965. Box 33, File 7, Ford Collection.
Letter to Thomas F. Divine, May 1, 1965. Box 20, File 18, Ford Collection.
Note to Paul VI. November 30, 1965. Box 25, File 13, Ford Collection.
Notes on private audiences with Paul VI, November 22–23, 1965, handwritten. Box 26, File 5, Ford Collection.
Pro Memoria, November 30, 1965. Box 25, File 5, Ford Collection.
Draft statement on Catholic conscientious objection, typewritten. January 16, 1965. Box 46, File 5, Ford Collection.

1966

Interim Statement, typewritten manuscript. Box 25, file 14, Ford Collection.
Journal entry, April 28, 1966, typewritten. Ford Collection (no reference number).

Letter to Cardinal Alfredo Ottaviani, March 9, 1966. Box 23 File 2, Ford Collection.

Letter to Andre' J. de Béthune, January 24, 1966. Box 20, file 16, Ford Collection.

Letter to George Klubertanz, January 16, 1966. Box 21, file 5, Ford Collection.

Letter to Thomas Higgins, March 2, 1966. Box 30, file 2, Ford Collection.

On absolution, handwritten notes, February 12, 1966. Box 30, file 1, Ford Collection.

"Response to a talk by Bernard Häring at Brown University on Planned Parenthood, 15 March 1966." Typewritten manuscript. Ford Collection (Box 21, File 8).

"State of the Question: More on the Council and Contraception." *America* 114:553–57.

Statement of Position, typewritten manuscript, May 25, 1966. Ford Collection (no reference number).

1968

Christmas card to Cardinal Heenan, December 19, 1968. Box 32, file 7, Ford Collection.

Letter to Paul Molinari, March 29, 1968. Box 32, file 7, Ford Collection.

Letter to Steve, October 31, 1968. Box 32, file 7, Ford Collection.

"The State of the Question: The Doctrine of the Church and its Authority." In *The Birth Control Debate*, edited by Robert G. Hoyt, Kansas City, MO: National Catholic Reporter.

with John Lynch. "Contraception: A Matter of Practical Doubt?" *Homiletic and Pastoral Review* 68:563–74

1969

Letter to William Guindon, January 6, 1969. Box 32, file 7, Ford Collection.

1970

Letter to William Guindon, March 16, 1970. Box 33, file 15b, Ford Collection.

Letter to William Guindon, March 23, 1970. Box 33, file 15b, Ford Collection.

"Theory and Practice in Pastoral Dealing with Compulsives," typewritten manuscript, October 13, 1970. Box 7, file 9, Ford Collection.

1978

Letter to George L., August 2, 1978. Quoted in Oliver Morgan. "'Chemical Comforting' and the Theology of John Ford, SJ." *Journal of Ministry in Addiction and Recovery* 6 (1): 57, n.18.

with Germain Grisez. "Contraception and the Infallibility of the Ordinary Magisterium." *Theological Studies* 39:258–312.

1988

"Response of Father John C. Ford to the Award of the Cardinal O'Boyle Medal." *Fellowship of Catholic Scholars Newsletter* 12 (1): 14.

n.d.

Fragment of a manuscript on manifestation of conscience, n.d. Box 10, file 9, Ford Collection.

WORKS BY OTHER AUTHORS

B., Dick. *Utilizing Early A.A.'s Spiritual Roots for Recovery Today.* Kihei, HI: Paradise Research Publications, 1999. www. dickb.com/archives/aaroots.shtml (accessed December 26, 1999).

Buck v. Bell 274 U.S. 200 (1927). http://carver.law.cuny.edu/cases/buck.html (accessed January 10, 2007)

Callahan, Daniel. "Authority and the Theologian." *Commonweal* 80 (1964): 319–23.

Catholic Theological Society of America. "Recipients of the Cardinal Spellman Award." 2006. www.jcu.edu/ctsa/recipients_CSA.html (accessed September 19, 2006).

Cicognani, A. G. Letter to John Ford, October 10, 1964. Ford Collection (Box 23, File 8).

Congregation for the Doctrine of the Faith (CDF). 1993. Responses to Questions Proposed Concerning "Uterine Isolation" and Related Matters. www.vatican.va/roman_curia/congregations/cfaith/documents/rc_con_cfaith_doc_31071994_uterine-isolation_en.html (October 27, 2003).

Curran, Charles E. and Robert E. Hunt. *Dissent In and For the Church: Theologians and Humanae Vitae.* New York: Sheed & Ward, 1969.

Davis, Henry. *Moral and Pastoral Theology.* New York: Sheed & Ward, 1938.

Fahey, Michael A. "Farewell from the Editor's Desk." *Theological Studies* 66 (2005): 735–38.

Fuchs, Josef. "Situation Ethics and Theology." *Theology Digest* 2 (1954): 25–30.

———. *General Moral Theology, Pt. I.* Rome: Pontificia Universitatis Gregoriana, 1963.

———. *Natural Law: A Theological Investigation.* Translated by Helmut Reckter and John Dowling. New York: Sheed and Ward, 1965.

———. "The Question Is Not Closed: The Liberals Reply." In *The Birth Control Debate.* Edited by Robert G. Hoyt. Kansas City, MO: National Catholic Reporter, 1968.

———. "Responsible Parenthood." In *Turning Point.* Edited by Robert McClory. New York: Crossroad, 1995.

Gallagher, John A. *Time Past, Time Future: A Historical Study of Catholic Moral Theology.* New York: Paulist Press, 1990.

Graham, Mark. *Josef Fuchs on Natural Law.* Washington, DC: Georgetown University Press, 2002.

Grisez, Germain. "Presentation of the Cardinal O'Boyle Award for Defense of the Faith to John C. Ford, SJ, by the Fellowship of Catholic Scholars." *Fellowship of Catholic Scholars Newsletter* 12(1): 14.

Guindon, William. Letter to John Ford, March 18, 1970. Ford Collection (Box 33, File 15b).

Harty, J. M. *The Catholic Encyclopedia,* s.v. "Probabilism." www.newadvent.org/cathen/12441a.htm (accessed October 8, 2003).

Holmes, Oliver Wendell. *Collected Legal Papers.* New York: Harcourt Brace & Co., 1920.

———. *Justice Oliver Wendell Holmes: His Book Notices, Uncollected Letters and Papers.* Edited and annotated by Harry S. Shriver. New York: Central Book Co., 1936

———. *The Common Law.* Boston: Little Brown and Co., 1938.

Holy Office. Letter on *amplexus reservatus*. *Acta apostolicae sedis* 44 (1952): 546. Quoted in John Ford and Gerald Kelly, *Contemporary Moral Theology, Vol. II: Marriage Questions*, 213. Westminster, MD: Newman Press, 1963.

Hoyt, Robert G., ed. *The Birth Control Debate*. Kansas City, MO: National Catholic Reporter, 1968.

Jonsen, Albert and Stephen Toulmin. *The Abuse of Casuistry: A History of Moral Reasoning*. Berkeley: University of California Press, 1988.

Kaiser, Robert Blair. *The Politics of Sex and Religion*. Kansas City, MO: Leaven Press, 1985.

———. *The Encyclical That Never Was: The Story of the Pontifical Commission on Population and Birth, 1964–66*. London: Sheed & Ward, 1987.

Keenan, James F. "The Return of Casuistry." *Theological Studies* 57 (1996): 123–39.

———. "Josef Fuchs and the Question of Moral Objectivity in Roman Catholic Ethical Reasoning." *Religious Studies Review* 24 (1998): 253–58.

Keenan, James F. and Peter Black. "The Evolving Self-Understanding of the Theologian: 1900–2000." *Studia Moralia* 39 (2001): 291–327.

Komonchack, Joseph A. Ordinary Papal Magisterium and Religious Assent. Quoted in Charles Curran and Richard McCormick *Readings in Moral Theology No. 3: The Magisterium and Morality*, New York: Paulist Press.

Kuhn, J. J. "Rhythm: Medical Aspects." *New Catholic Encyclopedia* vol. 12. Washington, DC: Catholic University Press, 1967.

Langan, John. "Catholic Moral Rationalism and the Philosophical Basis of Moral Theology." *Theological Studies* 50 (1989): 25–43.

Lynch, John E. "The Magistery and Theological Reforms from the Apostolic Fathers to the Gregorian Reforms." *Chicago Studies* 17 (1978): 188–209.

Mahoney, John. *The Making of Moral Theology: A Study of the Roman Catholic Tradition*. Oxford: Clarendon Press, 1987.

McClory, Robert. *Turning Point: The Inside Story of the Papal Birth Control Commission, and How Humanae Vitae Changed the Life of Patty Crowley and the Future of the Church*. New York: Crossroad, 1995.

McCormick, Richard. Letter to John Ford, February 22, 1965. Ford Collection (Box 23, File 8).

———. "Notes on Moral Theology." *Theological Studies* 27 (1966): 647–54.

———. "Notes on Moral Theology." *Theological Studies* 28 (1967): 749–800.

———. *Notes on Moral Theology: 1965–1980*. Washington, DC: University Press of America, 1981.

———. "Moral Theology 1940–1989: An Overview." *Theological Studies* 50 (1989): 3–24.

Morgan, Oliver J. "'Chemical Comforting' and the Theology of John C. Ford, SJ: Classical Answers to a Contemporary Problem." *Journal of Ministry in Addiction and Recovery* 6 (1999, no. 1): 29–66.

National Clergy Conference on Alcoholism. *The Best of the Blue Book Vol. 2 1960–97*. Ithaca, NY: NCCA, 1999.

Noonan, John. *The Scholastic Analysis of Usury*. Cambridge, MA: Harvard University Press, 1957.

———. Contraception: A History of Its Treatment by Catholic Theologians and Canonists. Cambridge, MA: Harvard University Press, 1965.

———. Letter to John Ford, May 4, 1965. Ford Collection (Box 21, File 5).

———. "Authority, Usury and Contraception." Cross Currents 16 (1966): 55–79.

———. The Church and Contraception: The Issues at Stake. New York: Paulist Press, 1967.

———. "The Pope's Conscience." Commonweal 85 (1967): 559–60.

———. 1993. "Development in Moral Doctrine." Theological Studies 54 (1993): 662–77.

Odozor, Paulinuis Ikechukwu. Richard McCormick and the Renewal of Moral Theology. Notre Dame, IN: University of Notre Dame Press, 1995.

Paul VI. "Address to Cardinals and Bishops during the Second Vatican Council." Acta Apostolicae Sedis 56 (1964): 588–89. Quoted in Ford and Lynch, "Contraception: A Matter of Practical Doubt?" Homiletic and Pastoral Review 68 (1968): 564.

———. "Address to the XIII Congress of the Italian Feminine Center." Acta Apostolicae Sedis 58 (1966): 219.

———. "Statement on Birth Control to the Fifty-second National Congress of the Italian Society of Obstetrics and Gynecology." Acta Apostolicae Sedis 58 (1966): 1169.

Pius XI. Casti connubii. Acta Apostolicae Sedis 22 (1930): 561. Quoted in John Ford and Gerald Kelly, Contemporary Moral Theology, Vol. II: Marriage Questions, 386. Westminster, MD: Newman Press, 1963.

Pius XII. Humani generis. 1950. www.vatican.va/holy_father/pius_xii/encyclicals/documents/hf_p-xii_enc_12081950_humani-generis_en.html (accessed November 3, 2003).

———. "Address to Midwives." Acta apostolicae sedis 43 (1951): 835–54.

———. Magnificate dominum. (1954) Quoted in John Ford and Gerald Kelly. Contemporary Moral Theology, Vol. I: Questions in Fundamental Moral Theology, 33. Westminster, MD: Newman Press.

———. "Christmas Message." Acta apostolicae sedis 49 (1956): 21–22.

———. Si diligis. (1958) Quoted in John Ford and Gerald Kelly. Contemporary Moral Theology, Vol. I: Questions in Fundamental Moral Theology, 33. Westminster, MD: Newman Press.

Pizzardo, Guiseppe. "Letter to all Ordinaries." April 21, 1955. Box 28, file 30, Ford Collection.

Place, Michael D. "From Solicitude to Magisterium: Theologians and Magisterium from the Council of Trent to the First Vatican Council." Chicago Studies 17 (1978): 225–41.

Pontifical Council on the Family. Vademecum for Confessors Concerning Some Aspects of the Morality of Conjugal Life. February 12, 1997. www.vatican.va/roman_curia/pontifical_councils/family/documents/rc_pc_family_doc_12021997_vademecum_en.html (accessed January 25, 2004).M

Pope, Stephen. "Overview of the Ethics of Thomas Aquinas." In The Ethics of Thomas Aquinas, 30–53. Washington, DC: Georgetown University Press, 2002.

Riedmatten, Henri de. Letter to John Ford, June 18, 1965. Box 23, file 8, Ford Collection.

Shaw, Russell. "The Making of a Moral Theologian." *The Catholic World Report*, March, 1996. www.ewtn.com/library/HOMELIBR/GRISEZ.TXT (accessed December 28, 2003).

Slater, Thomas. *A Manual of Moral Theology for English Speaking Countries*, Vol. I, 2nd ed. New York: Benzinger Brothers, 1908.

United States Conference of Catholic Bishops. *Declaration on Conscientious Objection and Selective Conscientious Objection*. 1971. www.usccb.org/sdwp/peace/declarat.htm (accessed June 20, 2007).

Valsecchi, Ambroglio. *Controversy: The Birth Control Debate 1958–1968*. Washington, DC: Corpus Books, 1968.

Walsh, Maurice. Interview by Eric Genilo, April 23, 2003. Transcript in the author's posssession.

Wilson, Bill. *Twelve Steps and Twelve Traditions*. New York: Alcoholics Anonymous Publishing, Inc., 1953.

———. *Alcoholics Anonymous Comes of Age*. New York: Harper, 1957.

Witherspoon, J. P. "Holmes, Oliver Wendell." *New Catholic Encyclopedia*, vol. 7. Washington, DC: Catholic University Press, 1967.

INDEX